HARDPRESS.NET
HOME OF HARD-TO-FIND BOOKS

The New Life
by Horace Bushnell

THE NEW LIFE

By HORACE BUSHNELL, D.D.
AUTHOR OF "THE VICARIOUS SACRIFICE"

Anchora Spei

ALEXANDER STRAHAN, PUBLISHER
LONDON AND NEW YORK
1866

CONTENTS.

I.

EVERY MAN'S LIFE A PLAN OF GOD.

II.

DIGNITY OF HUMAN NATURE SHEWN FROM ITS RUINS.

III.

THE HUNGER OF THE SOUL.

IV.

THE REASON OF FAITH.

V.

REGENERATION.

VI.

THE PERSONAL LOVE AND LEAD OF CHRIST.

VII.

LIGHT ON THE CLOUD.

VIII.

THE CAPACITY OF RELIGION EXTIRPATED BY DISUSE.

IX.

UNCONSCIOUS INFLUENCE.

X.

OBLIGATION A PRIVILEGE.

XI.

HAPPINESS AND JOY.

CONTENTS.

vi CONTENTS.

THE NEW LIFE.

I.

ISAIAH xlv. 5—"*I girded thee, though thou hast not known me.*"

So beautiful is the character and history of Cyrus, the person here addressed, that many have doubted whether the sketch given by Xenophon was not intended as an idealising, or merely romantic picture. And yet, there have been examples of as great beauty unfolded, here and there, in all the darkest recesses of the heathen world; and it accords entirely with the hypothesis of historic verity in the account given us of this remarkable man, that he is designated and named by our prophet, even before he is born, as a chosen foster-son of God. "I have surnamed thee," He declares; "I have girded thee, though thou hast not known me." And what should he be but a model of all princely beauty, of bravery, of justice, of impartial honour to the lowly, of greatness and true magnanimity in every form, when God has girded him, unseen, to be the minister of His own great and sovereign purposes to the nations of his time?

Something of the same kind will also be detected in the history and personal consciousness of almost every great and remarkable character. Christ himself testifies to the girding of the Almighty when He says—"To this end was I born, and for this purpose came I into the world." Abraham was girded for a particular work and mission, in what is otherwise denominated his call. Joseph, in Egypt, distinguishes the girding of God's hand, when he comforts his guilty brothers in the assurance—"So it was not you that sent me hither, but God."

Moses and Samuel were even called by name, and set to their great life-work in the same manner.   And what is Paul endeavouring, in all the stress and pressure of his mighty apostleship, but to perform the work for which God's Spirit girded him at his call and to apprehend that for which he was apprehended of Christ Jesus?   And yet these great master-spirits of the world are not so much distinguished, after all, by the acts they do, as by the sense itself of some mysterious girding of the Almighty upon them, whose behests they are set on to fulfil.   And all men may have this; for the humblest and commonest have a place and a work assigned them, in the same manner, and have it for their privilege to be always ennobled in the same lofty consciousness.   God is girding every man for a place and a calling, in which, taking it from Him, even though it be internally humble, he may be as consciously exalted as if he held the rule of a kingdom.   The truth I propose, then, for your consideration is this—

That God has a definite life-plan for every human person, girding him, visibly or invisibly, for some exact thing, which it will be the true significance and glory of his life to have accomplished.

Many persons, I am well aware, never even think of any such thing.   They suppose that, for most men, life is a necessarily stale and common affair.   What it means for them they do not know, and they scarcely conceive that it means anything.   They even complain, venting heavy sighs, that, while some few are set forward by God to do great works and fill important places, they are not allowed to believe that there is any particular object in their existence.   It is remarkable, considering how generally this kind of impression prevails, that the Holy Scriptures never give way to it, but seem, as it were, in all possible ways, to be holding up the dignity of common life, and giving a meaning to its appointments which the natural dullness and lowness of mere human opinion cannot apprehend.

They not only shew us explicitly, as we have seen, that God has a definite purpose in the lives of men already great, but they shew us how frequently, in the conditions of obscurity and depression, preparations of counsel going on, by which the commonest offices are to become the necessary first chapter of a great and powerful history.   David among the sheep; Elisha following after the plough; Nehemiah bearing the cup; Hannah, who can say nothing less common than that she is the wife of Elkanah and a woman of a sorrowful spirit,—who, that looks on these humble people, at their humble post of service, and discovers, at last, how dear a purpose God was cherishing in them, can be justified in thinking that God has no particular plan for him, because he is not signalised by any kind of distinction?

Besides, what do the Scriptures shew us, but that God has a particular care for every man, a personal interest in him, and a sympathy with him and his trials, watching for the uses of his one talent as attentively and kindly, and approving him as heartily, in the right employment of it, as if He had given him ten; and what is the giving out of the talents itself, but an exhibition of the fact that God has a definite purpose, charge, and work, be it this or that, for every man?

They also make it the privilege of every man to live in the secret guidance of God; which is plainly nugatory, unless there is some chosen work, or sphere, into which he may be guided; for how shall God guide him, having nothing appointed or marked out for him to be guided into, no field opened for him, no course set down which is to be his wisdom?

God also professes in His Word to have purposes prearranged for all events; to govern by a plan which is from eternity even, and which, in some proper sense, comprehends everything. And what is this but another way of conceiving that God has a definite place and plan adjusted for every human being? And, without such a plan, He could not even govern the world intelligently, or make a proper universe of the created system; for it becomes a universe only in the grand unity of reason, which includes it. Otherwise, it were only a jumble of fortuities, without counsel, end, or law.

Turning now from the Scriptures to the works of God, how constantly are we met here by the fact, everywhere visible, that ends and uses are the regulative reasons of all existing things? This we discover often, when we are least able to understand the speculative mystery of objects; for it is precisely the *uses* of things that are most palpable. These uses are to God, no doubt, as to us, the significance of His works. And they compose, taken together, a grand reciprocal system, in which part

B

answers actively to part, constructing thus an all-comprehensive and glorious whole. And the system is, in fact, so perfect, that the loss or displacement of any member would fatally derange the general order. If there were any smallest star in heaven that had no place to fill, that oversight would beget a disturbance which no Leverrier could compute; because it would be a real and eternal, and not merely casual or apparent, disorder. One grain, more or less, of sand would disturb, or even fatally disorder the whole scheme of the heavenly motions. So nicely balanced, and so carefully hung, are the worlds, that even the grains of their dust are counted, and their places adjusted to a correspondent nicety. There is nothing included in the gross, or total sum, that could be dispensed with. The same is true in regard to forces that are apparently irregular. Every particle of air is moved by laws of as great precision as the laws of the heavenly bodies, or, indeed, by the same laws; keeping its appointed place, and serving its appointed use. Every odour exhales in the nicest conformity with its appointed place and law. Even the viewless and mysterious heat, stealing through the dark centres and impenetrable depths of the worlds, obeys its uses with unfaltering exactness, dissolving never so much as an atom that was not to be dissolved. What now shall we say of man, appearing, as it were, in the centre of this great circle of uses. They are all adjusted for him: has he, then, no ends appointed for himself? Noblest of all creatures, and closest to God, as he certainly is, are we to say that his Creator has no definite thoughts concerning him, no place prepared for him to fill, no use for him to serve, which is the reason of his existence?

There is, then, I conclude, a definite and proper end, or issue, for every man's existence; an end which, to the heart of God, is the good intended for him, or for which he was intended; that which he is privileged to become, called to become, ought to become; that which God will assist him to become, and which he cannot miss, save by his own fault. Every human soul has a complete and perfect plan cherished for it in the heart of God—a divine biography marked out, which it enters into life to live. This life, rightly unfolded, will be a complete and beautiful whole, an experience led on by God and unfolded by His secret nurture, as the trees and the flowers, by the secret nurture of the world; a drama cast in the mould of a perfect art, with no part wanting; a divine study for the man himself, and for others; a study that shall for ever unfold, in wondrous beauty, the love and faithfulness of God; great in its conception, great in the Divine skill by which it is shaped; above all, great in the momentous and glorious issues it prepares. What a thought is this for every human soul to cherish! What dignity does it add to life! What support does it bring to the trials of life! What instigations does it add to send us onward in everything that constitutes our excellence! We live in the Divine thought. We fill a place in the great everlasting plan of God's intelligence. We never sink below His care, never drop out of His counsel.

But there is, I must add, a single but very important and even fearful qualification. Things all serve their uses, and never break out of their place. They have no power to do it. Not so with us. We are able, as free beings, to refuse the place and the duties God appoints; which, if we do, then we sink into something lower and less worthy of us. That highest and best condition for which God designed us is no more possible. We are fallen out of it, and it cannot be wholly recovered. And yet, as that was the best thing possible for us in the reach of God's original counsel, so there is a place designed for us now, which is the next best possible. God calls us now to the best thing left, and will do so till all good possibility is narrowed down and spent. And then, when He cannot use us any more for our own good, He will use us for the good of others— an example of the misery and horrible desperation to which any soul must come, when all the good ends, and all the holy callings of God's friendly and fatherly purpose are exhausted. Or it may be now that, remitting all other plans and purposes in our behalf, He will henceforth use us, wholly against our will, to be the demonstration of His justice and avenging power before the eyes of mankind; saying over us, as He did over Pharaoh in the day of His judgments, "Even for this same purpose have I raised thee up, that I might shew my power in thee, and that my name might be declared throughout all the earth." Doubtless He had other and more genial plans to serve in this bad man, if only he could have accepted such; but knowing his certain rejection of these, God turned His mighty

counsel in him wholly on the use to be made of him as a reprobate. How many Pharaohs in common life refuse every other
use God will make of them, choosing only to figure, in their
small way, as reprobates, and descending, in that manner, to a
fate that painfully mimics his.

God has, then, I conclude, a definite life-plan set for every
man; one that, being accepted and followed, will conduct him
to the best and noblest end possible. No qualification of this
doctrine is needed, save the fearful one just named; that we,
by our perversity, so often refuse to take the place and do the
work He gives us.

It follows, in the same way, that, as God, in fixing on our end
or use, will choose the best end or use possible, so He will ap-
point for us the best manner possible of attaining it; for, as it
is a part of God's perfection to choose the best things, and not
things partially good, so it will be in all the methods He prescribes for their attainment. And so, as you pass on, stage by
stage, in your courses of experience, it is made clear to you that,
whatever you have laid upon you to do or to suffer, whatever to
want, whatever to surrender or to conquer, is exactly best for
you. Your life is a school exactly adapted to your lesson, and
that to the best, last end of your existence.

No room for a discouraged or depressed feeling, therefore, is
left you. Enough that you exist for a purpose high enough to
give meaning to life, and to support a genuine inspiration. If
your sphere is outwardly humble, if it even appears to be quite
insignificant, God understands it better than you do, and it is a
part of His wisdom to bring out great sentiments in humble
conditions, great principles in works that are outwardly trivial,
great characters under great adversities and heavy loads of in-
cumbrance. The tallest saints of God will often be those who
walk in the deepest obscurity, and are even despised or quite
overlooked by man. Let it be enough that God is in your
history and that the plan of your biography is His, the issue
He has set for it is the highest and the best. Away, then, O
man, with thy feeble complaints and feverish despondencies.
There is no place left for this kind of nonsense. Let it fill
thee with cheerfulness and exalted feeling, however deep in obscurity your lot may be, that God is leading you on, girding
you for a work, preparing you to a good that is worthy of His

divine magnificence. If God is really preparing us all to become that which is the very highest and best thing possible, there ought never to be a discouraged or uncheerful being in the world.

Nor is it any detraction from such a kind of life that the helm of its guidance is, by the supposition, to be in God, and not in our own will and wisdom. This, in fact, is its dignity; it is a kind of divine order, a creation moulded by the loving thoughts of God; in that view to the man himself a continual discovery, as it is unfolded, both of himself and God. A discovery of some kind it must be to all; for, however resolutely or defiantly we undertake to accomplish our own objects, and cut our own way through to a definite, self-appointed future, it will never be true, for one moment, that we are certain of this future, and will almost always be true that we are met by changes and conditions unexpected. This, in fact, is one of the common mitigations even of a selfish and self-directed life, that its events come up out of the unknown and overtake the subject, as discoveries he could not shun, or anticipate. Evil itself is far less evil, even to the worldly man, that it comes by surprises. Were the scenes of necessary bitterness, wrong, trial, disappointment, self-accusation, every such man has to pass through in his life, distinctly set before him at the beginning, how forbidding generally, and how dismal the prospect. We say, therefore, how frequently, "I could not have endured these distasteful, painful years, these emptinesses, these trials and torments that have rent me, one after another, if I had definitely known beforehand what kind of lot was before me." And yet, how poor a comfort it is to such pains and disasters that they overtook the sufferer as surprises and sorrows not set down beforehand in the self-appointed programme of life! How different, how inspiring and magnificent, instead, to live, by holy consent, a life all discovery; to see it unfolding, moment by moment, a plan of God, our own life-plan conceived in His paternal love; each event, incident, experience, whether bright or dark, having its mission from Him, and revealing, either now or in its future issues, the magnificence of His favouring counsel; to be sure, in the dark day, of a light that will follow, that loss will terminate in gain, that trial will issue in rest, doubt in satisfaction, suffering in patience, patience in purity, and all in a consummation of greatness and dignity that even God will look on with a smile! How magnificent, how strong in its repose, how full of rest is such a kind of life! Call it human still, decry it, let it down by whatever diminutives can be invented, still it is great; a charge which ought even to inspire a dull-minded man with energy and holy enthusiasm.

But, the inquiry will be made, supposing all this to be true, in the manner stated, how can we ever get hold of this life-plan God has made for us, or find our way into it? Here, to many, if not all, will be the main stress of doubt and practical suspense.

Observe, then, first of all, some negatives that are important, and must be avoided. They are these:—

You will never come into God's plan if you study singularity; for, if God has a design or plan for every man's life, then it is exactly appropriate to his nature; and, as every man's nature is singular and peculiar to himself,—as peculiar as his face or look,—then it follows that God will lead every man into a singular, original and peculiar life, without any study of singularity on his part. Let him seek to be just what God will have him, and the talents, the duties, and circumstances of his life will require him to be, and then he will be just peculiar enough. He will have a life of his own; a life that is naturally and, therefore, healthily peculiar; a simple, unaffected, unambitious life, whose plan is not in himself, but in God.

As little will he seek to copy the life of another. No man is ever called to be another. God has as many plans for men as he has men; and, therefore, He never requires them to measure their life exactly by any other life. We are not to require it of ourselves to have the precise feelings, or exercises, or do the works, or pass through the trials of other men; for God will handle us according to what we are, and not according to what other men are. And whoever undertakes to be exercised by any given fashion, or to be any given character, such as he knows or has read of, will find it impossible, even as it is to make himself another nature. God's plan must hold, and we must seek no other. To strain after something new and peculiar is fantastic and weak, and is also as nearly wicked as that kind of weakness can be. To be a copyist, working at the reproduction of a human model, is to have no faith in one's significance.

to judge that God means nothing in his particular life, but only in the life of some other man. Submitting himself, in this manner, to the fixed opinion that his life means nothing, and that nothing is left for him but to borrow or beg a life-plan from some other man, what can the copyist become but an affectation or a dull imposture ?

In this view, also, you are never to complain of your birth, your training, your employments, your hardships ; never to fancy that you could be something if only you had a different lot and sphere assigned you. God understands His own plan, and He knows what you want, a great deal better than you do. The very things that you most deprecate, as fatal limitations or obstructions, are probably what you most want. What you call hindrances, obstacles, discouragements, are probably God's opportunities ; and it is nothing new that the patient should dislike his medicines, or any certain proof that they are poisons. No ; a truce to all such impatience ! Choke that devilish envy which gnaws at your heart, because you are not in the same lot with others ; bring down your soul, or, rather, bring it up to receive God's will and do His work, in your lot, in your sphere, under your cloud of obscurity, against your temptations ; and then you shall find that your condition is never opposed to your good, but really consistent with it. Hence it was that an apostle required his converts to abide each one in that calling wherein he was called ; to fill his place till He opens a way, by filling it, to some other ; the bondman to fill his house of bondage with love and duty, the labourer to labour, the woman to be a woman, the men to shew themselves men,—all to acknowledge God's hand in their lot, and seek to co-operate with that good design which He most assuredly cherishes for them.

Another frequent mistake, to be carefully avoided, is that, while you surrender and renounce all thought of making up a plan, or choosing out a plan, for yourself, as one that you set by your own will, you also give up the hope or expectation that God will set you in any scheme of life, where the whole course of it will be known, or set down beforehand. If you go to Him to be guided, He will guide you ; but He will not comfort your distrust, or half-trust of Him, by shewing you the chart of all His purposes concerning you. He will only shew you into a way where, if you go cheerfully and trustfully forward, He will shew you on still further.   No contract will be made with you, save that He engages, if you trust Him, to lead you into the best things, all the way through.   And if they are better than you can either ask or think beforehand, they will be none the worse for that.

But we must not stop in negatives.   How, then, or by what more positive directions can a man, who really desires to do it, come into the plan God lays for him, so as to live it and rationally believe that he does?   You are on the point of choosing, it may be, this or that calling, wanting to know where duty lies, and what the course God himself would have you take.   Beginning at a point most remote, and where the generality of truth is widest.

Consider, 1. The character of God, and you will draw a large deduction from that ; for all that God designs for you will be in harmony with His character.   He is a being infinitely good, just, true.   Therefore, you are to know that He cannot really seek anything contrary to this in you.   You may make yourselves contrary, in every attribute of character, to God ; but He never made you to become anything different from or unworthy of Himself.   A good being could not make another to be a bad being, as the proper issue and desired end of his existence ; least of all could one infinitely good.   A great many employments or callings are, by these first principles, for ever cut off. No thought is permitted you, even for a moment, of any work or calling that does not represent the industry, justice, truth, beneficence, mercy of God.

2. Consider your relation to Him as a creature.   All created wills have their natural centre and rest in God's will.   In Him they all come into a play of harmony, and the proper harmony of being is possible only in this way.   Thus, you know that you are called to have a will perfectly harmonised with God's and rested in His, and that gives you a large insight into what you are to be, or what is the real end of your being.   In fact, ninetenths of your particular duties may be settled, at once, by a simple reference in this manner to what God wills.

3. You have a conscience, which is given to be an interpreter of His will, and thus of your duty, and, in both, of what you are to become.

4. God's law and His written Word are guides to present duty, which, if faithfully accepted, will help to set you in accordance with the mind of God and the plan He has laid for you. "I am a stranger in the earth," said one; "hide not Thy commandments from me;" knowing that God's commandments would give him a clue to the true meaning and business of his life.

5. Be an observer of providence; for God is shewing you ever, by the way in which He leads you, whither He means to lead. Study your trials, your talents, the world's wants, and stand ready to serve God now, in whatever He brings to your hand.

Again, 6. Consult your friends, and especially those who are most in the teaching of God. They know your talents and personal qualifications better, in some respects, than you do yourself. Ask their judgment of you, and of the spheres and works to which you are best adapted.

Once more, 7. Go to God himself, and ask for the calling of God; for, as certainly as He has a plan or calling for you, He will somehow guide you into it. And this is the proper office and work of His Spirit. By this private teaching He can shew us, and will, into the very plan that is set for us. And this is the significance of what is prescribed as our duty—viz., living and walking in the Spirit; for the Spirit of God is a kind of universal presence, or inspiration, in the world's bosom; an unfailing inner light, which, if we accept and live in, we are guided thereby into a consenting choice, so that what God wills for us we also will for ourselves,—settling into it as the needle to the pole. By this hidden union with God, or intercourse with Him, we get a wisdom or insight deeper than we know ourselves; a sympathy, a oneness with the Divine will and love. We go into the very plan of God for us, and are led along in it by Him, consenting, co-operating, answering to Him, we know not how, and working out, with nicest exactness, that good end for which His unseen counsel girded us and sent us into the world. In this manner, not neglecting the other methods just named, but gathering in all their separate lights, to be interpreted in the higher light of the Spirit, we can never be greatly at a loss to find our way into God's counsel and plan. The duties of the resent moment we shall meet as they rise, and these will open a gate into the next, and we shall thus pass on, trustfully and securely, almost never in doubt as to what God calls us to do.

It is not to be supposed that you have followed me, in such a subject as this, without encountering questions from within that are piercing. It has put you on reflection; it has set you to the inquiry, what you have been doing and becoming thus far in your course, and what you are hereafter to be? Ten, twenty, fifty, seventy years ago, you came into this living world, and began to breathe this mortal air. The guardian angel that came to take charge of you said, "To this end is he born, for this cause is he come into the world." Or, if this be a Jewish fancy, God said the same Himself. He had a definite plan for you, a good end settled and cherished for you in His heart. This it was that gave a meaning and a glory to your life. Apart from this, it was not, in His view, life for you to live; it was accident, frustration, death. What now, O soul, hast thou done? what progress hast thou made? how much of the blessed life-plan of thy Father hast thou executed? How far on thy way art thou to the good, best end thy God has designed for thee?

Do I hear thy soul confessing, with a suppressed sob within thee, that, up to this time, thou hast never sought God's chosen plan at all. Hast thou, even to this hour, and during so many years, been following a way and a plan of thine own, regardless, hitherto, of all God's purposes in thee? Well, if it be so, what hast thou gotten? How does thy plan work? Does it bring thee peace, content, dignity of aim and feeling, purity, rest; or, does it plunge thee into mires of disturbance, scorch thee in flames of passion, worry thee with cares, burden thee with bitter reflections, cross thee, disappoint, sadden, sour thee? And what are thy prospects? what is the issue to come? After thou hast worked out this hard plan of thine own, will it come to a good end? Hast thou courage now to go on and work it through?

Perhaps you may be entertaining yourself, for the time, with a notion of your prosperity, counting yourself happy in past successes, and counting on greater successes to come. Do you call it, then, success, that you are getting on in a plan of your own? There cannot be a greater delusion. You set up a plan that is not God's, and rejoice that it seems to prosper; not observing that you are just as much further off from God's plan for you and from all true wisdom, as you seem to prosper more. And the day is coming when just this truth will be revealed to you, as the bitterest pang of your defeat and shame.

No matter which it be, prosperity or acknowledged defeat, the case is much the same in one as in the other, if you stand apart from God and His counsel. There is nothing good preparing for any man who will not live in God's plan. If he goes a prospecting for himself, and will not apprehend that for which he is apprehended, it cannot be to any good purpose.

And really, I know not anything, my hearers, more sad and painful to think of, to a soul properly enlightened by reason and God's truth, than so many years of Divine good squandered and lost; whole years, possibly many years, of that great and blessed biography which God designed for you, occupied by a frivolous and foolish invention of your own, substituted for the good counsel of God's infinite wisdom and love. Oh, let the past suffice!

Young man, or woman, this is the day of hope to you. All your best opportunities are still before you. Now, too, you are laying your plans for the future. Why not lay them in God? Who has planned for you as wisely and faithfully as He? Let your life begin with Him. Believe that you are girded by your God for a holy and great calling. Go to Him and consecrate your life to Him, knowing assuredly that He will lead you into just that life which is your highest honour and blessing.

And what shall I say to the older man, who is further on in his course and is still without God in the world? The beginning of wisdom, my friend, you have yet to learn. You have really done nothing, as yet, that you were sent into the world to do. All your best opportunities, too, are gone or going by. The best end, the next best, and the next are gone, and nothing but the dregs of opportunity is left. And still Christ calls even you. There is a place still left for you; not the best and brightest, but an humble and good one. To this you are called, for this you are apprehended of Christ Jesus still. Oh, come, repent of your dusty, and dull, and weary way, and take the call that is offered.

All men living without God are adventurers out upon God's world, in neglect of Him, to choose their own course. Hence the sorrowful, sad-looking host they make. Oh, that I could shew them whence their bitterness, their dryness, their unutterable sorrows, come. Oh, that I could silence, for one hour, the noisy tumult of their works, and get them to look in upon that better, higher life of fruitfulness and blessing to which their God has appointed them. Will they ever see it? Alas! I fear!

Friends of God, disciples of the Son of God, how inspiring and magnificent the promise, or privilege, that is offered here to you! Does it still encounter only unbelief in your heart? Does it seem to you impossible that you can ever find your way into a path prepared for you by God, and be led along in it by His mighty counsel? Let me tell you a secret. It requires a very close, well-kept life to do this; a life in which the soul can have confidence always toward God; a life which allows the Spirit always to abide and reign, driven away by no affront of selfishness. There must be a complete renunciation of self-will. God and religion must be practically first; and the testimony that we please God must be the element of our peace. And such a disciple I have never known who did not have it for his joy that God was leading him on, shaping his life for him, bringing him along out of one moment into the next, year by year. To such a disciple, there is nothing strained or difficult in saying that God's plan can be found, or that this is the true mode and privilege of life. Nothing to him is easier or more natural. He knows God ever present, feels that God determines all things for him, rejoices in the confidence that the everlasting counsel of his Friend is shaping every turn of his experience. He does not go hunting after this confidence; it comes to him, abides in him, fortifies his breast, and makes his existence itself an element of peace. And this, my brethren, is your privilege, if only you can live close enough to have the secret of the Lord with you.

How sacred, how strong in its repose, how majestic, how nearly divine is a life thus ordered! The simple thought of a life which is to be the unfolding, in this manner, of a Divine plan, is too beautiful, too captivating, to suffer one indifferent or heedless moment. Living in this manner, every turn of your experience will be a discovery to you of God, every change a token of His fatherly counsel. Whatever obscurity, darkness, trial, suffering, falls upon you: your defeats, losses, injuries; your outward state, employment, relations; what seems hard, unaccountable, severe, or, as nature might say, vexatious—all these you will see are parts or constitutive elements in God's beautiful and good plan for you, and, as such, are to be accepted with a smile. Trust God! have an implicit trust in God! and these very things will impart the highest zest to life. If you were in your own will, you could not bear them; and if you fall, at any time, into your own will, they will break you down. But the glory of your condition, as a Christian, is, that you are in the mighty and good will of God. Hence it was that Bunyan called his hero Great Heart; for no heart can be weak that is in the confidence of God. See how it was with Paul: counting all things but loss for the excellency of the knowledge; enduring, with godlike patience, unspeakable sufferings; casting everything behind him, and following on to apprehend that for which he was apprehended. He had a great and mighty will, but no self-will: therefore, he was strong, a true lion of the faith. Away, then, with all feeble complaints, all meagre and mean anxieties. Take your duty, and be strong in it, as God will make you strong. The harder it is, the stronger, in fact, you will be. Understand, also, that the great question here is, not what you will get, but what you will become. The greatest wealth you can ever get will be in yourself. Take your burdens, and troubles, and losses, and wrongs, if come they must and will, as your opportunities, knowing that God has girded you for greater things than these. Oh, to live out such a life as God appoints, how great a thing it is!—to do the duties, make the sacrifices, bear the adversities, finish the plan, and then to say with Christ (who of us will be able?)—"It is finished!"

II.

DIGNITY OF HUMAN NATURE SHEWN FROM ITS RUINS.

ROMANS iii. 13–18—*"Their throat is an open sepulchre: with their tongues they have used deceit: the poison of asps is under their lips: whose mouth is full of cursing and bitterness: their feet are swift to shed blood: destruction and misery are in their ways: and the way of peace have they not known: there is no fear of God before their eyes."*

A MOST dark and dismal picture of humanity, it must be admitted; and yet it has two sides or aspects. In one view, it is the picture of weakness, wretchedness, shame, and disgust; all which they discover in it who most sturdily resent the impeachment of it. In the other, it presents a being higher than even they can boast; a fearfully great being; great in his evil will, his demoniacal passions, his contempt of fear, the splendour of his degradation, and the magnificence of his woe.

It is this latter view of the picture to which, at the present time, I propose to call your attention, exhibiting—

The dignity of man, as revealed by the ruin he makes in his fall and apostasy from God.

It has been the way of many, in our time, to magnify humanity, or the dignity of human nature, by tracing its capabilities and the tokens it reveals of a natural affinity with God and truth. They distinguish lovely instincts, powers, and properties allied to God, aspirations reaching after God; many virtues, according to the common use of that term; many beautiful and graceful charities; and, by such kind of evidences or proofs, they repel, sometimes with scorn, what they call the libellous, or even the insulting doctrine of total depravity. And this they do, as I will add, not without some show of reason, when the fact of our depravity is asserted in a manner that excludes the admission of any such high aspirations and amiable properties.

or virtues, as we certainly discover in human conduct, apart from any gifts and graces of religion. And it must be admitted that some teachers have given occasion for this kind of offence; not observing the compatibility of great aspirations and majestic affinities with a state of deep spiritual thraldom; assuming, also, with as little right, the want of all appropriate sensibilities and receptivities for the truth, as a necessary inference from the complete destitution of holiness. They make out, in this manner, a doctrine of human depravity, in which there is no proper humanity left.

I am not required by my subject to settle the litigation between these two extremes; one of which makes the gospel unnecessary, because there is no depravation to restore; and the other of which makes it impossible, because there is nothing left to which any holy appeal can be made; but I undertake, in partial disregard of both, to shew the essential greatness and dignity of man from the ruin itself which he becomes; confident of this, that in no other point of view will he prove the spiritual sublimity of his nature so convincingly.

Nor is it anything new, or a turn more ingenious than just, that we undertake to raise our conceptions of human nature in this manner; for it is in just this way that we are accustomed to get our measures and form our conceptions of many things; of the power, for example, of ancient dynasties, and the magnificence of ancient works and cities. Falling thus, it may be, on patches of paved road here and there, on lines leading out divergently from ancient Rome, uncovering and deciphering the mile-stones by their sides, marked with postal distances, here for Britain, here for Germany, here for Ephesus and Babylon, here for Brundusium, the port of the Appian Way, and so for Egypt, Numidia, and the provinces of the sun; imagining the couriers flying back and forth, bearing the mandates of the central authority to so many distant nations, followed by the military legions trailing on to execute them; we receive an impression of the empire, from these scattered vestiges, which almost no words of historic description could give us. So, if we desire to form some opinion of the dynasty of the Pharaohs, of whom history gives us but the faintest remembrances and obscurest traditions, we have only to look on the monumental mountains, piled up to moulder on the silent plain of Egypt, and these dumb historians in stone will shew us more of that vast and populous empire, measuring by the amount of realised impression, more of the imperial haughtiness of the monarchs, more of the servitude of their people, and of the captive myriads of the tributary nations, than even Herodotus and Strabo, history and geography, together.

The same is true, even more strikingly, of ancient cities. Though described by historians in terms of definite measurement, with their great structures and defences and the royal splendour of their courts, we form no sufficient conception of their grandeur, till we look upon their ruins. Even the eloquence of Homer describing the glory and magnificence of Thebes, the vast circuit of its walls, its hundred gates, and the chariots of war pouring out of all, to vanquish and hold in subjection the peoples of as many nations, yields only a faint, unimpressive conception of the city; but to pass through the ruins of Karnac and Luxor, a vast desolation of temples and pillared avenues that dwarf all the present structures of the world, solemn, silent, and hoary, covered with historic sculptures that relate the conquest of kingdoms—a journey to pass through, a maze in which even comprehension is lost—this reveals a fit conception of the grandest city of the world as no words could describe it. Beheld and judged by the majesty of its ruins, there is a poetry in the stones surpassing all majesty of song. So, when the prophet Jonah, endeavouring, as he best can, to raise some adequate opinion of the greatness of Nineveh, declares that it is an exceeding great city of three days' journey; and, when Nahum follows, magnifying its splendour in terms of high description that correspond; still, so ambiguous and faint is the impression made, that many were doubting whether, after all, "the exceeding great city" was anything more than a vast inclosure of gardens and pasture-grounds for sheep, where a moderate population subsisted under the protection of a wall. No one had any proper conception of the city till just now, when a traveller and antiquary digs into the tomb where it lies, opens to view, at points many miles asunder, its temples and palaces, drags out the heavy sculptures, shews the inscriptions, collects the tokens of art and splendour, and says, "This is Nineveh, the 'exceeding great city,'" and, then, judging of its extent from the vast and glorious ruin, we begin to have some fit impression of its magnitude and splendour. And so it is with Babylon, Ephesus, Tadmor of the Desert, Baalbec, and the nameless cities and pyramids of the extinct American race. All great ruins are but a name for greatness in ruins; and we see the magnitude of the structure in that of the ruin made by it in its fall.

So it is with man. Our most veritable, though saddest, impressions of his greatness, as a creature, we shall derive from the magnificent ruin he displays. In that ruin we shall distinguish fallen powers that lie as broken pillars on the ground; temples of beauty, whose scarred and shattered walls still indicate their ancient, original glory; summits covered with broken stones, infested by asps, where the palaces of high thought and great aspiration stood, and righteous courage went up to maintain the citadel of the mind,—all a ruin now—"archangel ruined!"

And exactly this, I conceive, is the legitimate impression of the Scripture representations of man, as apostate from duty and God. Thoughtfully regarded, all exaggerations and contending theories apart, it is as if they were shewing us the original dignity of man from the magnificence of the ruin in which he lies. How sublime a creature must that be, call him either man or demon, who is able to confront the Almighty and tear himself away from His throne. And, as if to forbid our taking his deep misery and shame as tokens of contempt, imagining that a creature so humiliated is inherently weak and low, the first men are shewn us living out a thousand years of lustful energy, and braving the Almighty in strong defiance to the last. "The earth also is corrupt before God, and the earth is filled with violence." We look, as it were, upon a race of Titans broken loose from order and making war upon God and each other; beholding, in their outward force, a type of that original majesty which pertains to the moral nature of a being endowed with a self-determining liberty, capable of choices against God, and thus of a character in evil that shall be his own. They fill the earth, even up to the sky, with wrath and the demoniacal tumult of their wrongs, till God can suffer them no longer, sending forth His flood to sweep them from the earth. So of the remarkable picture given by Paul, in the first chapter of the Epistle to the

C

Romans. In one view we are disgusted, in another shocked, doubting whether it presents a creature most foolish and vile or most sublimely impious and wicked : and coming out, finally, where the chapter ends—" who knowing the judgment of God that they which commit such things are worthy of death, not only do the same, but have pleasure in them that do them "—there to confess the certain greatness of a being whose audacity is so nearly infinite, whose adherence to the league with evil is maintained with a pertinacity so damnably desperate and relentless. And the picture of the text corresponds, yielding no impression of a merely feeble and vile creature, but of a creature rather most terrible and swift ; destructive, fierce, and fearless ; miserable in his greatness ; great as in evil. "Their throat is an open sepulchre : with their tongues they have used deceit : the poison of asps is under their lips : whose mouth is full of cursing and bitterness : their feet are swift to shed blood : destruction and misery are in their ways : and the way of peace have they not known : there is no fear of God before their eyes."

But we come to the ruin as it is, and we look upon it with our own eyes, to receive the true, original impression for ourselves.

We look, first of all, upon the false religions of the world; pompous and costly rites transacted before crocodiles and onions; magnificent temples built over all monkeyish and monstrous creatures, carved by men's hands ; children offered up by their mothers, in fire or in water; kings offered on the altars by their people to propitiate a wooden image ; gorgeous palaces and trappings of barbaric majesty, studded all over with beetles in gold, or precious stones, to serve as a protection against pestilences, poisons, and accidents. I cannot fill out a picture that so nearly fills the world. Doubtless it is a picture of ruin—yet of a ruin how visibly magnificent! For, how high a nature must that be, how intensely allied to what is divine, that it must prepare such pomps, incur such sacrifices, and can elevate such trifles of imposture to a place of reverence ! If we say that in all this it is feeling after God, if haply it may find Him, which in one view is the truth, then how inextinguishable and grand are those religious instincts by which it is allied to the holy, the infinite, the eternal, but invisible One!

The wars of the world yield a similar impression. What opinion should we have of the energy, ferocity, and fearful passion of a race of animals, could any such be found, who marshal themselves by the hundred thousand, marching across kingdoms and deserts to fight, and strewing leagues of ground with a covering of dead, before they yield the victory. One race there is that figure in these heroics of war, in a small way— viz., the tiny race of ants—whom God has made a spectacle to mock the glory and magnificence of human wars; lest, carried away by so many brave shows, and by the applauses of the drunken ages of the world, we pass, undiscovered, the meanness and littleness of that selfish ambition, or pride, by which human wars are instigated. These are men such as history, in all past ages, shews them to be; swift to shed blood, swifter than the tiger race, and more terrible. Cities and empires are swept by their terrible marches, and become a desolation in their path. Destruction and misery are in their ways—oh, what destruction! misery, how deep and long! And what shall we think of any creature of God displayed in signs like these? Plainly enough he is a creature in ruins, but how magnificent a creature! Mean as the ant in his passions, but erecting, on the desolations he makes, thrones of honour and renown, and raising himself into the attitude of a god before the obsequious ages of mankind; for who of us can live content, as we are tempered, without some hero to admire and worship?

Consider, again, the persecutions of the good; fires for the saints of all ages, dungeons for the friends of liberty and benefactors of their times, poison for Socrates, a cross for Jesus Christ. What does it mean? What face shall we put on this outstanding demonstration of the world? No other than this, that cursing and bitterness, the poison even of asps, and more, is entered into the heart of man. He hates with a diabolical hatred. Feeling "how awful goodness is," the sight of it rouses him to madness, and he will not stop till he has tasted blood. And what a being is this that can be stung with so great madness by the spectacle of a good and holy life. The fiercest of animals are capable of no such devilish instigation, because they are too low to be capable of goodness, or even of the thought. But here is a creature who cannot bear the reminder even of good, or of anything above the ruin where his desolated glory lies. Oh, how great is the nature which is capable of this dire frenzy!

The great characters of the world furnish another striking proof of the transcendent quality of human nature, by the dignity they are able to connect even with their littleness and meanness. On a small island of the southern Atlantic, is shut up a remarkable prisoner, wearing himself out there in a feeble mixture of peevishness and jealousy, solaced by no great thoughts and no heroic spirit; a kind of dotard before the time, killing and consuming himself by the intense littleness into which he has shrunk. And this is the great conqueror of the modern world, the man whose name is the greatest of modern names, or, some will say, of all names the human world has pronounced; a man, nevertheless, who carried his greatest victories and told his meanest lies in close proximity; a character as destitute of private magnanimity, as he was remarkable for the stupendous powers of his understanding, and the more stupendous and imperial leadership of his will. How great a being must it be that makes a point of so great dignity before the world, despite of so much that is really little and contemptible.

But he is not alone. The immortal Kepler, piloting science into the skies, and comprehending the vastness of heaven for the first time, in the fixed embrace of definite thought, only proves the magnificence of man as a ruin, when you discover the strange ferment of irritability and "superstition wild," in which his great thoughts are brewed and his mighty life dissolved.

So also Bacon proves the amazing wealth and grandeur of the human soul only the more sublimely that, living in an element of cunning, servility, and ingratitude, and dying under the shame of a convict, he is yet able to dignify disgrace by the stupendous majesty of his genius, and commands the reverence even of the world, as to one of its sublimest benefactors. And the poet's stinging line—

"The greatest, wisest, meanest of mankind,"

pictures, only with a small excess of satire, the magnificence of ruin comprehended in the man.

Probably no one of mankind has raised himself to a higher

pitch of renown by the superlative attributes of genius displayed in his writings, than the great English dramatist; flowering out, nevertheless, into such eminence of glory, on a compost of fustian, buffoonery, and other vile stuff, which he so magnificently covers with splendour, and irradiates with beauty, that disgust itself is lost in the vehemence of praise. And so we shall find, almost universally, that the greatness of the world's great men is proved by the inborn qualities that tower above the ruins of weakness and shame in which they appear, and out of which, as solitary pillars and dismantled temples, they rise.

But we must look more directly into the contents of human nature, and the internal ruin by which they are displayed. And here you may notice, first of all, the sublime vehemence of the passions. What a creature must that be, who, out of mere hatred, or revenge, will deliberately take the life of a fellow man, and then despatch his own to avoid the ignominy of a public execution. Suppose there might be found some tiger that, for the mere bitterness of his grudge against some other whelp of his mother, springs upon him in his sleep and rends him in pieces, and then deliberately tears open his own throat to escape the vengeance of the family. No tiger of the desert is ever instigated by any so intense and terrible passion, that, for the sweetness of revenge, is willing afterwards to rush on death itself. This kind of frenzy plainly belongs to none but a creature immortal, an archangel ruined, in whose breast a fire of hell may burn high enough and deep enough to scorch down even reason and the innate love of life. Or take the passion of covetousness, generally regarded as one essentially mean and degraded. After all, how great a creature must that be who is goaded by a zeal of acquisition so restless, so self-sacrificing, so insatiable. The poor, gaunt miser, starving for want that he may keep the count of his gold—whom do we more naturally pity and despise? And yet he were even the greatest of heroes, if he could deny himself with so great patience, in a good and holy cause. How grand a gift that immortality, how deep those gulfs of want in the soul, that instigate a madness so desolating to character, a self-immolation so relentless, a niggard suffering so sublime! The same is true even of the licentious and gluttonous lusts and their loathsome results. No race of animals can shew the parallel of such vices; because they are none of them instigated by a nature so insatiable, so essentially great, in the magnificence of wants that find no good to satisfy their cravings. The ruin, we say, is beastly, but the beasts are clear of the comparison; it requires a mould vaster than theirs to burst the limits of nature in excesses so disgusting.

Consider, again, the wild mixtures of thought displayed both in the waking life and the dreams of mankind. How grand! how mean! how sudden the leap from one to the other! how inscrutable the succession! how defiant of orderly control! It is as if the soul were a thinking ruin; which it verily is. The angel and the demon life appear to be contending in it. The imagination revels in beauty exceeding all the beauty of things, wails in images dire and monstrous, wallows in murderous and base suggestions that shame our inward dignity; so that a great part of the study and a principal art of life is to keep our decency, by a wise selection from what we think, and a careful suppression of the remainder. A diseased and crazy mixture, such as represents a ruin, is the form of our inward experience. And yet, a ruin how magnificent, one which a buried Nineveh or a desolated Thebes can parallel only in the faintest degree; comprehending all that is purest, brightest, most divine, even that which is above the firmament itself; all that is worst, most sordid, meanest, most deformed.

Notice, also, the significance of remorse. How great a creature must that be that, looking down upon itself from some high summit in itself, some throne of truth and judgment which no devastation of order can reach, withers in relentless condemnation of itself, gnaws and chastises itself in the sense of what it is! Call it a ruin, as it plainly is, there rises out of the desolated wreck of its former splendour that which indicates and measures the sublimity of the original temple. The conscience stands erect, resisting all the ravages of violence and decay, and by this we distinguish the temple of God that was; a soul divinely gifted, made to be the abode of His Spirit, the vehicle of His power, the mirror of His glory. A creature of remorse is a divine creature of necessity, only it is the wreck of a divinity that was.

So again you may conceive the greatness of man by the ruin he makes, if you advert to the dissonance and obstinacy of his evil will. It is dissonant as being out of harmony with God and the world, and all beside in the soul itself—viz., the reason, the conscience, the wants, the hopes, and even the remembrances of the soul. How great a creature is it that, knowing God, can set itself off from God and resist Him, can make itself a unit, separate from all beings beside, and maintain a persistent rebellion even against its own convictions, fears, and aspirations. Like a Pharaoh, it sits on its Egyptian throne, quailing in darkness under the successive fears and judgments of life, relenting for the moment, then gathering itself up again to reassert the obstinacy of its pride, and die, it may be, in its evil. What a power is this, capable of a dominion how sublime, a work and sphere how transcendent! If sin is weak, if it is mean, little, selfish, and deformed—and we are ready to set humanity down as a low and paltry thing of nothing worth—how terrible and tragic in its evil grandeur does it appear, when we turn to look upon its defiance of God, and the desperate obstinacy of its warfare? Who, knowing the judgment of God, that they which commit such things are worthy of death, not only do the same, but have pleasure in them that do them. Or as we have it in the text—"There is no fear of God before their eyes." In one view there is fear enough, the soul is all its life long haunted by this fear, but there is a desperation of will that tramples fear and makes it as though it were not.

Consider, once more, the religious aspirations and capacities of religious attraction that are garnered up, and still live in the ruins of humanity. How plain it is, in all the most forward demonstrations of the race, that man is a creature for religion; a creature secretly allied to God himself, as the needle is to the pole, attracted toward God, aspiring consciously, or unconsciously, to the friendship and love of God. Neither is it true that, in his fallen state, he has no capacity left for religious affection, or attraction, till it is first new created in him. All his capacities of love and truth are in him still, only buried and stifled by the smouldering ruin in which he lies. There is a capacity in him still to be moved and drawn, to be charmed and melted by the divine love and beauty. The old affinity lives, though smothered in selfishness and lust, and even proves itself

in sorrowful evidence, when he bows himself down to a reptile
or an idol. He will do his most expensive works for religion.
There is a deep panting still in his bosom, however suppressed,
that cries inaudibly and sobs with secret longing after God.
Hence the sublime unhappiness of the race. There is a vast,
immortal want stirring on the world and forbidding it to rest.
In the cursing and bitterness, in the deceit of tongues, in the
poison of asps, in the swiftness to shed blood, in all the destruction and misery of the world's ruin, there is yet a vast, insatiate
hunger for the good, the true, the holy, the divine; and a great
part of the misery of the ruin is that it is so great a ruin—a desolation of that which cannot utterly perish, and still lives,
asserting its defrauded rights and reclaiming its lost glories.
And therefore it is that life becomes an experience to the race
so tragic in its character, so dark and wild, so bitter, so incapable of peace. The way of peace we cannot know, till we find
our peace, where our immortal aspirations place it, in the fulness and the friendly eternity of God.

Regarding man, then, as immersed in evil, a being in disorder,
a spiritual intelligence in a state of ruin, we derogate nothing
from his dignity. Small conception has any one of the dignity
of human nature, who conceives it only on the side of praise, or
as set off by the figments of a merely natural virtue. As little
could he apprehend the tragic sublimity of Hamlet, considered
only as an amiable son ingenuously hurt by the insult done his
father's name and honour. The character is great, not here, but
in its wildness and its tragic mystery; delicate and fierce, vin-
dictive and cool, shrewd and terrible, a reasonable and a reason-
ing madness, more than we can solve, all that we can feel. And
so it is that we discover the true majesty of human nature itself, in the tragic grandeur of its disorders, nowhere else. Nothing do we know of its measures, regarded in the smooth plausibilities and the respectable airs of good breeding and worldly
virtue. It is only as a lost being that man appears to be truly
great. Judge him by the ruin he makes, wander among the
shattered pillars and fallen towers of his majesty, behold the
immortal and eternal vestiges, study his passions, thoughts,
aspirations, woes; behold the destruction and misery that are
in his ways,—destruction how sublime, misery how deep, clung
to with how great pertinacity, and then say,—this is man, this

is the dignity of human nature. It will kindle no pride in you, stimulate no pompous conceit, but it will reveal a terror, discover a shame, speak a true conviction, and, it may be, draw forth a tear.

Having reached this natural limit of our subject, let us pause a moment, and look about us on some of the practical issues to which it is related.

It is getting to be a great hope of our time, that society is going to slide into something better, by a course of natural progress—by the advance of education, by great public reforms, by courses of self-culture and philanthropic practice. We have a kind of new gospel that corresponds ; a gospel which preaches not so much a faith in God's salvation as a faith in human nature ; an attenuated, moralising gospel that proposes development, not regeneration ; shewing men how to grow better, how to cultivate their amiable instincts, how to be rational in their own light, and govern themselves by their own power. Sometimes it is given as the true problem, how to reform the shape and reconstruct the style of their heads, and even this it is expected they will certainly be able to do ! Alas, that we are taken, or can be, with so great folly. How plain is it that no such gospel meets our want. What can it do for us but turn us away, more and more fatally, from that gospel of the Son of God, which is our only hope. Man as a ruin, going after development, and progress, and philanthropy, and social culture, and, by this fire-fly glimmer, to make a day of glory ! And this is the doctrine that proposes shortly to restore society, to settle the passion, regenerate the affection, reglorify the thought, fill the aspiration of a desiring and disjointed world ! As if any being but God had power to grapple with these human disorders ; as if man, or society, crazed and maddened by the demoniacal frenzy of sin, were going to rebuild the state of order, and reconstruct the shattered harmony of nature, by such kind of desultory counsel and unsteady application as it can manage to enforce in its own cause ; going to do this miracle by its science, its compacts, and self-executed reforms ! As soon will the desolations of Karnac gather up their fragments and reconstruct the proportions out of which they have fallen. No, it is not progress, not reforms that are wanted as any principal thing. Nothing meets our case, but to come unto God, and be medicated in Him ; to be born of God, and so, by His regenerative power, to be set in Heaven's own order. He alone can rebuild the ruin, He alone set up the glorious temple of the mind ; and those divine affinities in us that raven with immortal hunger—He alone can satisfy them in the bestowment of Himself.

And this brings me to speak of another point, where the subject unfolded carries an important application. The great difficulty with Christianity in our time is that, as a fact, or salvation, it is too great for belief. After all our supposed discoveries of dignity in human nature, we have commonly none but the meanest opinion of man. How can we imagine or believe that any such history as that of Jesus Christ is a fact, or that the infinite God has transacted any such wonder for man ? a being so far below His rational concern, or the range of His practical sympathy. God manifest in the flesh ! God in Christ reconciling the world unto Himself ! the birth of the manger ! the life of miracle ! the incarnate dying ! and the world darkening in funeral grief around the mighty Sufferer's cross !—it is extravagant, out of proportion, who can believe it ? Any one, I answer, who has not lost the magnitude of man. No work of God holds a juster proportion than this great mystery of godliness ; and if we did but understand the great mystery of ungodliness, we should think so. No man will ever have any difficulty in believing the work of Christ who has not lost the measures of humanity. But for this, no man will ever think it reason to deny His divinity, explain away His incarnation, or reject the mystery of His cross. To restore this tragic fall required a tragic salvation. Nor did ever any sinner who had come to himself, felt the bondage of his sin, trembled in the sense of his terrible disorders, groaned over the deep gulfs of want opened by his sin, struggled with himself to compose the bitter struggles of his nature, heaved in throes of anguish to emancipate himself —no such person, however deep in philosophy, or scepticism, ever thought, for one moment, that Christ was too great a Saviour. Oh, it was a divine Saviour, an almighty Saviour, coming out from God's eternity, that he wanted ! none but such was sufficient ! Him he could believe in, just because He was

great,—equal to the measures of his want, able to burst the
bondage of his sin. "For God so loved the world that He
gave His only-begotten Son, that whosoever believeth in Him
should not perish, but should have everlasting life." Oh, it is
the word of reason to his soul. He believes, and on this Rock,
as a rock of adequate salvation, he rests.

Once more, it is another and important use of the subject we
have here presented, that the magnitude and real importance of
the soul are discovered in it, as nowhere else. For it is not by
any computations of reason, but in your wild disorders, your
suppressed affinities for God, the distempers and storms of your
passions, and the magnificent chaos of your immortality, that
you will get the truest opinion of your consequence to yourselves. Just that which makes you most oblivious and blindest
to your own significance ought to make you most aware of it
and press you most earnestly to God. I know not how it is
that the soul appears under sin, all selfish as it is, to shrink and
grow small in its own sight. Perhaps it is due, in part, to the
consciousness we have, in sin, of moral littleness and meanness.
We commonly speak of it in figures of this kind; we call it low,
and weak, and degraded, and fall into the impression that these
words are real measures of our natural magnitude. Whereas,
in another sense, the sin we speak of is mighty, terrible, God-
defying, and triumphant. Let this thought come to you, my
friends, as well as the other; and if sin is morally little, let it be,
in power, mighty as it really is. The shadow by which most
convincingly your true height is measured, is that which is cast
athwart the abyss of your shame and spiritual ignominy. Just
here is it that you will get your most veritable impressions of
your immortality; even as you get your best impression of
armies, not by the count of numbers, but by the thunder-shock
of battle, and the carnage of the field when it is over. We try
all other methods, but in vain, to rouse in men's bosoms some
barely initial sense of their consequence to themselves, and get
some hold, in that manner, of the stupendous immortality
Christ recognises in them, and throws off His glory to redeem.
We take the guage of your power as a mind, shewing what this
power of mind has been able, in the explorations of matter, and
light, and air, of sea and land, and the distant fields of heaven,

to do. We display its inventions, recount its victories over
nature. We represent, as vividly as we can, and by computations as vast and far-reaching as we are master of, in our finite
arithmetic, the meaning of the word eternity. All in vain.
What are you still but the insect of some present hour, in which
you live and flutter and die? But here we take another method,
we call you to the battle-field of sin. We shew you the vestiges. This, we say, is man, the fallen principality. In these
tragic desolations of intelligence and genius, of passion, pride,
and sorrow, behold the import of his eternity. Be no mere
spectator, turn the glass we give you round upon yourself, look
into the ruin of your own conscious spirit, and see how much it
signifies, both that you are a sinner and a man. Here, within
the soul's gloomy chamber, the loosened passions rage and
chafe, impatient of their law; here huddle on the wild and desultory thoughts; here the imagination crowds in shapes of
glory and disgust, tokens both and mockeries of its own creative power, no longer in the keeping of reason; here sits
remorse scowling and biting her chain; here creep out the
fears, a meagre and pale multitude; here drives on the will in
his chariot of war; here lie trampled the great aspirations,
groaning in immortal thirst; here the blasted affections weeping out their life in silent injury; all that you see without,
in the wars, revenges, and the crazed religions of the world, is
faithfully represented in the appalling disorders of your own
spirit. And yet, despite all this, a fact which overtops and
crowns all other evidence, you are trying and contriving still to
be happy—a happy ruin! The eternal destiny is in you, and
you cannot break loose from it. With your farthing bribes
you try to hush your stupendous wants, with your single drops,
(drops of gall and not of water,) to fill the ocean of your immortal aspirations. You call on destruction to help you, and
misery to give you comfort, and complain that destruction and
misery are still in all your ways. Oh, this great and mighty soul,
were it something less, you might find what to do with it; charm
it with the jingle of a golden toy, house it in a safe with ledgers
and stocks, take it about on journeys to see and be seen! Anything would please it and bring it content. But it is the god
like soul, capable of rest in nothing but God; able to be filled
and satisfied with nothing but His fulness and the confidence

of His friendship. What man that lives in sin can know it, or conceive it? who believe what it is?

O thou Prince of Life! come in Thy great salvation to these blinded and lost men, and lay Thy piercing question to their ear—"What shall it profit a man to gain the whole world and lose his own soul?" Breathe, oh, breathe on these majestic ruins, and rouse to life again, though it be but for one hour, the forgotten sense of their eternity—their lost eternity.

Even so, your lost eternity. The great salvation coming, then, is not too great; nought else, or less could suffice. For if there be any truth that can fitly appal you, rive you with conviction, drive you home to God, dissolve you in tears of repentance, it is here, when you discover yourself and your terrible misdoings, in the ruins of your desolated majesty. In these awful and scarred vestiges, too, what type is given you of that other and final ruin, of which Christ so kindly and faithfully warned you, when, describing the house you are building on these treacherous sands, He shewed the fatal storm beating vehemently against it, with only this one issue possible—And immediately it fell; and the ruin of that house was great.

III.

THE HUNGER OF THE SOUL.

LUKE xv. 17—"*And when he came to himself, he said, How many hired servants of my father's have bread enough and to spare, and I perish with hunger!*"

THIS gentleman's son that was, and is now a swine-herd, brings his meditation to a most natural and fit conclusion. His low occupation, and the husks on which he has been feeding to save his life, recall his father's house, and the hired servants there that have bread enough and to spare, and, no longer able to contain himself, he cries, in bitter desolation, "I perish with hunger." And so, in this story of the prodigal, Christ teaches all men their hunger, by means of that on which they feed, and the necessary baseness of their sin, by the lowness of the objects to which they descend for their life.

The swine, according to Jewish opinion, is an unclean animal, not to be eaten as food, and therefore is not raised, except by those idolaters and men of no religion who live as outcasts in their country. Hence it is looked upon as the lowest and most abject of all occupations to be a swine-herd. He is the disgust of all men, an unclean character, who is, among other men, what the swine is among other animals. He may not enter the temple, or even come near it.

By the husks on which the prodigal is said, in his hunger, to have fed himself, we are not to understand exactly what is meant by the English word *husks*, but a certain fruit, the fruit of the carob tree, which grows in pods, and has a mealy and sweet taste. It is described by Galen as a "woody kind of food, creating bile, and hard of digestion;" useful, as acorns are with us, in the feeding of swine, and sometimes eaten by the poorer sort of men, to escape starvation. Still it can work no injury, since this kind of fruit is unknown to us, to retain the word *husks;* a word that comes nearer producing the true impression of the parable, which is the principal thing, than any other which might be substituted.

The important thing to be noted, as regards my present object, is the prodigal's hunger. About this central point, or fact, all the other incidents of the parable are gathered. And by this wretched figure of destitution, the Saviour of the world represents man under sin; he is one who forsakes the life of duty and religion, to go after earthly things. He is, therefore, reduced to the lowest condition of want, or spiritual hunger. His food is not the proper food of a man, but of a swine rather. A highborn creature, as being in God's image, he descends to occupations that are unclean, and feeds his starving nature on that which belongs only to a reprobate, or unclean class of animals. In this lot of deep debasement and bitter privation, there is no language in which he may so naturally vent his misery as when he cries, "I perish with hunger!"

What I propose, then, for our meditation, is the truth here expressed, *that a life separated from God is a life of bitter hunger, or even of spiritual starvation.*

My object will be, not so much to prove this truth as to make it apparent, or visible, as a real fact, by means of appropriate illustrations. But, in order to this, it will be necessary,

I. To exhibit the true grounds of the fact stated; for, as we discover how and for what reasons the life of sin must be a life of hunger, we shall see the more readily and clearly the force of those illustrations by which the fact is exhibited.

The great principle that underlies the whole subject and all the facts pertaining to it is, *that the soul is a creature that wants food, in order to its satisfaction, as truly as the body.* No principle is more certain, and yet there is none so generally overlooked, or hidden from the sight of men.

Of course it is not meant, when the soul is said to be a creature wanting food, that it receives by a literal mastication, and has a palate to be gratified in what it receives. I only mean to universalise the great truth that pertains to all vital creatures and organs—viz., that they differ from all dead substances, stones for example, in the fact that they subsist in a healthy state of vital energy and development, by receiving, appropriating, or feeding upon something out of themselves. Every tree and plant is, in this view, a feeding creature, and grows by that which feeds it; that, viz., which it derives from the air and clouds, from the soil, and the changing influence of day and night. In this larger sense, every organ of the body is a receptive and feeding organ. Sometimes it is fed by other organs, which prepare and furnish to it the food that is needful for its growth and subsistence. In this manner even the bones are feeding creatures. So the senses are fed by the elements appropriate, the ear by sounds, the eye by the light. And so true is this, that an eye shut up in total darkness, and probably an ear cut off from all sound, will finally die, or become an exterminated sense; even as that whole tribe of fishes discovered in the cave are found to have no eyes. Now what I mean to say is, that all these vital creatures, vegetable and animal, are only so many types of the soul, which is the highest, purest form of vital being we know; and that, as they all subsist by feeding on something not in themselves, and die for hunger without that food, just so the soul is a creature wanting food, and fevering itself in bitter hunger when that food is denied.

Hence it is that, in that most unnatural of all modes of punishment, regarded unaccountably with so great favour by many, the punishment I mean of absolute solitary confinement, a very large proportion of the prisoners become idiotic. Cut off from all the living sights and sounds, the faces of friends, the voices of social interchange, and the works and interests of life; shut away thus from all that enters into feeling, or quickens intelligence, or exercises judgment, or nerves the will to action, the soul has no longer anything to feed upon, and, for want of food, it dies—dies into blank idiocy.

Neither let this want of food in souls be regarded as a merely philosophic truth, or discovery. It is a truth so natural to the feeling of mankind, that it breaks into language every hour, and appears and reappears in the Scripture, in so many forms, that I cannot stay to enumerate half of them. Job brings it forward, by a direct and simple comparison, when he says, "For the ear trieth words, as the mouth tasteth meat;" where he means by the ear, you perceive, not the outward but the inward ear of the understanding. So the Psalmist says, "My soul shall be satisfied as with marrow and fatness." And so also the prophet, beholding his apostate countrymen dying for hunger and thirst in their

THE HUNGER OF THE SOUL.

sins, calls to them, saying, "Ho, every one that thirsteth, come ye to the waters; and he that hath no money, come ye, buy, and eat. Wherefore do ye spend money for that which is not bread? and your labour for that which satisfieth not? hearken diligently unto me, and eat ye that which is good, and let your soul delight itself in fatness." In the same way, an apostle speaks of them that have tasted the good word of God, and the powers of the world to come; and another, of them that have tasted that the Lord is gracious, and therefore desire the sincere milk of the Word, that they may grow thereby.

True, these are all figures of speech, transferred from the feeding of the body to that of the soul. But they are transferred because they have a fitness to be transferred. The analogy of the soul is so close to that of the body, that it speaks of its hunger, its food, its fulness, and growth, and fatness, under the images it derives from the body.

Hence you will observe that our blessed Lord appears to have always the feeling that He has come down into a realm of hungry, famishing souls. You see this in the parable of the prodigal son, and that of the feast or supper. Hence, also, that very remarkable discourse in the sixth chapter of John, where He declares Himself as the living bread that came down from heaven—that a man may eat thereof and not die. "Whoso eateth my flesh, and drinketh my blood, hath eternal life. My flesh is meat indeed, and my blood is drink indeed. He that eateth my flesh, and drinketh my blood, dwelleth in me and I in him. As the living Father hath sent me, and I live by the Father: so he that eateth me, even he shall live by me."

Many, I believe, are not able to read this language without a kind of revolted feeling. What can it mean, that they are to live by eating Christ? There is no difficulty, I answer, in the language, save in getting at the rational and true sense of the figure employed, and, when this is done, it becomes language strikingly significant. Suppose it were said that a tree can live, only as it eats the air and the light; the meaning, of course, would not be that it takes these elements by mastication, but that it has such a nature that it takes them into itself and gets a nutriment of growth out of them, and that without them, so appropriated, it would die. So, when Christ says, I will manifest myself unto him—we will come and make our abode with him, He means that He will be so received and appropriated by

D

the soul as to be its light, the breathing of its life, that which feeds it internally. He assumes, in all that He says, that as the tree has a nature requiring to be fed by air and light, so the soul has a nature inherently related to God the Infinite Spirit. Hence the deep hunger of the world in sin; because the sin is its attempt to live without God, and apart from God.

Accordingly, it is the grand endeavour of the gospel to communicate God to men. They have undertaken to live without Him, and do not see that they are starving in the bitterness of their experiment. It is not, as with bodily hunger, where they have a sure instinct compelling them to seek their food; but they go after the husks, and would fain be filled with these, not even so much as conceiving what is their real want or how it comes. For it is a remarkable fact that so few men, living in the flesh, have any conception that God is the necessary supply and nutriment of their spiritual nature, without which they famish and die. It has an extravagant sound; when they hear it, they do not believe it. How can it be that they have any such high relation to the eternal God, or He to them? It is as if the tree were to say, What can I, a mere trunk of wood, all dark and solid within, standing fast in my rod of ground—what can I have to do with the free, moving air, and the boundless sea of light that fills the world? And yet it is a nature made to feed on these, taking them into its body to supply, and vitalise, and colour every fibre of its substance. Just so it is that every finite spirit is inherently related to the Infinite, in Him to live, and move, and have its being. It wants the knowledge of God, the society of God, the approbation of God, the internal manifestation of God, a consciousness lighted up by His presence, to receive of His fulness, to be strong in His might, to rest in His love, and be centred everlastingly in His glory. Apart from Him, it is an incomplete creature, a poor, blank fragment of existence, hungry, dry, and cold. And still, alas! it cannot think so. Therefore Christ comes into the world to incarnate the Divine nature, otherwise unrecognised, before it; so to reveal God to its knowledge, enter Him into its faith and feeling, make Him its living bread, the food of its eternity. Therefore of His fulness we are called to feed, receiving of Him freely grace for grace. When He is received, He restores the consciousness of God, fills the soul with the Divine

light, and sets it in that connexion with God which is life—
eternal life.

Holding this view of the inherent relation between created
souls and God as their nourishing principle, we pass—

II. To a consideration of the necessary hunger of a state of
sin, and the tokens by which it is indicated. A hungry herd of
animals, waiting for the time of their feeding, do not shew their
hunger more convincingly, by their impatient cries, and eager
looks and motions, than the human race do theirs, in the works,
and ways, and tempers of their selfish life.

I can only point you to a few of these demonstrations. And
a very impressive and remarkable one you have in this—viz.,
the common endeavour to make the body receive double, so as
to satisfy both itself and the soul, too, with its pleasures. The
effort is, how continually, to stimulate the body by delicacies,
and condiments, and sparkling bowls, and licentious pleasures
of all kinds, and so to make the body do double service. Hence,
too, the drunkenness, and high feasting, and other vices of
excess. The animals have no such vices, because they have no
hunger save simply that of the body; but man has a hunger
also of the mind or soul, when separated from God by his sin,
and therefore he must somehow try to pacify that. And he
does it by a work of double feeding put upon the body. We
call it sensuality. But the body asks not for it. The body is
satisfied by simply that which allows it to grow and maintain
its vigour. It is the unsatisfied, hungry mind that flies to the
body for some stimulus of sensation, compelling it to devour so
many more of the husks, or carobs, as will feed the hungry
prodigal within. Thus it is that so many dissipated youths are
seen plunging into pleasures of excess—midnight feastings and
surfeitings, debaucheries of lust and impiety; it is because they
are hungry, because their soul, separated from God and the true
bread of life in Him, aches for the hunger it suffers. And so it
is the world over; men are hungry everywhere, and they compel the body to make a swine's heaven for the comfort of the
godlike soul.

Again, we see the hunger of sin by the immense number of
drudges there are in the world. It makes little difference generally, whether men are poor or rich. Some terrible hunger is

upon them, and it drives them madly forward, through burdens, and sacrifices, and toils that would be rank oppression put upon a slave. It is not simply that they are industrious—industry is a virtue—but they are drudges instigated by such a passion of want that they are wholly unable to moderate their plans by any terms of reason.

You see, too, what indicates the uneasiness of this hunger, in the constant shifting of their plans and arrangements. Even the more constant, stable characters, such as hold most firmly to their pursuits, are yet seen to be uneasy in them; comforting their uneasiness by one change or another; a new kind of crop, a new partner, a new stand, a wheeling about of counters, or a change of shelves, or a different way of transportation, or another place of banking,—nothing is ever quite right, because they are too uneasy in their hunger to be quiet long in anything.

Others shew their hunger by their closeness; the very look of their face is hungry, the gripe of their hand is hungry, the answer of their charity is the answer of hunger, the prices they pay for service are the grudged allowance of a heart that is pinched by its own stringent destitution.

Observe, again, the quarrels of debt and credit, the false weights, the fradulent charges, the habitual lies of false recom-.mendation, the arts, stratagems, oppressions of trade—how hungry do they look.

Notice, again, how men contrive, in one way or another, to get, if possible, some food of content for the soul that has a finer and more fit quality than the swine's food with which they so often overtask the body—honour, power, admiration, flattery, society, literary accomplishments. Works of genius are stimulated, how often, by a kind of superlative hunger. And the same is true even of the virtues that connect a repute of moderation, such as temperance, frugality, plainness, stoical superiority to suffering—a kind of subtle hunger for some consciousness of good is the secret root on which they grow.

There is no end to the diverse acts men practise to get some food for their soul; and to whatever course they turn themselves, you will see as clearly as possible that they are hungry. Nay, they say it themselves. What sad bewailings do you hear from them, calling the world ashes, wondering at the poverty of existence, fretting at the courses of Providence, and blaming their harshness, raging profanely against God's appointments, and venting their impatience with life in curses on its emptiness. All this, you understand, is the hunger they are in. Feeding on carobs only, as they do, what shall we expect but to see them feed impatiently?

This, also, you will notice as a striking evidence that, however well they succeed in the providing of earthly things, they are never satisfied. They say they are not, have it for a proverb that no man is, or can be. How can they be satisfied with lands, or money, or honour, or any finite good, when their hunger is infinite, reaching after God and the fulness of His infinite life—God, who is the object of their intelligence, their love, their hope, their worship; the complement of their weakness, the crown of their glory, the sublimity of their rest for ever. Such kind of hunger manifestly could not be satisfied with any finite good, and therefore it never is. Look, also, at some of the more internal and experimental evidences supplied by consciousness.

Consider, for example, the vice of envy, and the general propenseness of men to be in it. There are very few persons, however generous in their dispositions, who are not sometimes bitten by this very subtle and bitter sin. And the root of this misery is hunger of soul. Envy is only a malignant, selfish hunger, casting its evil eye on the elevation or supposed happiness of others. The bitterness of it is not simply that it really wants what others have, but that the soul, gnawed by a deep spiritual hunger which it thinks not of, is so profoundly embittered, that every kind of good it looks upon rasps it with a feeling of torment, and rouses a degree of impatience and ill-nature out of all terms of reason. It is the feeling of a prodigal or spendthrift, who, after he has spent all, vents his ill-nature on everybody but himself, and hates the good possessed by others because it is not his own. Oh, how many human souls are gnawed through and through all their lives long by this devilish hunger—envy!

Remorse differs from envy only in the fact that the soul here turns upon itself, just as they say it is the principal distress of extreme bodily hunger that the organs of digestion begin themselves to be gnawed and digested, in place of the food on which the digestive power is accustomed to spend its energy. Remorse,

in the same way, is a moral hunger of the soul. It is the bitter
wail of a famished immortality. It is your conscience lashing
your perverse will; your defrauded, hungry love weeping its
dry, pitchy tears on the desert your evil life has made for it.
It is your whole spiritual nature, famished by sin, muttering
wrathfully, and growling like a caged lion at the bars which shut
him up to himself. And as bodily hunger sometimes causes the
starving man to see devils in his ravings, so this hunger of
remorse fills the soul with angry demons and ministers of vengeance waiting to execute judgment. Sleep vanishes not seldom,
or comes only in dreams that scare the sleeper. The day lags
heavily. The look is on the ground. The walk is apart and
silent, and the man carries a load under which he stoops, a load
of selfish regret and worldly sorrow that worketh death.

Or, if we speak of care—the corroding, weary, ever-multiplying
care of which you are every day complaining—what, again, is
this but your hunger? We like to speak, however, not of care,
but, in the plural, of cares; for these, we imagine, are outside of
us, in things, not in ourselves. But these cares are all in ourselves, and of ourselves, and not in things at all—things are not
cares; cares are only cravings of that immortal hunger which
the swine's food of earthly things cannot satisfy. You say in
them all, What shall I do, for I perish with hunger? You look
up from the bitter husks or carobs, and say, I must have more
and better ; and these more and better things are your cares.
The very word *care* meant originally *want;* and these cares are
nothing but the wants of a hungry soul misnamed.

Sometimes, again, your feeling takes the turn of disgust. You
are disgusted with yourself and life, and all the employments
and objects of your pursuit—disgusted even with your pleasures.
How insipid, and dry, and foolish they appear. An air of distaste settles on all objects. They are all husks, acorns—food for
swine and not for men. Just so it is in the starvation of the
body. It creates a fever, and in that fever appetite dies. And
this, accordingly, is the rankest proof of hunger in the soul, that
it has run itself down to the starvation point of universal disgust. Life is cheap. It seems a very dull and mean thing to
live—as to live a prodigal and swine-herd's life it certainly is.
Sometimes, too, your disgust turns upon your own character and
feeling—your ambition, your pride, your very thoughts—and you

ache for the mortification that comes upon you. My ambition
—how low it creeps. My pride—what have I, or am I to be
proud of? My very thoughts are all trailing in the dust, and
dust is dry. O God! is it this to be a man?

I might speak also of your perpetual irritations, your fits of
anger, your animosities, your jealousies, your gloomy hypochon-
driac fears. These all, at bottom, are the disturbances of hunger
in the soul. How certainly is the child irritable when it is
hungry. Even the placidity of infancy vanishes when the body
is ravening for food. So it is with man. He is irritable, flies
to fits of passion, loses self-government, simply because the
placid state of satisfaction is wanting in his higher nature. He
is out of rest because of his immortal hunger. Three-quarters
of the ill-nature of the world is caused by the fact, that the
soul without God is empty, and so out of rest. We charge it,
more often than justice requires, to some fault of temperament;
but there is no temperament that would not be quieted and
evened by the fulness of God.

Now, the Spirit of God will sometimes shew you, in an
unwonted manner, the secret of these troubles, for He is the
interpreter of the soul's hunger. He comes to it whispering
inwardly the awful secret of its pains—"without God and
without hope in the world." He reminds the prodigal of his
bad history. He bids the swine-herd look up from his sensual
objects and works, and remember his home and his Father;
tells him of a great supper prepared, and that all things are now
ready, and bids him come. Conscious of the deep poverty he
is in; conscious of that immortal being whose deep wants have
been so long denied—wants that can be satisfied only by the
essential, eternal participation of the fulness of God—he hears
a gentle voice of love saying, "I am the bread of life. I am the
living bread that came down from heaven: if any man eat of
this bread, he shall live." Are there none of you to whom this
voice is calling now?

I will not pursue these illustrations further. Would that all
my hearers could but open their minds to the lesson they teach!
I know almost no subject or truth that will explain so many
things in the uneasy demonstrations of mankind; or that to any
thoughtful person, living without God, will resolve so many

mysteries concerning himself. Granting simply the fact that God is the want of the soul or created intelligence, what can it be, separated from God, but an element of uneasiness and bitter disturbance? If the soul, as a vital and organic nature, requires this Divine food or nutriment to sustain it, and in this highest, vastest want gets no supply, what else can you need to account for the unrest and the otherwise inexplicable frustration of your experience? And yet how many of you, goaded by this torment all your lives, do not understand it? You go after this or that objective circumstantial good, thrust on, as in some kind of madness, by the terrible impulsion of your hungry immortality, confessing all the time that you fail, even when in form you succeed, and shewing, by your demonstrations, that your objects, whether gained or lost, have no relation to your want. But your understandings are holden from any true discovery of your sin. It is as if you were under some dispossession, even as the Saviour intimates in His parable. He looks upon the prodigal described as one that has lost his reckoning or his reason; and when he discovers the secret of his misery, speaks of him as just then having come to himself. Could you come thus to yourselves, how quickly would you cease from your husks and return to your Father! How absurd the folly, then, of any attempt to satisfy or quiet your hunger by any inferior, merely external good!

O ye prodigals!—young and old, prodigals of all names and degrees—ye that have tasted the good word of God and the powers of the world to come, and have fallen away—ye that have always lived in the minding of earthly things—how clear is it here that no swine's food, no husks of money, pleasure, show, ambition, can feed you; that you have a divine part which none, or all of these dry carobs of sin can feed, which nothing can supply and satisfy but God himself!

And what should be a discovery more welcome than this? In what are you more ennobled, than in the fact that you are related thus, inherently, to God ; having a nature so high, wants so deep and vast, that only He can feed them, and not even He by any bestowment which does not include the bestowment of Himself? Would you willingly exterminate this want of your being, and so be rid eternally of this hunger? That would be to cease from being a man and to become a worm;

and even that worm, remembering what it was, would be a worm gnawing itself with eternal regrets. No; this torment that you feel is the torment of your greatness. It compliments you more, even by its cravings and its shameful humiliations, than all most subtle flatteries and highest applauses. Nay, there is nothing in which God himself exalts you more than by His own expostulation when He says—"Wherefore do ye spend money for that which is not bread? and your labour for that which satisfieth not? hearken diligently unto me, and eat ye that which is good. Incline your ear, and come unto me : hear, and your soul shall live." Why should we humble ourselves to so many things that are ashes, and call them bread—doubling our bodily pleasures in vices that take hold on hell—chasing after gains with cancerous appetite—torturing our invention to find some opiate of society, applause, or show that will quiet and content our unrest? All in vain. O ye starving minds! hearken for one hour to this, and turn yourselves to it as your misery points you. God—God—God alone is the true food. Ask it thus of God to give you the food that is convenient for you, and He gives you Himself. And that is bread—bread of life —bread of eternity! Take it for your true supply, and you hunger no more.

THE REASON OF FAITH.

JOHN vi. 36—"*But I said unto you, That ye also have seen me, and believe not.*"

IT is the grand distinction of Christianity, that by which it is separated from all philosophies and schemes of mere ethics, that it makes its appeal to faith, and upon that, as a fundamental condition, rests the promise of salvation. It is called the word of faith, the disciples are distinguished as believers, and Christ is published as the Saviour of them that believe.

But precisely this, which is the boast of apostles, is the scandal and offence of men. Were the word anything but a word of faith; a word of rhetoric, or of reason, or of absolute philosophy, or of ethics, or of grammar and lexicography, they could more easily accept it; but finding it instead a word of faith, they reject and scorn it. As if there were some merit, or could be some dignity in faith! What is it but an arbitrary condition, imposed to humble our self-respect, or trample our proper intelligence? For what is there to value or praise, say they, in the mere belief of anything? If we hold any truth by our reason, or by some act of perception, or by the shewing of sufficient evidence, what need of holding it by faith? If we undertake to hold it without such evidence, what is our belief in it but a surrender of our proper intelligence?

This kind of logic, so common as even to be the cant of our times, has all its plausibility in its own defect of insight, and nothing is wanting, in any case, to its complete refutation, but simply a due understanding of what faith is, and what the office it fills. In this view, I propose a discourse on the *reason of faith;* or to shew *how it is that we, as intelligent beings, are called to believe; and how, as sinners, we can, in the nature of things, be saved only as we believe.*

I select the particular passage, just cited, for my text, simply because it sets us at the point where seeing and believing are brought together; expecting to get some advantage, as regards the illustration of my subject, from the mutual reference of one to the other, as held in such proximity. In this verse, (the 36th,) they are brought together as not being united—"ye have seen me, and believe not." Shortly after, (in the 40th verse,) they are brought together as being, or to be united—"every one that seeth the Son, and believeth on Him."

Now, the first thing we observe, for it stands on the face of the language, is, that faith is not sight, but something different; so different that we may see and not believe. The next thing is, that sight does not, in the Scripture view, exclude faith, or supersede the necessity of it, as the common cavil supposes; for, after sight, faith is expected. And still, a third point is, that sight is supposed even to furnish a ground for faith, making it obligatory, and, where it is not yielded, increasing the guilt of the subject; which appears, both in the complaint of one verse, and the requirement of the other.

Thus much in regard to the particular case of the persons addressed; for they were such as had themselves seen Christ, witnessed His miracles, heard His teachings, and watched the progress of His ministry. In that respect, our case is different. We get by historic evidences what they got by their senses. The attestations we have are even more reliable evidences, I think, than those of sight; but they bring us to exactly the same point, viz., a settled impression of fact. That such a being lived they saw with their eyes, and we are satisfied that He lived by other evidences addressing our judging faculty, as sight addressed theirs. We take their case, accordingly, as the case proposed, and shape our argument to it.

Suppose, then, that you had lived as a contemporary in the days of Christ; that you had been privy to the dialogue between the angel and Mary, and also to all the intercourse of Mary and Elizabeth; that you had heard the song of the angels at the Nativity, and seen their shining forms in the sky; that you were entirely familiar with the youth of Jesus, were present at His baptism, saw Him begin His ministry, heard all His discourses, witnessed all His miracles, stood by His cross in the hour of His passion; that you saw Him, heard Him, ate with Him, touched

Him after His resurrection, and finally beheld His ascension from Olivet. You have had, in other words, a complete sense-view of Him, from His first breath onward. What now does all this signify to you?

Possibly much, possibly nothing. If received without any kind of faith, absolutely nothing; if with two kinds of faith, which are universally practised, it signifies the greatest fact of history; if with a third, equally rational and distinctively Christian, it signifies a new life in the soul, and eternal salvation.

Let us, in the first place, look at these two kinds of faith which are universally practised; for if faith is, in the nature of things, absurd or unintelligent, we shall be as likely to discover the fact here as anywhere. And we may discover, possibly, that the very persons who discard faith, as an offence to intelligence, are not even able to do the commonest acts of intelligence without it.

We begin, then, with the case of sight, or perception by sight. It has been, as some of you know, a great, or even principal question with our philosophers for the last hundred years, and these are commonly the people most ready to complain of faith, how it is that we perceive objects. The question was raised by Berkeley's denial that we see them at all, which, though it convinced nobody, puzzled everybody. He said, for example, that the persons who saw Christ did not really see Him, they had only certain pictures cast in the back of the eye; which pictures, he maintained, were mere subjective impressions, nothing more; that, by the supposition, spectators are never at the objects, but only at the images, which are all, intellectually speaking, they know anything about. If they take it as a fact, that they see real objects, they do it by a naked act of assumption, and, for aught that appears, impose upon themselves. The question, accordingly, has been, not whether real objects are perceived, for that is not often questioned now, but how we can imagine them to be? how, in other words, it is that we bridge the gulf between sensations and their objects? how it is that, having a tree-picture or a star-picture in the back of the eye, we make it to be a tree, really existing on some distant hill, or a real star, filling its measurable space many hundred millions of miles distant? Some deny the possibility of any solution; reducing even sight itself, and all that we call evidence in it, to a mystery for ever transcending intelligence. The best solutions agree virtually in this—they conceive the soul to be such a creature that, when it has these forms in the eye, it takes them, as it were, instinctively, to be more than forms—viz., objects perceived; which is the same as to say that we complete sensation itself, or issue it in perception, by assigning reality ourselves to the distant object. And what is this, but to say that we do it by a kind of sense-faith contributed from ourselves? In our very seeing we see by faith, and, without the faith, we should only take in impressions to remain as last things in the brain. Hence, perhaps, the word *perception*, a *through-taking*, because we have taken hold of objects through distances, and so have bridged the gulf between us and reality. Is, then, sight itself unintelligent, because it includes an act of faith? Or if we believe in realities, and have them by believing, would it be wiser and more rational to let alone realities and live in figures and phantasms painted on the retina of our eyes?

But there is another kind of faith, less subtle than this, which also is universally practised, and admitted universally to be intelligent. It is that kind of faith which, after sensation is past, or perception is completed, assigns truth to the things seen, and takes them to be sound historic verities. Thus, after Christ had been seen in all the facts of His life, it became a distinct question what to make of the facts—whether possibly there could have been some conspiracy in the miracles, some collusion or acting in the parts of Mary and her Son, some self-imposition or hallucination that will account for His opinions of Himself and the remarkable pretensions He put forth?—whether, possibly, there was any mistake in the senses, or any sleight-of-hand by which they were imposed upon? Before, the difficulty was natural, and related to the laws of sensation. Here it is moral, and respects the verity or integrity of the agents. For it is a remarkable fact that the mere seeing of any wonder never concludes the mind of the spectator. How many, for example, are testifying, in our time, that they have seen, with their own eyes, the most fantastic and extravagant wonders wrought by the modern necromancy; and yet they very commonly conclude by saying, that they know not what to make of them, evidently doubting whether, after all, the sleight-of-hand tricks of jugglery, ventriloquism, and magic, and the sometimes wondrous cunning of a lying character, will not account for all they saw. These doubts are not the ingenious doubts of philosophy, but the practical misgivings, questions, and withholding of good sense. And here, again, we perceive, as before, that the mere seeing of Christ concludes nothing in the spectator, as regards His verity. He does not stand before the mind as a necessary truth of arithmetic or geometry; there the seeing ends debate, the mind is *ipso facto* concluded, and there is no room for faith, either to be given or withholden. As the philosopher doubted whether the objects seen had any real existence out of him, so the practical spectator doubts, after all Christ's wonders, whether everything was genuine, and the Christ who lived just such a being as He seemed to be. Probably the evidence, to one who saw, was as perfect as it could be; but if we could imagine it to be increased in quantity and power a thousandfold, remaining the same in kind, the mere seeing would conclude nothing. All you could say, in such a case, would be that a given impression has been made; but that impression is practically naught, till an act of intellectual assent, or credence, is added on your part, which act of assent is also another kind of faith. If God were to burn Himself into souls by lenses bigger than worlds, all you could say would be that so much impression is made, which impression is no historic verity to the mind, till the mind assents, on its part, and concludes *itself* upon the impression. Then the impression becomes to it a real and historic fact, a sentence of credit passed.

We now come to the Christian, or third kind of faith, with some advantages already gained. Indeed, the argument against faith, as an offence to reason, or as being insignificant where there is evidence, and absurd where there is not, is already quite ended. We discover, in fact, two degrees or kinds of faith, going before and typifying and commending to our respect the higher faith that is to come after, as a faith of salvation. We discover, also, that we cannot even do the commonest acts of intelligence without some kind of faith. First, we complete an act of perception only by a kind of sense-faith, moving from ourselves, and not from the objects perceived. Next, we pass on to the historic verity, the moral genuineness of what we see, and our act of credit, so passed, is also a kind of faith moving from us, and is something over and above all the impressions we have received. A third faith remains that is just as intelligent, and, in fact, is only more intelligent than the others, because it carries their results forward into the true uses.

This, distinctively, is the Scripture faith, the faith of salvation, the believing unto life eternal. It begins just where the other and last-named faith ended. That decided the greatest fact of history—viz., that Christ actually *was*, according to all His demonstrations. It passed on the genuine truth of those demonstrations, and set them as accredited to the account of history. Let everything stop at that point, and we only have a Christ, just as we have a Gautamozin, or a Sardanapalus. The Christian facts are stored in history, and are scarcely more significant to us, than if they were stored in the moon. What is wanted, just here, in the case of Christ, and what also is justified and even required by the facts of His life, is a faith that goes beyond the mere evidence of propositions, or propositional verities about Christ—viz., the faith of a *transaction;* and this faith is Christian faith. *It is the act of trust by which one being, a sinner, commits himself to another being, a Saviour.* It is not mind dealing with notions, or notional truths. It is what cannot be a proposition at all. But it is being trusting itself to being, and so becoming other and different, by a relation wholly transactional.

If a man comes to a banker with a letter of credit from some other banker, that letter may be read and seen to be a real letter. The signature also may be approved, and the credit of the drawing party honoured by the other, as being wholly reliable. So far what is done is merely opinionative or notional, and there is no transactional faith. And yet there is a good preparation for this; just that is done which makes it intelligent. When the receiving party, therefore, accepts the letter, and intrusts himself actually to the drawing party in so much money, there is the real act of faith, an act which answers to the operative, or transactional faith of a disciple.

Another and perhaps better illustration may be taken from the patient or sick person as related to his physician. He sends for a physician, just because he has been led to have a certain favourable opinion of his faithfulness and capacity. But the suffering him to feel his pulse, investigate his symptoms, and tell the diagnosis of his disease, imports nothing. It is only the committing of his being and life to this other being, consenting to receive and take his medicines, that imports a real faith, the faith of a transaction.

In the same manner Christian faith is the faith of a transaction. It is not the committing of one's thought, in assent to any proposition, but the trusting of one's being to a being, there to be rested, kept, guided, moulded, governed, and possessed for ever.

In this faith many things are presupposed, many included; and, after it, many will follow.

Everything is *presupposed* that makes the act intelligent and rational. That Christ actually lived and was what He declared Himself to be. That He was no other than the incarnate Word of the Father. That He came into the world to recover and redeem it. That He is able to do it; able to forgive, regenerate, justify, and set in eternal peace with God; and that all we see, in His passion, is a true revelation of God's feeling to the world.

There was also a certain antecedent improbability of any such holy visitation, or regenerative grace, which has to be liquidated or cleared, before the supposed faith can be transacted. We live in a state under sin, where causes are running against us, or running destructively in us. We have also a certain scientific respect to causes, and expect them to continue. But Christ comes into the world as one not under the scheme of causes. He declares that He is not of the world, but is from above. He undertakes to verify His claim by His miracles, and His miracles by His transcendent character. Assuming all the attributes of a power supernatural, He declares that He can take us out of nature and deliver us from the bad causes loosened by our sin. Now that He really is such a being, having such a power supernatural, able thus to save unto the uttermost, we are to have accredited, before we can trust ourselves to Him.

But this will be less difficult, because we are urged by such a sense of bondage under sin, and have such loads of conscious want, brokenness, and helplessness upon us. Besides, if we look again into our disorders, we find that they are themselves abnormal disturbances only, by our sin, of the pure and orderly harmony of causes; so that Christ, in restoring us, does not break up, but only recomposes the true order of nature. Inasmuch, therefore, as our salvation, or deliverance from evil, implies a restoration, and not any breach of nature, the incredible thing appears to be already done by sin itself, and the credible, the restoration only, remains.

Having now all this previous matter cleared, we come to the transactional faith itself. We commit ourselves to the Lord Jesus by an act of total and eternal trust, which is our faith. The act is intelligent, because it is intelligently prepared. It is not absurd, as being something more than evidence. It is not superseded by evidence. It is like the banker's acceptance, and the patient's taking of medicine, a transactional faith that follows evidence.

The matters *included in* this act, for of these we will now speak, are the surrender of our mere self-care, the ceasing to live from our own point of separated will, a complete admission of the mind of Christ, a consenting, practically, to be modulated by His motives and aims, and to live, as it were, infolded in His Spirit. It is committing one's character wholly to the living character of Jesus, so that every willing and working and sentiment shall be pliant to His superior mind and spirit; just as a man, trusting himself to some superior man, in a total and complete confidence, allows that other to flow down upon him, assimilate him, and, as far as he may, with a superiority so slight, conform him to the subject of his trust. Only there is, in the faith of salvation, a trusting in Christ vastly more interior and searching, a presence internal to parts internal, a complete bathing of the trusting soul in Christ's own love and beauty.

Those things, which were just now named as presupposed matters, are all opinionative and prior to this which is the real faith, and this faith must go beyond all mere historic credences of opinion; it must include the actual surrender of the man to the Saviour. It must even include the eternity or finality of that surrender; for if it is made only as an experiment, and the design is only to try what the Saviour will do, then it is experiment, not faith. Anything and everything which is necessary to make the soul a total, final deposit of trust in the Lord Jesus.

must be included in the faith, else it is not faith, and cannot have the power of faith. It must be as if, henceforth, the subject saw his everything in Christ, his righteousness, his whole character, his life-work and death-struggle, and the hope of his eternity.

How great is the transaction! and *great results will follow*, such as these :—

He will be as one possessed by Christ, created anew in Christ Jesus. There will be a Christ-power resting upon him and operative in him; an immediate knowledge of Christ, as a being revealed in the consciousness. A Christly character will come over him, and work itself into him. All his views of life will be changed. The old disturbance will be settled into loving order, and a conscious and sweet peace will flow down, like a divine river, through the soul, watering all its dryness. It will be in liberty, free to good; wanting only opportunities to do God's will. Fear will be cast out, confidence established, hope anchored, and all the great eternity to come taken possession of. Christ will constrain every motion, in such a way that no constraint shall be felt, and the new man will be so exhilarated in obedience, and raised so high in the sense of God upon him, that sacrifice itself will be joy, and the fires of martyrdom a chariot to the victor soul.

But the most remarkable, because to some the most unaccountable and extravagant result of faith, is the creation of new evidence. The exercise of faith is itself a proving of the matter, or the being trusted. It requires, in order to make it intelligent, some evidence going before; and then more evidence will follow, of still another kind. As in trying a physician, or trusting one's life to him, new evidence is obtained from the successful management of the disease, so the soul that trusts itself to Christ knows Him with a new kind of knowledge, that is more immediate and clear, knows Him as a friend revealed within, knows Him as the real power of God, even God in sacrifice. He that believeth hath the witness in himself,—the proof of Jesus, in him, is made out and verified by trust. Everything in that text of Scripture, that stumbles so many of our wise reasoners, is verified to the letter :—"Now faith is the substance of things hoped for, the evidence of things not seen."

It is not said that faith goes before all evidence, but that, coming after some evidence, it discovers more and greater. It makes substance of what before stood in hope ; it proves things unseen, and knows them by the immediate evidence of their power in the soul. Hence it is that faith is described, everywhere, as a state so intensely luminous. Trust in God will even prove Him to be, more inevitably and gloriously than all scientific arguments. The taking immortality by trust and acting one's mighty nature into it proves it, as it were, by the contact of it. The faith itself evidences the unseen life, when all previous evidences wore a questionable look. And so the whole Christian life becomes an element of light, because the trust itself is an experience of Christ and of God.

And so truly intelligent is the process, that it answers exactly, in a higher plane, to the process of perception itself, already referred to. For when objects, that cast their picture in the eye, are accepted and trusted to as being more than pictures, solid realities, then, by that faith, is begun a kind of experiment. Taking, now, all these objects to be realities, we go into all the practical uses of life, handling them as if realities, and so, finding how they support all our uses and shew themselves to be what we took them for, we say that we know them to be real, having found them by our trust. Exactly so, only in a much higher and nobler sense, it is that faith is the substance of things hoped for, and the evidence of things not seen. Is there anything in this which scandalises intelligence ? I think not.

If, now, you have followed me in these illustrations, which I know are somewhat abstruse, you will not complain of their abstruseness, but will be glad, by any means, to escape from those difficulties which have been gathered round the subject of faith, by the unilluminated and superficial speculations of our times. Handling the subject more superficially, I might have seemed to some to do more, but should, in fact, have done nothing. Let us gather up now, in closing, some of the lessons it yields. And—

1. The mistake is here corrected of those who are continually assuming that the gospel is a theorem, a something to be thought out, and not a new premiss of fact communicated by God,—by men to be received in all the threefold gradations

of faith. To mill out a scheme of free will and responsibility, to settle metaphysically questions of ability and inability, to shew the scheme of regeneration as related to a theory of sin and not to the conscious fact, may all be very ingenious, and we may call it gospel ; but it is scarcely more than a form of rationalism. Feeding on such kind of notional and abstract wisdom, and not on Christ, the bread that came down from heaven, we grow, at once, more ingenious in the head, and more shallow in the heart, and, in just the compound ratio of both, more naturalistic and sceptical. Loosing out our robustness, in this manner, and the earnestness of our spiritual convictions, our ministry becomes, in just the same degree, more ambitious and more untransforming to the people, and the danger is that, finally, even the sense of religion, as a gift of God, a divine light in the soul, revealed from faith to faith, will quite die out and be lost. Our gospel will be nature, and our faith will be reason, and the true Christ will be nothing,—all the grand, life-giving truths of the incarnate appearing and cross are resolved into myths and legends.

2. We discover that the requirement of faith, as a condition of salvation, is not arbitrary, as many appear to suppose, but is only a declaration of the fact, before existing, that without faith there can be no deliverance from sin. The precise difficulty with us in our sin is, that we cannot make ourselves good and happy by acting on ourselves. Faith, accordingly, is not required of us, because Christ wants to humble us a little, as a kind of satisfaction for letting go the penalty of our sins, but because we cannot otherwise be cleared of them at all. What we want is God, God whom we have lost ; to be united being to being, sinner to Saviour ; thus to be quickened, raised up, and made again to partake, as before sin, the divine nature. And for just this reason, faith is required ; for we come into the power of God only as we trust ourselves to Him. And here it is, at this precise point, that our gospel excels all philosophies, proving most evidently its Divine origin. It sees the problem as it is, and shews, in the requirement of faith as the condition of salvation, that it comprehends the whole reason of our state. It has the sagacity to see that, plainly, there is no such thing as a raising of man, without God; also that there is no God save as we find Him by our trust, and have Him revealed within, by

resting our eternity on Him. And hence it is that all those Scripture forms of imputation spring up, as a necessary language of faith, under the gospel. We come, in our trust, unto God, and the moment we so embrace Him, by committing our total being and eternity to Him, we find everything in us transformed. There is life in us from God; a kind of Christ-consciousness is opened in us, testifying, with the apostle—Christ liveth in me. We see, therefore, in Him, the store of all gifts and graces. Everything flows down upon us from Him, and so we begin to speak of being washed, sanctified, justified, in Him. He is our peace, our light, our bread; the way, the truth, and the life. And in just the same manner, He is our righteousness; for He is, so to speak, a soul of everlasting integrity for us, and when we come in to be with Him, He becomes in us what He is to Himself. We are new created and clothed in righteousness from His glorious investiture. The righteousness of God, which is, by faith of Jesus Christ, unto all and upon all them that believe, is upon us, and the very instinct of our faith, looking unto God in this conscious translation of His nature to us, is to call Him the Lord our Righteousness, the justifier of him that believeth in Jesus.

Such now, my friends, is faith. It gives you God, fills you with God in immediate experimental knowledge, puts you in possession of all there is in Him, and allows you to be invested with His character itself. Is such faith a burden, a hard and arbitrary requirement? Why, it is your only hope, your only possibility. Shall this most grand and blessed possibility be rejected? So far it has been, and you have even been able, it may be, in your lightness, to invent ingenious reasons against any such plan of salvation. God forbid that you do not some time take the penalty of having just that salvation, without faith to work out, which you so blindly approve!

3. We perceive, in our subject, that mere impressions can never amount to faith. At this point, the unbelievers and all such as are waiting to have convictions and spiritual impressions wrought in them that amount to faith, perfectly agree. The unbelievers and cavillers say that impressions, taken as evidences, are everything, and that, over and above these, faith is nonsense. You that are waiting to be in faith, by merely having your convictions and feelings intensified, say the same thing; for you

expect your impressions to coalesce in faith, and so to be faith.
That, as we have seen already, is for ever impossible. Faith is
more than impression; it moves from you, it is the trusting
of your being, in a total, final act of commitment, to the being
of Christ, your Saviour. Impressions shot into you, even by
thunderbolts, would not be faith in you. Ye also have seen
me, says Jesus, and believe not. No impression can be stronger
and more positive than sight, and yet not even this was equivalent to faith. It was a good ground of faith, nothing more.
Whatever drawings, then, impressions, convictions, evidences,
God in His mercy may give you, they will only ask your faith,
and wait for it. Will you, can you, then, believe? On that
question hangs everything decisive as regards your salvation.
This crisis of faith, can you ever pass it, or will you always be
waiting for a faith to begin in you which is not faith, and never
can be? Let the faith be yours, as it must; your own coming
to Christ, your own act of self-surrender, your coming over to
Him and eternal trust in Him for peace, life, truth, and bread;
knowing assuredly that He will be made unto you all these, and
more—wisdom, righteousness, sanctification, and redemption.

Finally, it is very plain that what is now most wanted in the
Christian world is more faith. We too little respect faith, we
dabble too much in reason; fabricating gospels where we ought
to be receiving Christ; limiting all faith, if we chance to allow
of faith, by the measures of previous evidence, and cutting the
wings of faith when, laying hold of God, and bathing in the
secret mind of God, it conquers more and higher evidence. Here
is the secret of our sects and schisms, that we are so much in
the head; for when we should be one in faith, by receiving our
one Lord, as soon as we go off into schemes and contrived sum-
maries of notions, reasoned into gospels, what can follow but
that we have as many gospels as we have heads and theories?
It never can be otherwise, till we are united by faith. The word
of reason is a word of interminable schism and subdivision, and
the propagation of it, as in those animals that multiply by divid-
ing their own bodies, will be a fissiparous process to the end of
the world. Oh, that the bleeding and lacerated body of Christ
could once more be gathered unto the Head, and fastened there
by a simple, vital trust; that His counsel and feeling and all
His divine graces might flow down upon it, as a sacred healing

and a vivifying impulse of love and sacrifice; and that so, fighting each other no more, we might all together fight the good fight of faith!

We shall never recover the true apostolic energy and be indued with power from on high, as the first disciples were—and this exactly is the prayer in which the holiest, most expectant, and most longing souls on earth are waiting now before God—till we recover the lost faith. As regards a higher sanctification, which is, I trust, the cherished hope of us all, nothing is plainer than the impossibility of it, except as we can yield to faith a higher honour and abide in it with a holier confidence. Every man is sanctified according to his faith; for it is by this trusting of himself to Christ that he becomes invested, exalted, irradiated, and finally glorified in Christ. Be it unto you according to your faith, is the true principle, and by that the whole life-state of the Church on earth always has been, always will be graduated. Increase our faith, then, Lord! be this our prayer.

That prayer, I believe, is yet to be heard. After we have gone through all the rounds of science, speculation, dialectic cavil, and wise unbelief, we shall do what they did not even in the apostolic times, we shall begin to settle conceptions of faith that will allow us, and all the ages to come, to stand fast in it and do it honour. And then God will pour Himself into the Church again, I know not in what gifts. Faith will then be no horseman out upon the plain, but will have a citadel manned and defended, whence no power of man can ever dislodge it again. Faith will be as much stronger now than science, as it is higher and more diffusive. And now the reign of God is established. Christ is now the creed, and the whole Church of God is in it, fulfilling the work of faith with power.

V.

REGENERATION.

JOHN iii. 3—"*Jesus answered and said unto him, Verily, verily, I say unto thee, Except a man be born again, he cannot see the kingdom of God.*"

THIS very peculiar expression, *born again*, is a phrase that was generated historically in the political state, then taken up by Christ, and appropriated figuratively to the spiritual use in which we find it. Thus foreigners, or Gentiles, were regarded by the Jewish people as unclean. Therefore, if any Gentile man wanted to become a Jewish citizen, he was baptized with water, in connexion with other appropriate ceremonies, and so, being cleansed, was admitted to be a true son of Abraham. It was as if he had been born, a second time, of the stock of Abraham; and becoming, in this manner, a native Jew, as related to the Jewish state, he was said, in form of law, to be born again. Our term *naturalisation* signifies essentially the same thing—viz., that the subject is made to be a natural-born American, or, in the eye of the law, a native citizen. Finding this Jewish ceremony on foot, and familiarly known, Christ takes advantage of it, (and the more naturally that a person so regenerated was, by the supposition, entered religiously into the covenant of Abraham,) as affording a good analogy, and a good form of expression, to represent the naturalisation of a soul in the kingdom of heaven. Regarding us in our common state under sin, as aliens, or foreigners, and not citizens in the kingdom; unclean in a deeper than ceremonial and political sense; He says, in a manner most emphatic—"Verily, verily, I say unto thee, Except a man be born again, he cannot see the kingdom of God." And again—"Marvel not that I said unto you, Ye must be born again." In this language, so employed, He gives us to understand that no man can ever be accepted before God, or entered into the kingdom of the glorified, who is not cleansed by a spiritual transformation, in that manner born of God, and so made native in the kingdom. He does not leave us to suppose that He is speaking merely of a ceremonial cleansing. He only takes the *water* by the way as a symbol, and adds *the Spirit* as the real cleansing power—"Except a man be born of water and *the Spirit*, he cannot enter into the kingdom of God. That which is born of the flesh is flesh, that which is born of the Spirit is spirit."

I propose, now, a deliberate examination of this great subject, hoping to present such a view of it as will command the respect of any thoughtful person, whatever may have been his previous difficulties and objections. My object will be to unfold the Scripture doctrine in a way to make it clear, not doubting that, when it is intelligibly shewn, it will also prove itself to be soundly intelligent, and will so command our assent as a proper truth of salvation. I believe, also, that many minds are confused to such a degree in their notions of this subject, as must fatally hinder them in their efforts to enter the gate which it opens.

I call your attention specially to three points :—

I. That Christ requires of all mankind, without distinction, some great and important change, as the necessary condition of their salvation.

II. The nature and definition of this change.

III. The manner in which it is, and is to be, effected.

I. That Christ requires of all some great and important change.

He does not, of course, require it of such as are already subjects of the change, and many are so even from their earliest years ; having grown up into Christ by the preventing or anticipating grace of their nurture in the Lord ; so that they can recollect no time when Christ was not their love, and the currents of their inclination did not run toward His word and His cause. The case, however, of such is no real exception ; and, besides this, there is even no semblance of exception. Intelligence, in fact, is not more necessary to our proper humanity, than the second birth of this humanity, as Christ speaks, to its salvation. Many cannot believe, or admit any such doctrine. It savours of hardness, they imagine, or undue severity, and does not correspond with what they think they see, in the examples of natural character among men.   There is too much amiability and integrity, too much of exactness, and even of scrupulousness in duty, to allow any such sweeping requirement, or the supposition of any such universal necessity.   How can it be said or imagined that so many moral, honourable, lovely, beneficent, and habitually reverent persons need to be radically and fundamentally changed in character before they can be saved?

That, according to Christ, depends on the question whether "the one thing" is really lacking in them or not.   If it be, not even the fact that He can look upon them with love will at all modify His requirement.   This is the word of Christ, this His new testament still—regeneration, universal regeneration, thus salvation.

We can see, too, for ourselves, that Christianity is based on the fact of this necessity.   It is not any doctrine of development or self-culture—no scheme of ethical practice or social reorganisation; but it is a salvation—a power moving on fallen humanity from above its level to regenerate, and so to save.   The whole fabric is absurd, therefore, unless there was something to be done in man, and for him, that required a supernatural intervention. We can see, too, at a glance, that the style of the transaction is supernatural from the incarnate appearing, onward.   Were it otherwise—were Christianity a merely natural and earthly product—then it were only a fungus growing out of the world, and, with all its high pretensions, could have nothing more to do for the world than any other fungus for the heap on which it grows. The very name, *Jesus*, is a false pretence unless He has something to do for the race which the race cannot do for itself— something regenerative and new-creative—something fitly called a salvation.

But how can we imagine, some of you will ask, that God is going to stand upon any such definite and rigid terms with us? Is He not a more liberal Being, and capable of doing better things?   Since He is very good and very great, and we are very weak and very much under the law of circumstances, is it not more rational to suppose that He will find some way to save us, and that if we do not come into any such particular terms of life, it will be about as well?   May we not safely risk the consequences?   It ought to be a sufficient answer to all such suggestions that Christ evidently understood what is necessary for us better than we do, and that we discover no disposition to uncharitableness or harshness in Him. He comes directly out from God, and knows the mind of God. He takes our case upon Him, and is so pressed by the necessities of our state, that He is even willing to die for us.

It ought also to be observed that all such kinds of argument are a plea for looseness, which is not the manner of God. Contrary to this, we discover, in all we know of Him, that He is the exactest of beings—doing nothing without fixed principles, and allowing nothing out of its true place and order. He weighs every world of the sky, even to its last atom, and rolls it into an orbit exactly suited to its uses and quantities. Nothing is smuggled out of place, or into place, because it is well enough anywhere. If a retreating army wants to cross a frozen river, the ice will not put off dissolving, but will run into the liquid state at a certain exact point of temperature. If a man wants to live, there is yet some diseased speck of matter, it may be, in his brain or heart, which no microscope even could detect, and by that speck, or because of it, he will die at a certain exact time, which time will not be delayed for a day simply because it is only a speck. Is, then, character a matter that God will treat more loosely? Will He decide the great questions of order and place dependent on it by no exact terms or conditions? If He undertakes to save, will He save us by accommodation or by some fixed law? If He undertakes to construct a beatific state, will He gather in a jumble of good and bad and call it heaven? How certainly will any expectation of heaven, based on the looseness of God and the confidence that He will stand for no very exact terms, issue in dreadful disappointment. And the more certainly, in this case, that the exactness supposed refers, not to any mere atoms of quantity, but to eternal distinctions of kind. His law of gravity will as soon put the sea on the backs of the mountains as His terms of salvation will gather into life them that are not quickened in His Son.

Do we not also see as clearly as possible for ourselves what signifies much—that some men, a very large class of men, are certainly not in a condition to enter the kingdom of God, or any happy and good state? They have no purity or sympathy with it. They are slaves of passion. They are cruel, tyrannical, brutal, and even disgusting to decency—fearful, unbelieving,

abominable. Who can think that these are ready to melt into
a perfectly blessed and celestial society? But if not these, then
there must be a division, and where shall it fall? If a line must
be drawn, it must be drawn somewhere, and what is on one side
of that line will not be on the other; which is the same as to say
that there must be exact terms of salvation if there are any.

Again, we know, we feel in our own consciousness, while living in the mere life of nature, that we are not in a state to enjoy
the felicities of a purely religious and spotlessly sinless world.
We turn from it with inward pain. Our heart is not there. We
want the joys of that state; we feel a certain hunger, at times,
after God himself; and that hunger is to us an assured evidence
that we have Him not. I do not undertake to press this argument further than it will bear. I only say that we feel conscious of something uncongenial in our state toward God and
heaven. We seem to ourselves not to be in the kingdom of God,
but without, and can hardly imagine how we shall ever find any
so great felicity in the employments of holy minds.

It is also a very significant proof that some great change is
needed in us, that, when we give ourselves to some new purpose
of amendment, or undertake to act up more exactly to the ideals
of our mind, we are consciously legal in it, and do all by a kind
of constraint. Something tells us that we are not spontaneous
in what we do; that our currents do not run this way, but the
contrary. A sad kind of heaven will be made by this sort of
virtue! How dry it is! and if we call it service, how hard a
service! What we want is liberty, to be in a kind of inspiration,
to have our inclinations run the way of our duty, to be so deep
in the spirit of it as to love it for its own sake. And this
exactly is what is meant by the being born of God. It is having
God revealed in the soul, moving in it as the grand impulse of
life, so that duty is easy and, as it were, natural. Then we are
in the kingdom as being naturalised in it, or native-born. Our
regeneration makes us free in good. How manifest is it that,
without this freedom, this newly-generated inclination to good,
all our supposed service is mockery, our seeming excellence
destitute of sound reality.

There is, then, a change, a great spiritual change, required by
Christianity as necessary to salvation; and we find abundant
reason, in all that we know of ourselves and the world, to admit

the necessity of some transformation quite as radical. In presence of a truth so momentous and serious, we now raise the question—

II. What is the nature of this change, how shall it be conceived?

To make the answer as clear as possible, let some things which only confuse the mind, and which often enter largely into the discussion, be excluded.

Thus a great deal of debate is had over the supposed instantaneousness of the change. But that is a matter of theory, and not of necessary experience. If we call the change a change from bad in kind to good in kind, from a wrong principle of life to a right, the change will imply a beginning of what is good and right, and a gradual beginning of anything would seem to be speculatively impossible. Still the change is, in that view, only an instantaneous beginning. But, however this may be in speculation, there is often, or even commonly, no consciousness of any such sudden transition. The subject often cannot tell the hour or the day; he only knows, it may be, looking back over hours or days, or even months, that he is a different man.

Some persons hold impressions of the change which suppose, or even require it to be gradual. This is an error quite as likely to confuse the mind; for then they set out, almost of course, to make it a change only of degrees, in the old plane of the natural character. The true, practical method is to drop out all considerations and questions of time, and look at nothing but the simple fact of the change itself, whenever and however accomplished.

Much, again, is said in this matter of previous states and exercises—conviction, distress, tumult; then of light, peace, hope, bursting suddenly into the soul. Let no one attempt to realise any such description. Something of the kind may be common among the inductive causes, or the consequences of the change, but has nothing to do with its radical idea.

Excluding now all these points, which are practically immaterial and irrelevant, as regards a definite conception of the change, let us carefully observe, first of all, how the Scriptures speak of it, or what figure it makes in their representations; and more especially the fact that they never speak of it as being a change of degrees, an amendment of the life, an improvement or growing better in the plane of the old character. Contrary to this, they use bold, sweeping contrasts, and deal as it were in totalities. It is the being born again, or born over; as if it were a spiritual reproduction of the man. They describe him as one new created in Christ Jesus unto good works. Old things they declare to be passed away; behold all things are become new. It is passing from death to its opposite, life. It is dying with Christ, to walk with Him in newness of life. That which is born of the flesh is declared to be flesh; and, in the same sense, that which is born of the Spirit to be spirit; as if a second nature, free to good, were inbreathed by the Divine Spirit, partaking His own quality.

It is called putting off the old man and putting on the new man, which after God is created in righteousness and true holiness; as if there was even a substitution of one man for another in the change, a new divine man in the place of the old.

Again, it is called being transformed, and that by a renewing even of the mind, or intelligent principle.

Again, as if for ever to exclude the idea of a mere growing better by care, and duty, and self-improvement, an apostle says, "Not by works of righteousness which we have done, but according to His mercy He saved us, by the washing of regeneration and renewing of the Holy Ghost."

Now, you understand that a change of this kind can be spoken of, or described, only in figures. Therefore none of these expressions are to be taken as literal truths. But the great question under them is this—Is the change spoken of a change merely of degree, or is it a change of kind? Is it simply the improving of principles already planted in the soul, or is it the passing into a new state under new principles, to be started into a life radically different from the former? I have not one doubt which of the two alternatives to accept as the true answer. Had it been the matter in hand, in redeeming the world, simply to make us better in degree, it would have been the easiest thing in the world to say it. The gospel does not say it. On the contrary, it labours after terms in which to set forth a change of kind, of principle,—a grand *anakainosis*, renovation, new creation, spiritually speaking, of the man.

Nor is there anything contrary to this, in those expressions which require a process of growth and gradual advancement. For it is only potentially that the new life is regarded as a complete or total renovation. As the child is potentially a man, as the seed planted is potentially the full-grown plant, so it is with the regenerated life in Christ. It is a beginning, the implanting of a new seed, and then we are to see, first the blade, then the ear, and after that the full corn in the ear. All such conceptions of growth fall into place *under* the fact that the new character begun is only begun, and that, while it is the root and spring of a complete renovation, it must needs unfold itself and fill itself out into completeness by a process of holy living. On the other hand, there could be no growth if there were not something planted, and it is everywhere assumed and taught that, until the new man is born, or begotten, there is not so much as a seed of true holiness, no principle that can be unfolded ; that, without faith, the soul abideth even in death, and therefore cannot grow.

Advancing, now, from this point, let us see if we can accurately conceive the interior nature of the change.

Every man is conscious of this, that when he acts in any particular manner of wrong-doing, or sin, or neglect of God, there is something in the matter besides the mere act or acts. There is a something back of the action which is the reason why it is done. In the mere act itself there is, in fact, no character at all. In striking another, for example, the mere thrust of the arm, by the will, is the act ; and, taken in that narrow mechanical sense, there is no wrong in it, more than there is in the motion that dispenses a charity. The wrong is back of the act, in some habit of soul, some disposition, some *status* of character, whence the action comes. Now, this something, whatever it be, is the wrong of all wrong, the sin of all sin, and this must be changed—which change is the condition of salvation.

Sometimes this change is conceived to be a really organic change in the subject. The strong expressions just referred to in the Scripture, are taken literally, as if there was and must needs be a literal re-creation of the man. The difficulty back of the wrong action is conceived to be the man himself, as a malconstructed and constitutionally evil being, who can never be less evil, till something is taken out of him and replaced by a new insertion, which is, in fact, a new creation, by the fiat of

Omnipotence. But this, it is plain, would be no proper regeneration of the man, but the generation rather of another man in
his place. Personal identity would be overthrown. The man
would not, or should not, be consciously the same that he was.
Besides, we are required to put off the old man ourselves and
put on the new, and even to make ourselves a new heart, and a
new spirit, which shews, as clearly as possible, that we are to act
concurrently in the change ourselves, whatever it be. But how
can we act concurrently in a literal re-creation of our nature?

Sometimes, again, the change is conceived to be only a change
of purpose, a change of what is called the governing purpose.
You determined this morning, for example, to attend worship in
this place. This determination, or purpose, being made, it, in
one view, passed out of mind; you did not continue to say and
repeat, "I will do it," till you reached the place and took your
seat; and yet it was virtually in you, governing all your thousand
subordinate volitions, in rising, preparing, walking, choosing
your way, and the like, down to that moment. Just so there is,
it is said, a bad governing purpose of sin, or self-devotion, back
of the whole life, making it what it is; and what Christianity
does or requires is the change of that purpose; which being
changed, a change is wrought in the whole life and character.
And this, it is conceived, is to be born again. The change of the
governing purpose is the regeneration of the man.

The illustration, somewhat popularly taken, has truth in it,
and it may be used, in many cases, with advantage. Still it is
not exactly a bad governing purpose that we find, when we look
for the seat of our disorder, but a something rather which we
call a bad mind, state, or disposition. Having a certain quality
of freedom, this bad mind, state, or disposition, may be represented analogically by a bad governing purpose, though it cannot
be identified with that. It is to the character what the will is
dynamically to the actions, a bad affinity that distempers and
carnalises the whole man. I know not how to describe it better
than to call it a *false love*, a *wrong love*, a *downward, selfish love*.
How this love gets dominion, or becomes established in us, is
not now the question. Enough to know that this wrong love is
in us, and, being in us, is the source of a wrong life, much as the
bad governing purpose is said to be. Only it is a more real and
fatal condition of bondage, and a less superficial evil. When we

speak of a purpose that needs to be changed, we have only to will it, and the change is wrought. But when we speak of changing one's reigning love, so that his life shall be under another love, a right love, a heavenly, a divine love, that is quite another and deeper and more difficult matter.

Every man's life, practically speaking, is shaped by his love. If it is a downward, earthly love, then his actions will be tinged by it, all his life will be as his reigning love. This love, you perceive, is not a mere sentiment, or casual emotion, but is the man's settled affinity; it is that which is, to his character, what the magnetic force is to the needle, the power that adjusts all his aims and works, and practically determines the man. It only must be either a downward love or an upward love; for, being the last love and deepest of the man, there cannot be two last and deepest, it must be one or the other. And then, as this love changes, it works a general revolution of the man.

Hence it is that so much is said of the heart in the gospel, and of a change of the heart; for it is what proceeds out of the heart that defileth the man. The meaning is, not that Christianity proposes to give us a new organ of soul, or to extract one member of the soul and insert another, but that it will change the love of the heart. A man's love is the same thing as a man's heart.

Thus it is declared that God will write His laws in the hearts of men, which is saying that He will bring His laws into their love. In accordance also with this, it is declared that love is of God, and every one that loveth is born of God; that is, that every one that has the right love, the heavenly, or divine love, established in him, has the change on which salvation hangs.

I have brought you on thus far, in a simple and direct line of thought, to what may be called a scriptural and correct view of the change. And yet there is another and higher which is also scriptural, and which needs to be held in view, in order to a right understanding of our next point, the manner in which the change is effected.

Thus far, you will observe, I have looked directly at the subject of the change, regarding only what transpires in him as a man. He is not re-created, he is not simply changed in his governing purpose, he is changed in his ruling love. Still he could not be so changed as a man in his own spirit, without and

F

apart from another change, of which this is only an incident. After all, the principal stress of the change is not in himself, as viewed by himself, but in his personal relation to God, a being external to himself. In his prior, unregenerate state as a sinner, he was separated from God, and centred in himself, living in himself, and to himself. And he was not made to live in this manner. He was made to live in God, to be conscious of God, to know Him by an immediate knowledge, to act by His divine impulse, in a word, to be inspired by Him. By this I mean not that he is to be inspired in the same sense and manner as a prophet is, or a writer of Scripture, which is the sense commonly attached to the word; I only mean that he is made to be occupied, filled, governed, moved, exalted by His all-containing Spirit; so that all his tempers, actions, ends, enjoyments, will be from God. A tree can as well live out of the light, or out of the air, as a finite soul out of God, and separate from God. Here, then, is the grand overtowering summit of the change, that the man is born of God. He is born into God, restored to the living connexion with God that was lost by his sin, made to be a partaker of the Divine nature, and live a life hid with Christ in God. He acts no more by his mere human will, as before; he says, yet not I, but Christ, liveth in me. God is now revealed in him; he is not a sole, simple, human nature; but he is a human nature occupied by the Divine, living and acting in an inspired movement—all which is signified by the declaration, "That which is born of the Spirit is spirit." He is more than a human person, he is spirit; a human person that is pervaded, illuminated, swayed, exalted, empowered, and finally to be glorified by the life and spirit of God developed freely in him. This emphatically is regeneration. It cannot be fully defined by looking simply at the man himself. He must be regarded as in relation to another being. He is really parted from sin, and quickened in a spirit of life, only as he is restored to God, and received into the glorious occupancy of the Divine nature.

But whether we regard the change as a change in the soul's ruling love, or in the higher form of it here recognised, makes little difference; for, in fact, neither of these two will be found separated from the other. If a man's ruling love is changed, he will, of course, be altered in his relation to God, and restored to oneness with Him. And if he is restored to that oneness, his ruling love will be changed. There will be no precedence of time in one to the other. They will be rigidly coincident. They will even be mutual conditions one of the other. No man will ever be united to God, except in and by a love that embraces or entemples God. No man ever will be changed in his ruling love, except in the embrace of God, and His revelation in the soul. The consequences, therefore, of the change will be such as belong to both. The soul is now entered into rest—rest in love, rest in God. It is flooded also with a wondrously luminous joy; its whole horizon is filled with light; the light of a new love, the light of God revealed within. It has the beginning of true blessedness; because God himself and the principle of God's own blessedness are in it. It settles into peace; for now it is at one with God and all the creatures of God. It is filled with the confidence of hope; because God, who is wholly given Himself to a right love, will never forsake it, in life or death. It is free to good, inclined to good; for the good love reigns in it, and it would even have to deny itself not to do the works of love. It consciously knows God within; for God is there now in a new relation, love present to love, love answering to love. There is no alienation, or separation, but oneness. "If a man love me," says the Saviour, "he will keep my words: and my Father will love him, and we will come unto him, and make our abode with him." That abode in the soul is a new condition of Divine movement; for it is in the movement of God. All things, of course, are new. Life proceeds from a new centre, of which God is the rest and prop. The Bible is a new book, because there is a light in the soul by which to read it. Duties are new, because the Divine love the soul is in has changed all the relations of time and the aims of life. The saints of God on earth are no longer shunned, but greeted in new terms of celestial brotherhood. The very world itself is revealed in new beauty and joy to the mind, because it is looked upon with another and different love, and beheld as the symbol of God.

But let this one caution be observed. You are likely to be more attracted by the consequences of the change than by the change itself. But with the consequences you have nothing to do. God will take care of these. It may be that your mind will be so artificial, or so confused, as to miss the consequences

for a time, after the reality is past.   But God will bring them
out in His own good time, perhaps gradually, certainly in the
way that is best for you.   Let Him do His own work, and be it
yours to look after nothing but the new love.   This brings me
to speak, as I shall do in the briefest manner possible,—

III. Of the manner in which the change, already described,
is to be effected.

To maintain that such a change can be manipulated, or offici-
ally passed by a priest, in the rite of baptism, is no better than
a solemn trifling with the subject.   Indeed, so plain is this, that
a sober argument, instituted to prove the contrary, is itself a
half surrender of the truth.   "Born of water and of the Spirit,"
says our Lord, and the language is a Hebraism, which presents
the water as the symbol and the Spirit as the power of the
change.

Equally plain is it that the change is not to be effected by
waiting for some new creating act of God to be literally passed
on the soul.   Whoever thinks to compliment the sovereignty of
God in that manner, mocks both himself and God.   The change,
as we have seen, passes only by consent and a free concurrence
with God.   God will never demolish a sinner's personality.

As little is it to be accomplished by any mere willing, or
change of purpose, apart from God.   There must be a change of
purpose, a final, total, sweeping change of all purpose, but that
of itself will not change the soul's love, least of all will it be a
birth of God into the soul.   A man can as little drag himself
up into a new reigning love, as he can drag a Judas into paradise.   Or, if we say nothing of this, how can he execute a
change, that consists in the revelation of God, by acting on
himself ?   "Born of God," remember, is the Christian idea, not
born of self-exercise; "created anew in Christ Jesus," not self-
created.   You must get beyond your own mere will, else you
will find, even though you strain your will to the utmost
for a hundred years, that, while to will is present, you perform
not.   You cannot lift this bondage, or break this chain, or
burst open a way into freedom through this barrier, till you
can say, "I thank God through Jesus Christ my Lord.   For the
law of the spirit of life hath made me free from the law of sin
and death."

The question then recurs, how shall this change be effected? The whole endeavour, I answer, on your part must be Godward. In the first place, you must give up every purpose, end, employment, hope, that conflicts with God and takes you away from Him. Hence what is said in so many forms of self-renunciation. Hence the requirement to forsake all. It is on the ground that, in your life of sin, you are altogether in self-love—centred in yourself, living for yourself, making a god of your own objects and works. These occupy the soul, fill it, bear rule in it, and God cannot enter. You must make room for God, create a void for Him to fill—die to yourself that Christ may live within.

But this negative work of self-clearing is not enough. There must be a positive reaching after God, an offering up of the soul to Him, that He may come and dwell in it and consecrate it as His temple. For, as certainly as the light will pour into an open window, just so certainly will God reveal Himself in a mind that is opened to His approach. Now, this opening of the mind, this reaching after God, is faith; and hence it is that so much is made of faith. For God is revealed outwardly, in the incarnate life and death of Jesus, in order that He may present Himself in a manner level to our feeling, and quickening to our love, and so encourage that faith by which He may come in to re-establish His presence in us. For God, who commanded the light to shine out of darkness, hath shined in our hearts, to give the light of the knowledge of the glory of God in the face of Jesus Christ. Oh, it is there that the true God shines—let Him shine into our hearts! Jesus, if we understand Him, is the true manifestation of God, and He is manifested to be the regenerating power of a new divine life. By His beautiful childhood, by His loving acts and words, by His sorrowful death, God undertakes to impregnate our dead hearts with His love, and so to establish Himself eternally in us. What is said of the Spirit is said of Him, as being also the Spirit of Jesus. For, in highest virtuality, they are one, even as Christ himself declares, when discoursing of the promised Spirit,—"I will come to you . . . . but ye see me." Receive Him, therefore, as receiving Christ, and Him as the accepted image of God, and this will be your faith, this the regeneration of your love, and this the token of your new connexion with God.

Allow no artificial questions of before and after to detain you here, as debating whether Christ, or the Spirit, or the faith, or the new-born love, must be first. Enough to know that, if your faith is conditioned by the Spirit, so is the victory of the Spirit conditioned by your faith; that here you have all these mercies streaming upon you, and that nothing effectual can be done till your faith meets them and they are revealed in your faith. Enough to know that, if the faith is to be God's work, it is also to be your act, and it cannot be worked *before* it is acted. Let Christ also be your help in this acting of faith and this receiving of God, even as He set Himself to give it in His conversation with Nicodemus; going directly on to speak of Himself and the grace brought down to sinners in His person, declaring that, "as Moses lifted up the serpent in the wilderness, even so must the Son of man be lifted up: that whosoever believeth in Him should not perish, but have everlasting life." He brings the Divine love down to this most wondrous attitude, the cross, that we may there drop out our sin, and receive into our faith the love the God of love expressed. And therefore it is represented that Christ ever stands before the door and knocks for admission, with a promise that, "if any man open the door (which is faith), He will come in and sup with him." Christianity is God descending to the door to get admission; this is the grand philosophy of the incarnation. God is just what you see Him here; and He comes to be revealed *in* you as He is presented *before* you. Thus received, you are born again, born of God. A new love enters—God enters, and eternal life begins.

Shall He enter thus with you? How many of you are there that ought to hear this call? And no one of you is excluded. You may have come hither to-day with no such high intention. Still the call is to you. If you ask who? how many? when? All, I answer, all, and that to-day. Do you not see a glorious simplicity in this truth of regeneration? How beautiful is God in the light of it, how deep in love Christ Jesus and His cross, how close, in all this, come the tenderness and winning grace of your God! No matter if you did not think of receiving Him, are you going to reject Him? Is it nothing to be so exalted, so divinely ennobled? Have you fallen so low that no such greatness can attract you?

Then be it so. Have it as confessed that, when you saw the

true gate open, you would not enter. Go back to your sins.
Plunge into your little cares, fall down to your base idols, creep
along through the low affinities of your sin, make a covenant
with hunger and thirst, and hide it from you, if you can, that
you were made for God, made to live in the consciousness of
Him, as a mind irradiated by His Spirit, quickened by His life,
cleared by His purity.   But if you cannot be attracted by this,
let it be no wonder, call it no severity, that Christ has not
opened heaven to you.   No wonder is it to Him, even if it be to
you, and therefore He says, whispers it to you kindly, but faithfully, as you turn yourself away, "Marvel not that I said unto
you, Ye must be born again."

VI.

THE PERSONAL LOVE AND LEAD OF CHRIST.

JOHN x. 3—"*And He calleth His own sheep by name, and leadeth them out.*"

IN this parable, Christ is a shepherd, and His people are His flock. And two points, on which the beauty and significance of the parable principally turn, are referred to in the text, which might not be distinctly observed by one who is not acquainted with the peculiar manner of the eastern shepherds. They have, in the first place, a name for every sheep, and every sheep knows its name when it is called. And then the shepherd does not drive the flock, as we commonly speak, but he leads them, going before. To these two points, or to the instruction contained under these two analogies, I now propose to call your attention.

I. " He calleth His own sheep by name." As we have names for dogs and other animals, which they themselves know, so it was with the eastern shepherds and their flocks. This fact is shewn, historically, by many references. It is to this, for example, that Isaiah refers when he represents the Almighty Creator as leading out the starry heavens, like a shepherd leading his flock,—" Lift up your eyes, and behold who hath created these things, that bringeth out their host by number : He calleth them all by names." The shepherd, in this view, is not as one who keeps a hive of bees, knowing well the hive, but never any particular bee in it, but he has a particular recognition of every sheep, has a name for every one, teaches every one to know that name and follow at the call. This also is signified in the words that immediately follow—"The sheep follow Him, for they know His voice,"—words that refer, not so much to the mere tones of His voice, as to the fact that He is able, as a stranger is not, to call the names they are wont to answer as their own.

—

Under this analogy stands the tender and beautiful truth, *that Christ holds a particular relation to individual persons ; knows them, loves them, watches for them, leads them individually, even as if calling them by name.*

In this respect, the parable is designed to counteract and correct, what has in all ages been the common infirmity of Christian believers; they believe that God has a real care of the Church and of all great bodies of saints, but how difficult is it to imagine that He ever particularly notes, or personally recognises them. They know that God has a vast empire, and that the cares and counsels of His love include immense numbers of minds, and they fall into the impression that He must needs deal with them in the gross, or as noting only generals, just as they would do themselves. They even take an air of philosophy in this opinion, asking how we can imagine that so great a Being takes a particular notice of, and holds a particular and personal relation to individual men. There could not be a greater mistake, even as regards the matter of philosophy ; for the relation God holds to objects of knowledge is different, in all respects, from that which is held by us. Our general terms, *man, tree, insect, flower,* are the names of particular or single specimens, extended, on the ground of a perceived similarity, to kinds or species. They come, in this manner, to stand for millions of particular men, trees, insects, flowers, that we do not and never can know. They are, to just this extent, words of ignorance ; only we are able, in the use, to hold right judgments of innumerable particulars we do not know, and have the words, so far, as words of wisdom. But God does not generalise in this manner, getting up general terms under which to handle particulars, which, as particulars, He does not know. He is not obliged to accommodate His ignorance or shortness of perception by any such splicing process in words. His knowledge of wholes is a real and complete knowledge. It is a knowledge of wholes as being a distinct knowledge of particulars. Indeed, whatever particulars exist, or by Him are created, He must first have thought ; and therefore they were known by Him, as being thought, even before they became subjects of knowledge in the world of fact. Holding in His thought the eternal archetypes of kinds and species, He also thought each individual in its particular type, as dominated by the common archetype.

So that all things, even things most particular, are known or thought by Him eternally, before they take existence in time. When He thinks of wholes or kinds therefore—of society, the Church, the nation, the race—He knows nothing of them in our faint, partial way of generalisation, but He knows them intuitively, through and through; the wholes in the particulars, the particulars in the wholes; knows them in their types, knows them in their archetypes, knows them in their genesis out of both; so with a knowledge that is more than verbal, a solid, systematic, specific knowledge. Nay, it is more, a necessary, inevitable knowledge; for the sun can no more shine on the world, as in the gross, without touching every particular straw and atom with his light, than God can know, or love whole bodies of saints, without knowing and loving every individual saint. In one view, it requires no particular act of tenderness or condescension in Him; it is the sublime necessity of His perfect mind. Being a perfect mind, and not a mere spark of intelligence like us, He cannot fall into the imperfections and shorten Himself to the half-seeing of our contrivance, when we strain ourselves to set up generals in a way to piece out and hide our ignorance.

And yet we could not wean ourselves of this folly, could not believe that our God has a particular notice of us, and a particular interest in our personal history. And this was one of the great uses of the incarnation; it was to humanise God, reducing Him to a human personality, that we might believe in that particular and personal love in which He reigns from eternity. For Christ was visibly one of us, and we see, in all His demonstrations, that He is attentive to every personal want, woe, cry of the world. When a lone woman came up in a crowd to steal, as it were, some healing power out of His person, or out of the hem of His garment, He would not let her off in that impersonal, unrecognising way; He compelled her to shew herself and to confess her name, and sent her away with His personal blessing. He pours out, everywhere, a particular sympathy on every particular child of sorrow; He even hunts up the youth He has before healed of his blindness, and opens to him, persecuted as he is for being healed, the secrets of His glorious Messiahship. The result, accordingly, of this incarnate history is that we are drawn to a different opinion of God; we have seen that He can love as a man loves another, and that such is the way of His love. He has tasted death, we say, not for all men only, but for every man. We even dare to say, for me,—who loved me and gave Himself for me. Nay, He goes even further than this Himself, calling us friends, and claiming that dear relationship with us ; friends, because He is on the private footing of friendship and personal confidence : "The servant knoweth not what his lord doeth : but I have called you friends." He even goes beyond this, promising a friendship so particular and personal, that it shall be a kind of secret, or cipher of mutual understanding, open to no other—a new white stone given by his King, "and in the stone a new name written, which no man knoweth saving he that receiveth it."

Indeed, I might go on to shew, from every particular work and turn of this gospel, how intensely personal it is. What is communion that is not communion with particular souls ? Is it the communion or fellowship of God that He reaches only great bodies of men ? If He promises comfort or support, whom does He comfort or support, when He touches no individual person ? The promises to prayer—whom does He hear, when He hears the prayer of nobody in particular, and for nothing in particular ? The work of the Holy Spirit in souls—what is it, in all its degrees and modes ? in their calling, their guidance, their sanctification ? what can it be imagined that He does which is not personal—the bestowment of a convincing, illuminating, drawing, renovating grace, exactly tempered to, and by, the individual blessed ? a visiting of His intelligent person, at just the point of his particular want, sin, sorrow, prejudice, so as to exactly meet his personality at that particular time ? We speak, indeed, of the Holy Spirit as falling on communities, or assemblies, but we must not suppose that He touches the general body and no particular person. On the contrary, if we understand ourselves, He reaches the general body only by and through individuals, save that there is an effect of mutual excitement, which is secondary, and comes from their sense of what is revealed in each other, under the power of the Spirit in each. How then can it be imagined that God effectually calls any person by His Spirit, without dispensing a grace most distinctly and even adaptively personal ?

So it is, in short, with everything included in the gospel as a grace of salvation; everything in the renewing, fashioning, guidance, discipline, sanctification, and final crowning of an heir of glory. His Saviour and Lord is over him and with him, as the good Shepherd, calling him by name; so that he is finally saved, not as a man, or some one of mankind, led forth by his Lord in the general flock, but as the Master's dear Simon, or James, or Alpheus, or Martha, whose name is so recorded in the Lamb's book of life.

And in this view it is, I suppose, that the Church, in baptizing her children, takes there at the font, with a most beautiful and touching propriety, what she calls the " Christian name ; " as if it were Christ's own gift ; a name bestowed by Him, in which He recognises the child's discipleship, and which, as often as it is spoken, he is himself to recognise as the calling of his Master's voice : " And He calleth His own sheep by name."

Consider now the

II. Point of the text, " He leadeth them out." It is not said, you observe, that the Shepherd driveth them out, for that was not the manner of shepherds, but that He leadeth them, going before to call them after Him. This, indeed, is expressly and formally said in the next verse,—" And when he putteth forth his own sheep, he goeth before them, and the sheep follow him." Hence those poetic figures of the Old Testament,—" The Lord is my shepherd ; he leadeth me beside the still waters ; " " Thou leddest thy people like a flock by the hand of Moses and Aaron ; " " Give ear, O shepherd, thou that leadest Joseph like a flock." The same custom of going before the flock pertains even now, it is said, in the sheep-walks of Spain.

What a beautiful image, or picture, to represent the attitude and personal relationship of Jesus among His followers—*That He does not drive them on before, as a herd of unwilling disciples, but goes before Himself, leading them into paths that He has trod, and dangers He has met, and sacrifices He has borne Himself, calling them after Him, and to be only followers.* He leadeth them out.

If driving could do any good, He might well enough drive His flock as a body, caring nothing for any one of them in particular ; but, if He is going to draw them after Him, He must work upon their inclinations, draw them by their personal favour to Him, and must therefore know them personally, and call them to fol-

low, as it were, by name.   Just the difference will be observed
in this matter that pertains between the eastern shepherds and
those of the west and north.   No sooner do we come upon this
latter fashion of driving flocks a-field, than we see the noting,
knowing, and calling of particular sheep disappear.   When the
driving and thrusting on before becomes the manner, there is
no need of getting any one of them under a power of confidence
and attraction, no need of noting them individually at all.   So,
if driving were in place, Christ might well enough let fall the
fires of Sodom behind His flock, and drive them out, as He
drove Lot's family, or his vain-hearted wife, out of the city
But the best use that could be made of such a flock, after all,
would be to turn them into pillars of salt and let them stand.
No disciple is a real disciple till he becomes a follower, going
after the Shepherd, as one that follows by name, and is drawn
by love.

Here, then, is the beauty and glory of Christ as a Redeemer
and Saviour of lost man, that He goes before, always before, and
never behind His flock.   He begins with infancy, that He may
show a grace for childhood.   He is made under the law, and
carefully fulfils all righteousness there, that He may sanctify
the law to us, and make it honourable.   He goes before us in
the bearing of temptations, that we may bear them after Him,
being tempted in all points like as we are, yet without sin.   He
taught us forgiveness by forgiving Himself His enemies.   He
went before us in the loss of all things, that we might be able
to follow, in the renouncing of the world and its dominion.
The works of love that He requires of us, in words, are preceded
and illustrated by real deeds of love, to which He gave up all His
mighty powers from day to day.   He bore the cross Himself
that He commanded us to take up and bear after Him.   Requiring us to hate even life for the gospel's sake, He went before
us in dying for the gospel ; suffering a death most bitter at the
hand of enemies exasperated only by His goodness, and that
when, at a word, He might have called to His aid whole legions
of angels, and driven them out of the world.   And then He went
before us in the bursting of the grave and the resurrection from
it ; becoming, in His own person, the first-fruits of them that
slept.   And, finally, He ascended and passed within the veil before us, as our forerunner, whom we are to follow even there.

In all which He is our shepherd, going before us, and never behind; calling, but never driving; bearing all the losses He calls us to bear; meeting all the dangers, suffering all the cruelties and pains which it is given us to suffer, and drawing us to follow where He leads.

And then we see what kindred spirit entered into the teachers that He gave to lead His flock. They were such as followed Him in the regeneration; going up at last, according to His promise, to sit on thrones of glory with Him. And it is remarkable that the apostles took it as incumbent on them always, in their Master's law, to require nothing of others in which they were not forward themselves. Thus, when Paul says, once and again, I beseech you, be ye followers of me; brethren, be followers together of me; it has a sound, taken as it may be taken, of conceit, or vanity; but, when we look upon him as a man who goes after Christ, in the ways of scorn and suffering patience; in labours more abundant, in stripes above measure, in prisons more frequent, in deaths oft, receiving more than once his forty stripes save one, beaten with rods and stoned out of cities, running the gauntlet through all sorts of perils, in weariness and painfulness, in watchings often, in hunger and thirst, in fastings often, in cold and nakedness, accounted as the filth of the world and the offscouring of all things—when we see him tramping on heavily thus, bearing his Master's dark flag of patience and loss, and calling others to follow, we only see that he has taken Christ's own spirit and despises even to send the flock before him, where he does not lead himself.

Ah! we have seen things different from this: teachers that bind heavy burdens and lay them on men's shoulders, which they themselves will not so much as lighten with the touch of their fingers; priests and confessors that feed their lusts out of the charities extorted from the poor, imposing on them loads of penance in turn to humble them and keep them in subjection; philanthropists publishing theories and great swelling words of equality, and tapering off in the commendation of virtues they themselves do not practise, and even inwardly distaste. All such are men that drive a flock. But Christ, the true Shepherd, the eternal Son of God, wants nothing in His flock that He does not shew in Himself. He goes before them, bearing all the bitterest loads of sacrifice, and facing all the fiercest terrors Himself, only calling them gently to come and follow. "Come unto me, all ye that labour and are heavy laden, and I will give you rest. Take my yoke upon you, and learn of me. My yoke is easy, and my burden light."

The uses and applications of this subject are many. The time allows me to name only a few that are most practical.

1. A great mistake or false impression held by most worldly minds, and even by some who profess to be disciples, is here corrected—viz., the mistake of regarding the Christian life as a legal and constrained service. It is as if the flock were driven by the shepherd, and not as if it were led by the shepherd's call, going before. In this image or figure is beautifully represented the freedom of the disciple. He is one who is led by a personal influence—one who hears the voice and answers to the name by which he is called. He could not be thrust on, as in a crowd, by mere force or fear. Christ wants to lead men by their love, their personal love to Him, and the confidence of His personal love to them. And therefore the representation is, not that He is a shepherd going behind with dogs to gather in the flock, and keep them before Him, but that He draws them after Him, and gets them into such a training of confidence that they will hear His call and follow. The whole relation, therefore, of discipleship is a relation of liberty. No one goes to his duty because he must, but only because his heart is in it. His inclinations are that way, for his heart is in the Master's love, and he follows Him gladly. It no doubt seems to you, my friends, when you look on, only as strangers to Christ, that this must be a hard and dry service, for you see no attraction in it. But the reason is that your heart is not in it. With a new heart, quickened by the grace of Christ, all this would be changed. It will then seem wholly attractive. All the currents of your love will run that way, and the freest freedom of your nature will be to go after Christ. No sacrifice will be hard—no service a burden. The wonder now will be that all men do not rush in after Christ to be His eager followers. God grant that even to-day, you may have this truth as an experience in the choice of Christ, and the renewing of His promised Spirit.

Brethren, are there some of you that hold this same impression of the life of duty? If so, if you have no knowledge of this freedom in Christ, the sign is a dark one for you. Perhaps it is not exactly the same impression that you hold. It may be that you have it only in a degree, accordingly as you are over-legal in your conceptions of duty, and rob yourself, in that manner, of its comforts. Let your mistake be now corrected. See, in particular, that Christ is not behind you but before, calling and drawing you on. He wants your faith, wants your love—not a minute, and scrupulous, and careful piling up of legalities. You are not to stand off, doing something for Him that He is to examine and report upon as accepted by statute conditions, but you are to go after Him, and be with Him, and keep along in His train, feeding in His pasture, and following where He leads. This is the liberty—the beautiful liberty of Christ. Claim your glorious privilege in the name of a dis-ciple ; be no more a servant when Christ will own you as a friend.

2. We discover, in this subject, what to think of that large class of disciples who aspire to be specially faithful, and hold a specially high-toned manner of life, but are, after all, principally strenuous in putting others forward, and laying burdens upon others. Christ, we have seen, goes before when He leads, and so did His apostles, calling on the saints to follow. But there is a cheaper way some have, in which they beguile even them-selves. It is a kind of righteousness with them that they have such stern principles of duty and sacrifice. How greatly are they scandalised, too, by the self-indulgence, the parsimony, the show, the pleasures, the vanities of others who profess the Christian name ! And in all this they may be sincere, and not hypocritical. They only find it so much easier to be stiff in their judgments, and self-renouncing in their words and exhor-tations, that they slide over, only the more unwittingly, their own looseness and deficiency in the very things they insist on. How many preachers of Christ fall into just this snare ! Pray for us, brethren, for our temptation is great. Christians of this class commonly have it as a kind of merit; and how many Christian ministers repeat the same thing, that they never ask it of others to follow them. God forbids that they should in-dulge in any such conceit as that ! Yes, God forbid, indeed, the conceit, for it would be one ; and, what is more, God forbid that others be ever found as their followers ! and for just the

reason that they do not follow Christ.   They half-consciously know it themselves—hence their modesty.   Would they could also understand how great a thing it is in Christ and His first messengers, that they go before, to lead in all sacrifice and suffering; doing first themselves whatsoever they lay upon others.   I believe, my brethren, that there are almost none of us who do not slide into this infirmity, complimenting ourselves on the high principles we hold, and the severe standards we set up, in our words and judgments, when, in our practice, we fall low enough to require some such kind of comfort to piece out our evidence and satisfaction.   And then we compliment, again, our modesty, that we do not propose to be examples to others! How much more and more genuinely modest should we be, if we judged only as we practised and set forward others in words, only as we fortify words by example.   Let us understand ourselves in this; that we are not what we talk, or stand for with our words, but what we do and become.

3. Consider, in this subject, what is true of any real disciple, who is straying from Christ—viz., that his holy Shepherd, folding the flock and caring for it as a shepherd should, does not let him go, nor take it only as a fact that the flock is diminished by one, not caring by what one.   He knows what one it is, and, if the wanderer will listen, he may hear the Shepherd calling his name.   The love of Christ, as we have seen, is personal and particular, and He watches for His flock with a directly personal care.   Do not imagine, then, if you consciously begin to fall off, or stray, that you are no longer cared for by the Shepherd.   Christ follows you with His personal and particular love, and will not let you go.   That same tenderness which melted the heart of an apostle, when he said, "who loved me, and gave Himself for me," pursues you still.   It is faithful, patient, forgiving, and true; it waits and lingers, it whispers and calls, saying, "Will ye also go away?" holding on upon you by a personal and persistent love, that will not be content till you are gathered back into the fold, to be, as before, a follower. And the same is true where the love of many waxes cold, and whole bodies of disciples are chilled by worldliness, or carried away by common temptations; it is not the mass only, or the general flock, that Christ regards.   Each one He follows and calls, as truly as if he were the only one.   The wrong they do

G

Him, and the grief He feels, is personal. By name and privately He deals with each, gathering him back, if possible, to prayer and holy living, to faith, and sacrifice, and works of love. By these private reproofs, and these tender and personal remonstrances, brethren, He is calling after all you that stray from Him to-day. And if you think you have personal apologies, or have been stolen away by temptations you could not detect, He knows exactly what is true, and will every true allowance make, and, as being faithful to you, He will make no other. Whatever grace you want to bind you up and establish you, He waits to bestow. He will not only forgive you, readily and completely, but He will embrace you heartily, and take you again to His confidence ; the same sweet, personal confidence in which you stood before. Oh, thou wavering, faltering, failing disciple ! come thou, at His call, and see !

Finally, consider the close understanding with Christ, the ennobled confidence and dignity of a true discipleship. To be a disciple, is to have the revelation of Christ, and the secret witness of His love in the soul. It implies a most intimate and closely reciprocal state. According to the representation of the parable, the holy Shepherd knows His own sheep with a particular knowledge, and calleth them by name ; while they, on their part, know His voice and follow. A stranger will they not follow, but flee from him ; for they know not the voice of strangers. And He also says Himself, " I am the good shepherd, and know my sheep, and am known of mine." Oh, this deep and blessed knowledge—the knowledge of Christ—to be in the secret witness of His love, to be in His guidance, to be strong in His support, to be led into the mind of God by Him, and have our prayers shaped by His inward teaching ; so to be set in God's everlasting counsel, and be filled with the testimony that we please Him, this, all this it is to know Christ's voice. Happy are we, brethren, if the sense of this knowledge be in us.

And what can fill us with a loftier inspiration, or lift us into a more sublime and blessed confidence than this—the fact that Christ, the eternal Shepherd, has a personal recognition of us, leading us on by name, and calling us to follow? No matter whether He call us into ways of gain or of suffering, of honour or of scorn; it is all one, with such a Leader before us. Nay, if we go down to sound the depths of sorrow, and ennoble the pains of sacrifice, and perfume the grave of ignominy, what are these but a more inspiring and more godlike call, since He is now our leader even here?   O my brethren! here is our misery: that we think to go above Christ, and find some cheaper way; when, if we could truly descend to His level of sacrifice, and take His cross to follow, we should be raised in feeling and power, ennobled in impulse, glorified with Him in His joy. After all, the secret of all our dryness, the root of all our weakness, our want of fruit and progress, our dearth and desolation, is, that we cannot follow Christ.   First, we cannot believe that He has any particular care of us, or personal interest in our life; and then, falling away, at that point, from His lead, we drop into ourselves to do a few casual works of duty, in which neither we nor others are greatly blessed.   God forbid that we sacrifice our peace so cheaply!   Let us hear—oh, let us hear to-day the Shepherd's voice; and, as He knows us in our sin, so let us go after Him in His sacrifice.   Let us claim that inspiration, that ennobled confidence, that comes of being truly with Him.   Folded thus in His personal care, and led by the calling of His voice, for which we always listen, let us take His promise and follow, going in and out, and finding pasture.

VII.

LIGHT ON THE CLOUD.

JOB xxxvii. 21—"*And now men see not the bright light which is in the clouds; but the wind passeth, and cleanseth them.*"

THE argument is, let man be silent when God is dealing with him; for he cannot fathom God's inscrutable wisdom. Behold, God is great, and we know Him not. God thundereth marvellously with His voice; great things doeth He which we cannot comprehend. Dost thou know the wondrous works of Him that is perfect in knowledge? Teach us what we shall say unto Him, for we cannot order our speech by reason of darkness. If a man speak, surely he shall be swallowed up.

Then follows the text, representing man's life under the figure of a cloudy day. The sun is in the heavens, and there is always a bright light on the other side of the clouds, but only a dull, pale beam pierces through. Still, as the wind comes at length to the natural day of clouds, clearing them all away, and pouring in from the whole firmament a glorious and joyful light, so will a grand clearing come to the cloudy and dark day of life, and a full effulgence of light from the throne of God will irradiate all the objects of knowledge and experience.

Our reading of the text, you will observe, substitutes for *cleansing, clearing away,* which is more intelligible. Perhaps also it is better to read "on the clouds," and not "in." Still the meaning is virtually the same. The words, thus explained, offer three points which invite our attention.

I. *We live under a cloud, and see God's way only by a dim light.*

II. *God shines at all times with a bright light, above the cloud, and on the other side of it.*

III. *This cloud of obscuration is finally to be cleared away.*

I. We live under a cloud, and see God's way only by a dim light. As beings of intelligence, we find ourselves hedged in by mystery on every side. All our seeming knowledge is skirted. close at hand, by dark confines of ignorance. However drunk with conceit we may be, however ready to judge everything, we still comprehend almost nothing.

What, then, does it mean? Is God jealous of intelligence in us? Has He purposely drawn a cloud over His ways to baffle the search of our understanding? Exactly contrary to this. He is a Being who dwelleth in light, and calls us to walk in the light with Him. He has set His works about us to be a revelation to us always of His power and glory. His Word He gives us to be the expression of His will and character, and bring us into acquaintance with Himself. His Spirit He gives us to be a teacher and illuminator within. By all His providential works He is training intelligence in us and making us capable of knowledge.

No view of the subject, therefore, can be true that accuses Him. The true account appears to be, that the cloud under which we are shut down is not heavier than it must be. How can a Being Infinite be understood or comprehended by a being finite? And when this Being Infinite has plans that include infinite quantities, times, and relations, in which every present event is the last link of a train of causes reaching downward from a past eternity, and is to be connected also with every future event of a future eternity, how can a mortal, placed between these two eternities, without knowing either, understand the present fact, whatever it be, whose reasons are in both?

Besides, we have only just begun to be; and a begun existence is, by the supposition, one that has just begun to know, and has everything to learn. How then can we expect, in a few short years, to master the knowledge of God and His universal kingdom? What can He be to such but a mystery? If we could think Him out, without any experience, as we do the truths of arithmetic and geometry, we might get on faster and more easily. But God is not a mere thought of our own brain, as these truths are, but a Being in the world of substance, fact, and event, and all such knowledge has to be gotten slowly, through the rub of experience. We open, after a few days, our infantile eyes and begin to look about, perceive, handle, suffer, act and be acted on, and, proceeding in this manner, we gather in, by degrees, our data and material of knowledge; and so, by trial, comparison, distinction, the study of effects and wants, of rights and wrongs, of uses and abuses, we frame judgments of things, and begin to pass our verdict on the matters we know. But how long will it take us to penetrate, in this manner, the real significance of God's dealings with us and the world, and pass a really illuminated judgment on them? And yet, if we but love the right, as the first father did before his sin, God will be revealed in us internally, as the object of our love and trust, even from the first hour. He will not appear to be distant, or difficult. We shall know Him as a friendly presence in our heart's love, and we shall have such a blessed confidence in Him that if, in the outer world of fact and event, clouds and darkness appear to be round about Him, we shall have the certainty within that justice and judgment are the habitation of His throne. Meanwhile, He will be teaching us graciously, and drawing us insensibly, through our holy sympathies, into the sense of His ways, and widening, as fast as possible, the circle of our human limitation, that we may expatiate in discoveries more free. And thus it comes to pass that, as the eyelids of the infant are shut down, at first, over his unpractised eyes, which are finally strengthened for the open day, by the little, faint light that shines through them, so our finite, childish mind, saved from being dazzled, or struck blind, by God's powerful effulgence, and quickened by the gentle light that streams through His cloud, is prepared to gaze on the fulness of His glory, and receive His piercing brightness undimmed.

But there is another fact less welcome that must not be forgot when we speak of the darkness that obscures our knowledge of God. There is not only a necessary, but a guilty limitation upon us. And therefore we are not only obliged to learn, but, as being under sin, are also in a temper that forbids learning, having our mind disordered and clouded by evil. Hence, come our perplexities; for, as the sun cannot shew distinctly what it is in the bottom of a muddy pool, so God can never be distinctly revealed in the depths of a foul and earthly mind. To understand a philosopher requires, they tell us, a philosopher; to understand patriotism, requires a patriot; to understand purity, one that is pure; so, to understand God requires a godlike spirit. Having this, God will as certainly be revealed in the soul, as light through a transparent window. "He that loveth knoweth God, for God is love." What darkness, then, must be upon a mind that is not congenially tempered, a mind unlike to God, opposite to God, selfish, lustful, remorseful, and malignant! Even as an apostle says : " Having the understanding darkened, being alienated from the life of God through the ignorance that is in them, because of the blindness of their heart."

The very activity of reason, which ought to beget knowledge, begets only darkness now, artificial darkness. We begin a quarrel with limitation itself, and so with God. He is not only hid behind thick walls of mystery, but He is dreaded as a power unfriendly, suspected, doubted, repugnantly conceived. Whatever cannot be comprehended—and how very little can be—is construed as one construes an enemy, or as an ill-natured child construes the authority of a faithful father. An evil judgment taken up yesterday prepares another to-day, and this another to-morrow, and so a vast complicated web of false judgments, in the name of reason, is spread over all the subjects of knowledge. We fall into a state thus of general confusion, in which even the distinctions of knowledge are lost. Presenting our little mirror to the clear light of God, we might have received true images of things, and gotten by degrees a glorious wealth of knowledge, but we break the mirror, in the perversity of our sin, and offer only the shivered fragments to the light ; when, of course, we see distinctly nothing. Then, probably enough, we begin to sympathise with ourselves, and justify the ignorance we are in, wondering if there be a God that He should be so dark to us, or that He should fall behind these walls of silence, and suffer Himself to be only doubtfully guessed, through fogs of ignorance and obscurity. Reminded that He is and must be a mystery, we take it as a great hardship, or, it may be, an absurdity, that we are required to believe what we cannot comprehend. We are perplexed by the mode of His existence and action—how can He fill all things, and yet have no dimensions? How is it that He knows all things, before the things known exist ? Foreknowing what we will do, how can we be blamed for what we were thus certain beforehand to do? How is it that He creates, governs, redeems, and yet never forms a new purpose, or originates a new act, which is not from eternity? How is He infinitely happy, when a great many things ought to be, and are declared to be, repugnant or abhorrent to His feeling? How does He produce worlds out of nothing, or out of Himself, when nothing else exists? How did He invent forms and colours, never having seen them?

Entering the field of supposed revelation, the difficulties are increased in number, and the mysteries are piled higher than before. God is here declared to be incarnate, in the person of Jesus Christ, and the whole history of this wonderful Person is made up of things logically incompatible. He is the eternal Son of God, and the Son of Mary; He is Lord of all, and is born in a manger; stills the sea by His word, and, travelling on foot, is weary; asks, "Who convinceth me of sin?" and prays like one wading through all the deepest evils of sin; dies like a man, and rises like a God, bursting the bars of death by His power. Even God himself is no more simply God, but a three-fold mystery that mocks all understanding—Father, Son, and Holy Ghost. Is it revelation, then, that only burdens faith with mysteries more nearly impossible? Exactly so; nothing is more clear to any really thoughtful person than that, until some high point is passed, God ought to be enveloped in greater mystery, and will be, the closer He is brought to the mind. Knowing nothing of Him, He is no mystery at all; knowing a little, He is mystery begun; knowing more, He is a great and manifold deep, not to be fathomed. We are, and ought to be, overwhelmed by His magnitudes, till we are able to mount higher summits of intelligence than now. Or, if it be answered, that in some of these things we have contradictions, and not mere difficulties, it is enough to reply that the highest truths are wont to be expressed in forms of thought and language that, as forms, are repugnant. Nor is it any fault of these mere instrumental contradictions that we cannot reconcile them, if only they roll upon us senses of God's deep majesty and love, otherwise impossible. Our amazement itself is but the vehicle of His truth.

Turning next to the creative works of God, we find the cloud also upon these. The Lord by wisdom hath founded the earth, by understanding hath He established the heavens, there is no searching of His understanding; why He created the worlds when He did, and not before; what He could have been doing, or what enjoyment having, previous to their creation; and, if all things are governed by inherent laws, what more, as the universal Governor, He can find any place to do since—these are questions, again, before which speculative reason reels in amazement. If the baffled inquirer then drops out the search after God, as many do, and says—I will go down to nature, and it shall, at least, be my comfort that nature is intelligible, and even a subject of definite science, he shortly discovers that science only changes the place of mystery and leaves it unresolved. Hearing, with a kind of scientific pity, Job's question about the thunder—who can understand "the noise of His tabernacle?" he at first thinks it something of consequence to say that thunder is the noise of electricity, and not of God's tabernacle at all. But he shortly finds himself asking, who can understand electricity? and then, at last, he is with Job again. So, when he hears Job ask, "Knowest thou the ordinances of heaven?"—he recollects the great Newtonian discovery of gravity, and how, by aid of that principle, even the weights of the stars have been exactly measured, and their times predicted, and imagines that, now the secrets of astronomy are out, the ordinances of Heaven are understood. But here, again, it finally occurs to him to ask, what is gravity? and forthwith he is lost in a depth of mystery as profound as that of Job himself. And so, asking what is matter—what is life, animal and vegetable— what is heat, light, attraction, affinity—he discovers that, as yet, we really comprehend nothing, and that nature is a realm as truly mysterious even as God. Not a living thing grows out of the earth, or walks upon it, or flies above it; not an inanimate object exists, in heaven, earth, or sea, which is not filled and circled about with mystery as truly as in the days of Adam or Job, and which is not really as much above the understanding of science as the deepest things of God's eternity or of His secret life.

But there is, at least, one subject that he must understand and know even to its centre—viz., himself. Is he not a self-conscious being, and how can there be a cloud over that which is comprehended even by consciousness itself? Precisely contrary to this, there are more mysteries and dark questions grouped in his own person than he has ever met in the whole universe beside. He cannot even trace, with any exactness, the process by which he has been trained to be what he is, or the subtle forces by which his character has been shaped. Only

the smallest fraction of his past history can he distinctly remember, all the rest is gone. Even the sins for which he must
answer before God are gone out of his reach, and can no more
be reckoned up in order, till the forgotten past gives up its dead
things, to be again remembered. As little can he discover the
manner of his own spirit, how he remembers, perceives objects,
compares them, and, above all, how he wills and what it is that
drives him to a sentence against himself when he wills the
wrong. He knows, too, that in wrong, he is after self-advan-
tage; and every wrong, he also knew at the time, must be to his
disadvantage; why, then, did he do it? He cannot tell. The
sin of his sin will be, when he is judged before God, that he cannot tell. Even the familiar fact of his connexion with a body
is altogether inexplicable; and why any act of his will should
produce a motion of his body, he can no more discover than
why it should produce a motion among the stars. The beating
of his heart and the heaving of his lungs are equally mysterious.
In his whole nature and experience, he is, in fact, a deep and
inscrutable mystery to himself. God breathes unseen in his
heart, and yet he wonders that God is so far off. Death comes
in stealthily, and distills the fatal poison that will end his life,
unseen and unsuspected. He goes down to his grave, not knowing, by any judgment of his own, apart from God's promise
(which he does not believe), that he shall live again. What
shall be the manner of his resurrection, and with what body he
shall come, he can as little comprehend, as he can the mystery
of the incarnation.

Finding, therefore, God, nature, himself, overhung with this
same cloud, it is not wonderful that he suffers bitter afflictions,
and galls himself against every corner of God's purposes. Why
is society a weight so oppressive on the weak and the poor? If
sin is such an evil, as it certainly is, why did the Creator, being
almighty, suffer it? Indeed, there is almost nothing that meets
us, between our first breathing and our graves, that does not, to
an evil mind, connect, in one way or another, some perplexity,
some accusing or questioning thought, some inference that is
painful, or perhaps atheistical. Can it be? Why should it be?
How can a good God let it be? If He means to have it otherwise, is He not defeated? If defeated, is He God? If He has
no plan, how can I trust Him? If His plan will suffer such

things, how then can I trust Him ?—these are the questions that are continually crowding upon us. The cloud is all the while over us. He hath made darkness His pavilion, and thick clouds of the skies. This man's prosperity is dark ; that man's adversity is dark. The persecutions of the good, the afflictions of the righteous, the desolations of conquest, the fall of nations and their liberties, the extinction of churches, the sufferings of innocence, the pains of animals, the removal by death of genius and character just ripened to bless the world—there is no end to our dark questions. There are times, too, when our own personal experience becomes enveloped in darkness. We not only cannot guess what it means, or what God will do with us in it, but it wears a look contrary to what appear to be our just expectations. We are grieved, perplexed, confounded. Other men are blessed in things much worse. We ourselves have been successful in things far more questionable, and when our deserts were less. What does it mean, that God is covering His way under these thick clouds of mystery and seeming caprice ? In short, we may sum it up, as a general truth, that nothing in the world is really luminous to a mind unilluminated by religion ; and if we say that the Christian walks in the light, it is not so much that he can always understand God, as it is that he has confidence in Him, and has Him always near.

Thus we live. Practically, much is known about God and His ways, all that we need to know ; but, speculatively, or by the mere understanding, almost nothing, save that we cannot know. The believing mind dwells in continual light ; for, when God is revealed within, curious and perplexing questions are silent. But the mind that judges God, or demands a right to comprehend Him before it believes, stumbles, complains, wrangles, and finds no issue to its labour. Still there is light, and we pass on now to shew—

II. That there is abundance of light on the other side of the cloud, and above it.

This we might readily infer, from the fact that so much of light shines through. When the clouds overhead are utterly black, too black to be visible, we understand that it is night, or that the sun is absent ; but, when there is a practical and sufficient light for our works, we know that the sun is behind them, and we call it day. So it is when God spreadeth a cloud upon His throne. We could not see even the mystery, if there were no light behind it, just as we could not see the clouds if no light shone through.

The experience of every soul that turns to God is a convincing proof that there is light somewhere, and that which is bright and clear. Was it a man struggling with great afflictions, an injured man crushed by heavy wrongs; was it a man desolated and broken down by domestic sorrows; was it a rich man stripped by sore losses and calamities; was it a proud man blasted by slander; was it an atheist groping after curious knowledge, and starving on the chaff of questions unresolved—be it one or other of these, for all alike were tormented in the same perplexities of the darkened understanding, everything was dark and dry, and empty; but when they come to Christ and believe in Him, it is their common surprise to find how suddenly everything becomes luminous. Speculatively, they understand nothing which before was hidden, and yet there is a wondrous glory shining on their path. God is revealed within, and God is light. The flaming circle of eternal day skirts the horizon of the mind. Their dark questions are forgot, or left behind. They are even become insignificant. Their dignity is gone, and the soul, basking in the blessed sunshine of God's love, thinks it nothing, any more, if it could understand all mysteries. In all which it is made plain that, if we are under the cloud, there is yet a bright light above.

It will also be found, as another indication, that things which, at some time, appeared to be dark—afflictions, losses, trials, wrongs, defeated prayers, and deeds of suffering patience, yielding no fruit—are very apt, afterward, to change colour and become visitations of mercy. And so where God was specially dark, He commonly brings out, in the end, some good or blessing in which the subject discovers that his heavenly Father only understood his wants better than he did himself. God was dark in His way, only because His goodness was too deep in counsel for him to follow it to its mark. It is with him as with Joseph, sold into slavery, and so into the rule of a kingdom; or as it was with Job, whose latter end, after he had been stripped of everything, was more blessed than his beginning; or as with Nehemiah, whose sorrowing and disconsolate look itself brought him the opportunity to restore the desolations over which he sorrowed. Even the salvation of the world is accomplished through treachery, false witness, and a cross. All our experience in life goes to shew that the better understanding we have of God's dealings, the more satisfactory they appear. Things which seemed dark or inexplicable, or even impossible for God to suffer without wrong in Himself, are really bright with goodness in the end. What, then, shall we conclude, but that on the other side of the cloud, there is always a bright and glorious light, however dark it is underneath.

Hence it is that the Scriptures make so much of God's character as a light-giving Power, and turn the figure about into so many forms. "In God," they say, "is light, and no darkness at all." According to John's vision of the Lord, "His countenance was as the sun that shineth in his strength." The image of Him given by another apostle is even more sublime, "Who only hath immortality, dwelling in the light that no man can approach unto;" language, possibly, in which he had some reference to his own conversion; when a light, above the brightness of the sun, bursting upon him and shining round about him, seared his eye-balls; so that afterward there fell off from them, as it had been scales of cinder. God, therefore, he conceives to be light inapproachable, as figured in that experience. And probably enough he would say, that as the astronomers in looking at the sun arm their sight with a smoky or coloured medium, so the very clouds we complain of are mercifully interposed, in part, and rather assist than hinder our vision.

It is little therefore to say, and should never be a fact incredible, that however dark our lot may be, there is light enough on the other side of the cloud, in that pure empyrean where God dwells, to irradiate every darkness of the world; light enough to clear every difficult question, remove every ground of obscurity, conquer every atheistic suspicion, silence every hard judgment; light enough to satisfy, nay, to ravish the mind for ever. Even the darkest things God has explanations for; and it is only necessary to be let into His views and designs, as when we are made capable of being we certainly shall, to see a transcendent wisdom and beauty in them all. At present, we have no capacity broad enough to comprehend such a revelation. We see through a glass darkly, but we see what we can.

When we can see more, there is more to be seen. On the other side of the cloud there is abundance of light. This brings me to say—

III. That the cloud we are under will finally break way and be cleared.

On this point we have many distinct indications. Thus it coincides with the general analogy of God's works, to look for obscurity first, and light afterward. According to the Scripture account of the creation, there was, first a period of complete darkness; then a period of mist and cloud, where the daylight is visible, but not the sun; then the sun beams out in a clear open sky, which is called, in a way of external description, the creation of the sun. How many of the animals begin their life at birth with their eyes closed, which are afterward opened to behold the world into which they have come. How many myriads of insects begin their existence underground, emerging afterward from their dark abode, to take wings and glitter in the golden light of day. If we observe the manner, too, of our own intellectual discoveries, we shall generally see the inquirer groping long and painfully under a cloud, trying and experimenting in a thousand guesses to no purpose, till finally a thought takes him and behold the difficulty is solved! At a single flash, so to speak, the light breaks in, and what before was dark is clear and simple as the day. Darkness first and light afterward, this is the law of science universally. By so many and various analogies, we are led to expect that the cloud, under which we live in things spiritual, will finally be lifted, and the splendour of eternal glory poured around us.

Our desire for knowledge, and the manner in which God manages to inflame that desire, indicate the same thing. This desire He has planted naturally in us, as hunger is natural in our bodies, or the want of light in our eyes. And the eye is not a more certain indication that light is to be given, than our desire to know divine things is that we shall be permitted to know them. And the evidence is yet further increased, in the fact that the good have a stronger desire for this knowledge than mere nature kindles. And if we say, with the Scripture, that "the fear of the Lord is the beginning of knowledge," doubtless the body of it is to come after.

It is the glory of God, indeed, to conceal a thing, but not absolutely, or for the sake of concealment. He does it only till a mind and appetite for the truth is prepared, to make His revelation to. He gives us a dim light, and sets us prying at the walls of mystery, that He may create an appetite and relish in us for true knowledge. Then it shall be a joyful and glorious gift—"drink to the thirsty, food to the hungry, light to the prisoner's cell." And He will pour it in from the whole firmament of His glory. He will open his secret things, open the boundaries of universal order, open His own glorious mind and His eternal purposes.

The Scriptures also notify us of a grand assize, or judgment, when the merit of all His doings with us, as of our doings toward Him, will be revised; and it appears to be a demand of natural reason, that some grand exposition of the kind should be made, that we may be let into the manner of His government far enough to do it honour. This will require Him to take away the cloud in regard to all that is darkest in our earthly state. Every perplexity must now be cleared, and the whole moral administration of God, as related to the soul, must be sufficiently explained. Sin, the fall, the pains and penalties and disabilities consequent, redemption, grace, the discipline of the righteous, the abandonment of the incorrigibly wicked—all these must now be understood. God has light enough to shed on all these things, and He will not conceal it. He will shine forth in glorious and transcendent brightness, unmasked by cloud, and all created minds, but the incorrigible outcasts and enemies of His government, will respond— "Alleluia; Salvation, and glory, and honour, and power, be unto the Lord our God; for just and true are his judgments."

Precisely what is to be the manner and measure of our knowledge, in this fuller and more glorious revelation of the future, is not clear to us now; for that is one of the dark things or mysteries of our present state. But the language of Scripture is remarkable. It even declares that we shall see God as He is; and the intensity of the expression is augmented, if possible, by the effects attributed to the sight : "We shall be like Him; for we shall see Him as He is." We shall be so irradiated and penetrated, in other words, by His glory, as to be transformed into a spiritual resemblance, partaking His purity, reflecting His beauty, ennobled by His divinity. It is even declared that our knowledge of Him shall be complete. Now we know in part; then shall we know even as also we are known. To say that we shall know God as He knows us is certainly the strongest declaration possible, and it is probably hyperbolical; for it would seem to be incredible that a finite mind should at once, or even at any time in its eternity, comprehend the Infinite, as it is comprehended by the Infinite. It is also more agreeable to suppose that there will be an everlasting growth in knowledge, and that the blessed minds will be for ever penetrating new depths of discovery, clearing up wider fields of obscurity, attaining to a higher converse with God and a deeper insight of His works; and that this breaking forth of light and beauty in them by degrees and upon search, will both occupy their powers and feed their joy. Still, that there will be a great and sudden clearing of God's way, as we enter that world, and a real dispersion of all the clouds that darken us here, is doubtless to be expected; for when our sin is completely taken away (as we know it then will be), all our guilty blindness will go with it; and that of itself will prepare a glorious unveiling of God, and a vision of His beauty as it is.

In what manner we shall become acquainted with God's mind, or the secrets of His interior life, whether through some manifestation by the Eternal Word, like the incarnate appearing of Jesus, or partly in some way more direct, we cannot tell. But the Divine nature and plan will be open, doubtless, in some way most appropriate, for our everlasting study, and our everlasting progress in discovery. The whole system of His moral purposes and providential decrees, His penal distributions and redeeming works, will be accessible to us, and all the creatures and creations of His power offered to our acquaintance and free inspection. Our present difficulties and hard questions will soon be solved and passed by. Even the world itself, so difficult to penetrate, so clouded with mystery, will become a transparency to us, through which God's light will pour as the sun through the open sky. John knew no better way of describing the perfectly luminous state of the blessed minds than to say, "And there shall be no night there; and they need no candle, neither light of the sun; for the Lord God giveth them light." They dwell thus in the eternal daylight of love and reason; for they are so let into the mind of God, and the glorious mysteries of His nature, that everything is lighted up as they come to it, even as the earth and its objects by the sun: "The Lord God giveth them light."

In closing the review of such a subject as this, let us first of all receive a lesson of modesty, and particularly such as are most wont to complain of God, and boldest in their judgments against Him. Which way soever we turn in our search after knowledge, we run against mystery at the second or third step. And a a great part of our misery, a still greater of our unbelief, and all the lunatic rage of our scepticism, arises in the fact that we either do not, or will not see it to be so. Ignorance trying to comprehend what is inscrutable, and out of patience that it cannot make the high things of God come down to its own petty measures, is the definition of all atheism. There is no true comfort in life, no dignity in reason, apart from modesty. We wrangle with Providence and call it reason, we rush upon God's mysteries, and tear ourselves against the appointments of His throne, and then, because we bleed, complain that He cruelly mocks our understanding. All our disputings and hard speeches are the frothing of our ignorance maddened by our pride. Oh, if we could see our own limitations, and how little it is possible for us to know of matters infinite, how much less, clouded by the necessary blindness of a mind disordered by evil, we should then be in a way to learn; and the lessons God will teach would put us in a way to know what now is hidden from us. Knowledge puffeth up, charity buildeth up. One makes a balloon of us, the other a temple. And as one, lighter than the wind, is driven loose in its aerial voyage, to be frozen in the airy heights of speculation, or drifted into the sea to be drowned in the waters of ignorance, which it risked without ability to swim, so the other, grounded on a rock, rises into solid majesty, proportionate, enduring, and strong. After all his laboured disputings and lofty reasons with his friends, Job turns himself to God, and says: "I know that thou canst do every thing, and that no thought can be withholden from thee. Who is he that hideth counsel without knowledge? therefore have I uttered that I understood not; things too wonderful for me, that I knew not."

H

There is the true point of modesty—he has found it at last!
Whoever finds it has made a great attainment.

How clear is it also, in this subject, that there is no place for
complaint or repining under the sorrows and trials of life.
There is nothing in what has befallen, or befalls you, my friends,
which justifies impatience or peevishness. God is inscrutable,
but not wrong. Remember, if the cloud is over you, that there
is a bright light always on the other side ; also, that the time is
coming, either in this world or the next, when that cloud will
be swept away, and the fulness of God's light and wisdom
poured around you. Everything which has befallen you, whatever sorrow your heart bleeds with, whatever pain you suffer
—even though it be the pains of a passion like that which Jesus
endured at the hands of His enemies—nothing is wanting but
to see the light that actually exists, waiting to be revealed, and
you will be satisfied. If your life is dark, then walk by faith,
and God is pledged to keep you as safe as if you could understand everything. "He that dwelleth in the secret place of the
most High shall abide under the shadow of the Almighty."

These things, however, I can say with no propriety to many.
No such comforts or hopes belong to you that are living without God. You have nothing to expect from the revelations of
the future. The cloud that you complain of will indeed be
cleared away, and you will see that in all your afflictions, severities, and losses, God was dealing with you righteously and
kindly. You will be satisfied with God and with all that He
has done for you ; but, alas ! you will not be satisfied with
yourself. That is more difficult—for ever impossible ! And I
conceive no pang more dreadful than to see, as you will, the
cloud lifted from every dealing of God that you thought to be
harsh or unrighteous, and to feel that, as He is justified, you
yourself are for ever condemned. You can no more accuse your
birth, your capacity, your education, your health, your friends,
your enemies, your temptations. You still had opportunities,
convictions, calls of grace, and calls of blessing. You are
judged according to that you had, and not according to that
you had not. Your mouth is eternally shut, and God is
eternally clear.

Finally, it accords with our subject to observe that, while the
inscrutability of God should keep us in modesty and stay our

complaints against Him, it should never suppress, but rather sharpen our desire of knowledge. For the more there is that is hidden, the more is to be discovered and known, if not to-day, then to-morrow, if not to-morrow, when the time God sets for it is come. To know, is not to surmount God, as some would appear to imagine. Rightly viewed, all real knowledge is but the knowledge of God. Knowledge is the fire of adoration, adoration is the gate of knowledge. And when this gate of the soul is fully opened, as it will be when the adoring grace is complete in our deliverance from all impurity, what a revelation of knowledge must follow! Having now a desire of knowledge perfected in us, that is, clear of all conceit, ambition, haste, impatience, the clouds under which we lived in our sin are for ever rolled away, and our adoring nature, transparent to God as a window to the sun, is filled with His eternal light. No mysteries remain but such as comfort us in the promise of a glorious employment. The light of the moon is as the light of the sun, and the light of the sun sevenfold; and every object of knowledge, irradiated by the brightness of God, shines with a new celestial clearness and an inconceivable beauty. The resurrection morning is a true sunrising, the inbursting of a cloudless day on all the righteous dead. They wake, transfigured, at their Master's call, with the fashion of their countenance altered and shining like His own :—

> Creature all grandeur, son of truth and light,
> Up from the dust, the last great day is bright—
> Bright on the holy mountain round the throne,
> Bright where in borrow'd light the far stars shone !
> Regions on regions far away they shine,
> 'Tis light ineffable, 'tis light divine !
> Immortal light and life for evermore !

There was a cloud, and there was a time when man saw not the brightness that shined upon it from above. That cloud is lifted, and God is clear in His own essential beauty and glory for ever.

VIII.

THE CAPACITY OF RELIGION EXTIRPATED BY DISUSE.

MATTHEW xxv. 28—*" Take therefore the talent from him."*

MANY persons read this parable of the talents, I believe, very much as if it related only to gifts external to the person; or, if to gifts that are personal, to such only as are called talents in the lower and merely manward relations and uses of life—such as the understanding, reason, memory, imagination, feeling, and whatever powers are most concerned in discovery, management, address, and influence over others. But the great Teacher's meaning reaches higher than this, and comprehends more—viz., those talents, more especially, which go to exalt the subject in his God-ward relations. The main stress of His doctrine hinges, I conceive, on our responsibility as regards the capacity of religion itself; for this, in highest pre-eminence, is the talent—the royal gift of man. The capacity of religion, taken as the highest trust God gives us, He is teaching His disciples may be five-folded, tenfolded, indefinitely increased, as all other gifts are, by a proper use; or it may be neglected, hid, suppressed, and, being thus kept back, may finally be so reduced as to be even extirpated. This latter—the extirpation or taking away of the holy talent, is the fearful and admonitory close to which the parable is brought in my text. In pursuing the subject presented, two points will naturally engage our attention.

I. *That the capacity for religion is a talent—the highest talent we have.* And,

II. *That this capacity is one that, by total disuse and the overgrowth of others, is finally extirpated.*

I. The capacity for religion is a talent—the highest talent we have.

We mean by a talent the capacity for doing or becoming

something ; as for learning, speaking, trade, command. Our talents are as numerous, therefore, and various as the effects we may operate.

We have talents of the body, too, and talents of the mind or soul." Our talents of body are strength, endurance, grace, swiftness, beauty, and the like. Our mental or spiritual talents are more various, and, for the purpose we have now in hand, may be subdivided into such as belong in part to the natural life, and such as belong wholly to the religious and spiritual.

All those which can be used, or which come into play in earthly subjects, and apart from God and religion, are natural ; and those which relate immediately to God and things unseen, as connected with God, are religious. In the former class we may name intellect, judgment, reason, observation, abstraction, imagination, memory, feeling, affection, will, conscience, and all the moral sentiments. These all come into the uses and act a part in the activities of religion, but they have uses and activities in things earthly, where religion is wholly apart, or may be ; and therefore we do not class them as religious talents. An atheist can remember, reason, hate, and even talk of duty; and therefore these several kinds of talent are not distinctively religious.

The religious talents compose the whole God-ward side of faculty in us. They are such especially as come into exercise in the matter of religious faith and experience, and nowhere else. They include first the want of God, which is, in fact, a receptivity for God. All wants are capacities of reception, and in this view are talents according to their measure. Low grades of being want low objects, but the want of man is God. And as all great wants in things inferior, such as knowledge, honour, power, belong only to great men, what shall we consider this want of God to be, but the highest possible endowment ?

Nearly related to this talent of want is the talent of inspiration. By this we mean a capacity to be permeated, illuminated, guided, exalted by God or the Spirit of God within, and yet so as not to be any the less completely ourselves. This is a high distinction—a glorious talent. No other kind of being known to us in the works of God, whether animate or inanimate, has the capacity to admit in this manner and be visited by the inspirations of God. It requires a nature gloriously akin to God in its mould thus to let in His action, falling freely into chime with His freedom, and in consciously self-acting power receiving the impulsion of His eternal thought and character.

We have also another religious talent or God-ward capacity, which may be called the spiritual sense or the power of divine apprehension. Some kind of apprehensive or perceptive power belongs to every creature of life, as we may see in the distinguishing touch of the sensitive plant, in the keen auditory and scenting powers of many quadrupeds, in our own five senses, or, rising still higher, in that piercing insight of mind which distinguishes the intellectual and scientific verities of things. So also there is given to our spiritual nature a still higher talent —the spiritual sense—the power of distinguishing God and receiving the manifestation or immediate witness of God. I speak not here of a speculating up to God, or an inference that conducts to God, but of a window that opens directly on Him from within, lets in the immediate light or revelation of God, and makes the soul even conscious of His reality as of its own.

The capacity of religious love is another and distinct kind of talent. Other kinds of love are merely emotional or humanly social, involving no principle of life, either good or bad, and no particular spiritual condition. Whereas this love of God, and of men as related to God, is a determining force in respect to all character and all springs of action. We have it only as we have a certain talent or capacity of religious love—the capacity that is to let in or appropriate the love of God to us. Which if we do it comes, not as some rill or ripple of our human love, changing nothing in us, but it pours in as a tide with mighty floods of joy and power, and sets the whole nature beating with it, as the shores give answer to the ocean roll and roar. Now the man acts out of love and from it. He chimes with all good freely; for his love is the spirit of all good. His activity is rest, and a lubricating power of joy gladdens all the works of duty and sacrifice.

The power of faith also is a religious talent, which is to religion what the inductive or experimental power is to science. It is a power of knowing God, or finding God by experiment. It is the power in human souls of falling on God, and being recumbent on Him in trust, so as to prove Him out and find the answer of His personality. Reason cannot do it, but faith can.

It knows God, or may reciprocally, and finds a way into His secret will and mind so as to be of Him—a conscious partaker of His divine nature and life.

These now are the talents of religion—the highest, noblest, closest to Divinity of all the powers we have. And yet how many never once think of them as having any special consequence, or even as being talents at all, just because, living in separation from God, they are never once allowed to come into use.

If, then, you will see, in the plainest manner, what is their true place and order in the soul, you shall find them, first of all, at the head of all its other powers, holding them subordinate. They are like the capital city of an empire, flowing down upon all the other cities to regulate, animate, and, at the same time, appropriate them all. What we sometimes call the intellectual powers—observation, abstraction, reason, memory, imagination—submit themselves at once, when religion comes into the field, to be the servitors of religion. None of these faculties make use of the religious, but the religious use and appropriate them, in which we see at a glance their natural inferiority.

Next, you will see that all these other talents fall into a stunted and partially disabled state when they are not shone upon, kept in warmth, and raised in grade by the talents of religion. They sometimes grow intense, in their downward activity, on mere things : witness the scientific activity of the French people ; but this scientific intensity only makes the tenuity, the affectations, the sentimentalities substituted for love, the mock heroics of fame substituted for the heroics of faith, the barrenness of great thought, the pruriency of conceit, the more painfully evident. No people, emptied of religion, was ever genuinely great in anything.

How manifestly, too, are the subjects of the religious talents superior to those of the natural, even as " the heaven is high above the earth." History, science, political judgments, poetry as a mere growth of nature, philosophy as a development of reason, belong to these. The others look on God, embrace the infinite in God, receive the love of God, experience God, let in the inspirations of God, discover worlds beyond the world, seize the fact of immortality, deal in salvation, aspire to ideal and divine perfection.

Again, it will be seen that all the greatest things ever done in
the world have been done by the instigations and holy eleva-
tions of the religious capacity. We shall never have done
hearing, I suppose, of Regulus and Curtius, and such like specimens of the Roman virtue, great in death; but the whole army
of the martyrs, comprising thousands of women, and even many
small children, dying firmly in the refusal to deny the Lord
Jesus, are a full match and more, by the legion, for the bravest
of the Romans. What but the mighty mastership of religion
has ever led a people up through civil wars and revolutions, into
a regenerated order and liberty? What has planted colonies for
a great history but religion? The most august and most beautiful structures of the world have been temples of religion;
crystalisations, we may say, of worship. The noblest charities,
the best fruits of learning, the richest discoveries, the best insti-
tutions of law and justice, every greatest thing the world has
seen, represents, more or less directly, the fruitfulness and cre-
ativeness of the religious talents.

The real summit, therefore, of our humanity is here, as our
blessed Lord plainly understands in His parable of the talents.
He does not overlook other and inferior gifts, for God will
certainly hold us responsible for all gifts; but it is this, more
especially, that He holds in view, when He says, "Take therefore the talent from him." In the clause that follows, we are
not to understand, of course, that God will literally pass the
talent over to one who has been more faithful. The terms are
sufficiently met by understanding that God will so dispense the
talents as regularly to increase the gifts of the faithful, and
regularly diminish, or gradually extirpate, the gifts of those
who will not use them. We proceed, then,

II. To shew that the religious talent, or capacity, is one that,
by total disuse and the overgrowth of others, is finally extirpated.

Few men, living without God, are aware of any such possibility, and still less, of the tremendous fact itself. That they are
really reducing themselves in this manner to lower dimensions,
shortening in their souls, making blank spaces of all the highest
and divinest talents of their nature—alas! they dream not of it;
on the contrary, they imagine that they are getting above reli-

gion, growing too competent and wise to be longer subjected to its authority, or incommoded by its requirements. They do not see, or suspect, that this very fact is evidence itself of a process more radical and fearful, even that which Christ himself is teaching in the parable. Are you willing, my friends, to allow the discovery of this process, this dying process, this extirpating process, which, in your neglect of God, is removing, by degrees, the very talent for religion, your highest and most sacred endowment?

Hear, then, first of all, what is the teaching of the Scripture. That this is the precise point of the parable of the talents we have seen already. In close connexion, also, Christ reiterates His favourite maxim—"To him that hath shall be given, and from him that hath not shall be taken away even that which he hath." And here, also, the very point of meaning is, that neglected or abused talents will be shortened more and more by continued neglect and abuse, and, at last, will be virtually taken away or exterminated. What is said in the Scripture of spiritual blindness, or the loss of spiritual perception, will also occur to you. "For this people's heart is waxed gross," says the Saviour, "and their ears are dull of hearing, and their eyes have they closed." What is this closing of the eye, this loss of sight, but the judicial extirpation of sight? Even as He says in another place, "He hath blinded their eyes and hardened their heart, that they should not see with their eyes, nor understand with their heart." Hence, also, what is said derogatively of the wisdom of the wise and the understanding of the prudent— "That conceit of opinion, falsely called philosophy, which grows up in the neglect of God." The Word of God looks on it with pity, calls it folly and strong delusion, as if it were a kind of disability that comes on the soul in the gradual loss or extirpation of its highest powers. What is it but the uplifting littleness of opinion when these highest powers are taken away? These babblings of opinion, speculation, reason, are also presented in a more pathologic way, as a kind of cancerous activity in the lower functions, that will finally devour all the higher powers of godliness and love. "Shun profane and vain babblings, for they will increase unto more ungodliness, and their word will eat as doth a canker." How sadly verified is the picture, in the ever-increasing ungodliness of the over-curious and merely speculative spirit ; in the swelling bulk of its conceit, and the reduction, correspondently, of all highest function of insight.

Now this general view of a necessary taking away, or spiritual extirpation, of which we are admonished by the Scriptures under these various forms, is referrible, I conceive, to two great laws, or causes. It is due partly to the neglect of the higher talents of our religious nature, and partly to the over-activity or overgrowth of the other and subordinate talents.

1. To the neglect of the talents, or capacities of religion. All living members, whether of body or mind, require use, or exercise. It is necessary to their development, and, without it, they even die. Thus, if one of the arms be kept in free use, from childhood onward, while the other is drawn up over the head and made rigid there, by long and violent detention—a feat of religious austerity which the idolaters of the East often practise—the free arm and shoulder will grow to full size, and the other will gradually shrink and perish. So if one of the eyes were permanently covered, so as never to see the light, the other would be likely to grow more sharp and precise in its power, while this is losing its capacity, and becoming a discontinued organ, or inlet of perception. It is on the same principle that the fishes which inhabit the underground river of a great western cave, while in form and species they appear to correspond with others that swim in the surface waters of the region adjacent, have yet the remarkable distinction of possessing no eyes. Since there is no light in their underground element, the physical organism instinctively changes type. It will not even go on to make eyes, when they cannot be used. It therefore drops them out, presenting us the strange, exceptional product of an eyeless race.

So it is with all mental and spiritual organs. Not used, they gradually wither and die. The child, for example, that grows up in utter neglect, and without education, or anything to develop its powers, grows dull at last, and brutish ; and, by the time it is twenty or thirty years old, the powers it had appear to be very much taken away. The man, thus abridged in faculty, cannot learn to read without the greatest difficulty. The hand cannot be trained to grace, or the eye to exactness. The very conscience, disused as having any relation to God, is blunted and stupified. But, while we note this visible decay of the functions specified, let it be observed that here, in the case of the child, there is no such thing as a complete disuse. The most uneducated man has a certain necessary use of his common faculties of intelligence, and, in some low sense, keeps them in exercise. He cannot take care of his body, cannot provide for life, cannot act his part among men, without contrivance, thought, plan, memory, reason, all the powers that distinguish him as an intelligent being. Hence these faculties never can be wholly exterminated by disuse, however much reduced in scope and quality they may be. But it is not so with the religious talents. In a worldly life they are almost absolutely disused. They are kept under, suppressed, allowed no range or play. According to the parable, they are wrapped up in a napkin and hid. Refusing to know God, to let your deep want receive Him, to admit the holy permeations of His Spirit, to be flooded with His all-transforming love, to come into the secret discerning and acquaintance of His mind, and live in the mutuality of His personal fellowship, you command all these higher talents of your soul to exist in disuse. This is the fearful, horrible thing in your life of sin, that you sentence all your God-ward powers to a state of utter nothingness, to be ears that must not hear, eyes that must not see. And then, what must finally follow, but that they cannot? How is it possible for any talent or gift to survive that cannot be exercised? And this process of extirpation will be hastened, again,

2. By the operation of that immense overgrowth or overactivity which is kept up in the other powers. Thus it is that gardeners, when a tree is making wood too fast, understand that it will make no fruit—all the juices and nutritive fluids being carried off in the other direction to make wood; and therefore, to hasten the growth of fruit, they head in the branches. So when trees are growing rapidly upward, as in a forest, that growth calls away the juices from the lower and lateral branches, and leaves them to die. A healthy limb of our body, being checked by some disease, the other limbs or members call off the nutriment in their direction; when it begins to wither, and, at last, is virtually extirpated.

Just so it is when a child becomes preternaturally active in some particular faculty, under the stimulus of success or much applause, it turns out finally that the wonderful activity that made him a prodigy in figures or in memory, unless early arrested, has sunk him to a rank as much below mediocrity in everything else. His overgrowth in arithmetic or in the memorizing powers takes away the nutriment of all his other functions and leaves him to a miserable inferiority.

Just so it is again, when the pursuit of money grows to a monster passion of the soul, the mind dwindles, the affections wither, and sometimes even the nerve of hunger itself ceases to act, leaving the wretched miser to perish by starvation fast by his heap of gold. So if a man lives for the table, the organs of the mouth and chin change their expression, the eye grows dull, the gait heavy, the voice takes a coarse, animalised sound, and the higher qualities of intelligence he may once have manifested will be manifested nowhere save as purveyors to the organs of taste and the gastric energy.

In the same way a man who is brought up in mere conventionalities, and taught to regard appearances as the only realities, loses out the sense of truth. He blushes at the least defect in his toilet and lies to get away from an honest debt without any trace of compunction or shame for his baseness.

And so also the child, brought up as a thief, gets an infinite power of cunning and adroitness, and loses out just as much in the power of true perception.

In the same way a race of men, long occupied in ferocious wars, grow sharp in the hearing, keen as the beasts of prey in pursuit, sensitively shy of death when it can be avoided, and when it cannot, equally stoical in regard to it; but, while these talents of blood are unfolding so remarkably, they lose out utterly the sense of order, the instinct of prudence and providence, all the sweet charities, all the finer powers of thought, and become a savage race. Having lost a full half of their nature, and sunk below the possibility of progress, we for that reason call them savages.

By a little different process the Christian monks were turned to fiends of blood without being savages. Exercised, day and night, in a devotion that was aired by no outward social duties, waiting only on the dreams and visions of a cloistered religion, all the gentle humanities and social charities were absorbed or taken away. And then their very prayers would draw blood, and they would go out from the real Presence itself to bless the knife or kindle the fire.

Now just this extirpating process, which you have seen operating here on so large a scale, is going on continually in the overactive worldliness of all men that are living without God. An extravagant activity of some kind is always stimulating their inferior and merely natural faculties, and extirpating the higher talents of religion. Occupied with schemes that are only world-ward and selfish, there is an egregiously intense activity in that direction, coupled with entire inaction in all the highest perceptions and noblest affinities of their godlike nature. To say that these latter will be finally taken away, or extirpated in this manner is to say nothing which permits a doubt. It cannot be otherwise. All the laws of vital being, whether in body or mind, must be overturned to allow it to be otherwise. No man can live out a life of sin without also living out all the God-ward talent of his soul.

Let me come a degree nearer to you now, and lay the question side by side with your experience. Is it wrong to assume that your religious sense was proportionately much stronger and more active in childhood than it is now? Thus onward, during your minority, you felt the reality of God and things unseen, as you cannot now, by your utmost effort. It is as if these worlds beyond the world had faded away, or quite gone out. You have a great deal more knowledge than you then had—knowledge of books, men, business, scenes, subjects, a more practised judgment, a greater force of argument; but it troubles you to find that these higher things are just as much further off and less real. It even surprises you to find that you are growing sceptical, without any, the least, effort to be so. Perhaps you begin at times to imagine that it must be only because of some fatal weakness in the evidences of religion. Why else should it lose its power over your mind as you grow more intelligent? There is one very simple answer, my friends, to this inquiry—viz., that eyes disused gradually lose the power to see. If God gave you a religious talent, whereby to ally you to Himself, an eye to see Him and catch the light of unseen worlds, a want to long after Him, and you have never used this higher nature at all, what wonder is it that it begins to wither and do its functions feebly, as a perishing member? If your bodily eyes had, for so long a

time, been covered and forbidden once to see, what less could
have befallen them? Your very hand, held fast to your side for
only half the time, would be a perished member. And what
does it signify that your other faculties, or talents, have been
growing in strength so plausibly? What could be the result of
this selfish and world-ward activity, but a prodigious drawing
off of personal life and energy in that direction? Hence it is
that you grow blind to God. Hence that, when you undertake
to live a different life, you get on so poorly, and your very
prayers fly away into nothingness, finding only emptiness to
embrace, and darkness to see.

All this, my friends, which I gather out of your own experience, is but a practical version of Christ's own words—"Take
therefore the talent from him." It is being taken away rapidly,
and the shreds of it will very soon be all that is left. Your
religious nature will finally become a virtually exterminated
organ. Neither let it be imagined that, meaning no such thing,
but really intending, at some future time, to turn yourself to
God, no such thing will be allowed to befall you. It is befalling
you, and that is enough to spoil you of any such confidence.
Besides, it was not shewn in the parable that the servant who
disused his talent threw it away. He carefully wrapped it up,
and meant to keep it safe. But it was not safe to him. His
lord took it away, and the same thing is now befalling you.
The purpose you have, at some future time, to use your talent,
avails nothing. It is going from you, and, before you know it
will be utterly, irrecoverably gone.

The thoughts that crowd upon us, standing before a subject
like this, are practical and serious. And—

1. How manifestly hideous the process going on in human
souls, under the power of sin. It is a process of real and fixed
deformity. Who of us has not seen it even with his eyes?
The most beautiful natural character, in man or woman, changes,
how certainly, its type, when growing old in worldliness and
the neglect of religion. The grace perishes, the beautiful feeling
dries away, the angles grow hard, the sociality grows cold and
formal, the temper irritable and peevish, and the look wears a
kind of half expression, as if something once in it were gone
out for ever. It should be so, and so, in awful deed, it is; for

a whole side of the nature, most noble and closest in affinity with God, has been taken away. On the other hand, it will be seen that a thoroughly religious old person holds the proportions of life, and even grows more mellow and attractive as life advances. Indeed, the most beautiful sight on earth is an aged saint of God, growing cheerful in his faith as life advances, becoming mellowed in his love, and more and more visibly pervaded and brightened by the clear light of religion.

This deforming process, too, is a halving process, with all that are in it. It exterminates the noblest side of faculty in them, and all the most affluent springs of their greatness it for ever dries away. It murders the angel in us, and saves the drudge or the worm. The man that is left is but a partial being, a worker, a schemer, a creature of passion, thought, will, hunger, remorse, but no divine principle, no kinsman of Christ, or of God. And this is the fearful taking away of which our blessed Lord admonishes; a taking away of the gems and leaving the casket, a taking away of the great and leaving the little, a taking away of the godlike and celestial and a leaving of the sinner in his sin.

2. It follows, in the same manner, that there is no genuine culture, no proper education, which does not include religion. Much, indeed, of what is called education is only a power of deformity, a stimulus of overgrowth in the lower functions of the spirit, as a creature of intelligence, which overlooks and leaves to wither, causes to wither, all the metropolitan powers of a great mind and character. The first light of mind is God, the only genuine heat is religion, imaginative insight is kindled only by the fervours of holy truth, all noblest breadth and volume are unfolded in the regal amplitude of God's eternity and kingdom, all grandest energy and force in the impulsions of duty and the inspirations of faith. All training, separated from these, operates even a shortening of faculty, as truly as an increase. It is a kind of gymnastic for the arm that paralyses the spine. It diminishes the quantity of the subject, where all sovereign quantity begins, and increases it only in some lower point, where it ends; as if building the trunk of a lighthouse stanch and tall were enough, without preparing any light and revolving clockwork for the top. Hence it is that so many scholars, most bent down upon their tasks, and digging most

intently into the supposed excellence, turn out, after all, to be
so miserably diminished in all that constitutes power. Hence
also that men of taste are so often attenuated by their refine-
ments, and dwarfed by the overgrown accuracy and polish of
their attainments. No man is ever educated, in due form, save
as being a man ; that is, a creature related to God, and having all
his highest summits of capacity unfolded by the great thoughts,
and greater sentiments, and nobler inspirations of religion.

  ⁕ 3. Let no one comfort himself in the intense activity of his
mind on the subject of religion. That is one of the things to be
dreaded. To be always thinking, debating, scheming, in reference to the great questions of religion, without using any of the
talents that belong more appropriately to God and the receiving
of God, is just the way to extirpate the talents most rapidly,
and so to close up the mind in spiritual darkness. And no man
is more certainly dark to God than one who is always at work
upon His mystery, by the mere understanding. To be curious,
to speculate much, to be dinning always in argument, battle-
dooring always in opinions and dogmas, whether on the free
side of rationalistic audacity, or the stiff side of catechetic
orthodoxy, makes little difference ; all such activity is cancerous
and destructive to the real talents of religion. What you do
with the understanding never reaches God. He is known only
by them that receive Him into their love, their faith, their deep
want—known only as He is enshrined within, felt as a divine
force, breathed in the inspirations of His secret life. The
geometer might as well expect to solve his problems by the
function of smell, as a responsible soul to find God by the
understanding. How little does it signify, then, that you are
always thoughtful on religious subjects ? That, by itself, will
only be your ruin.

  4. Make as little of the hope that the Holy Spirit will some-
time open your closed or consciously closing faculties. It
requires a talent, so to speak, for the Holy Spirit, to entertain or
receive Him. A rock cannot receive the Holy Spirit. No more
can a mind that has lost, or extinguished, the talent for inspiration. The Holy Spirit, glorious and joyful truth, does find a
way into souls that are steeped in spiritual lethargy, does beget
anew the sense of holy things that appeared to be faded
almost away. But when the very faculty that makes His work-

ing possible is quite closed up, or so nearly closed that no living receptivity is left for Him to work in, when the soul has no fit room, or function, to receive His inspiring motions, more than a tree, half-dead, to receive the quickening sap of the spring, or an ossified heart to let the life-power play its action, then, manifestly, nothing is to be hoped for longer from His quickening visitations. The soul was originally made to be dwelt in, actuated, filled with God, but finally this high talent is virtually extirpated; when, of course, there is nothing to hope for longer. It may not be so with you, and it also may.

5. The truth we are here bringing into view wears no look of promise, in regard to the future condition of bad men. If we talk of their final restoration, what is going to restore them, when the very thing we see in them here is the gradual extinction of their capabilities of religion? Their want of God itself dies out, and they have no God-ward aspirations left. The talent of inspiration, of spiritual perception, of love, of faith, every inlet of their nature that was open to God, is closed and virtually extirpated. This is no figure of speech that merely signifies their habitual obscuration, it is fact. By what, then, are they going to be restored? Will God take them up, as they enter into the future life, and re-create their extirpated faculties of religion? Will the pains of hell burn a religion into their lower faculties, and so restore them?

But there is another hope, viz., that bad men will finally be themselves extirpated and cease; that the life of sin will finally burn them quite out, or cause them literally and totally to perish. But the difficulty here is that no such tendency is visible. It is only seen that the talent for religion, which is the higher and diviner side of the soul, is extirpated. The other parts are kept in some kind of activity, and are sometimes even overgrown by the stimulations of worldly or vicious impulse. If we sometimes look on a poor, imbruted mortal,—one who walks, looks, speaks, not as a proper man but as the vestiges only of a man,—asking in ourselves what is there left that is worth salvation?—as if there were nothing; still he lives, and, what is more, some of his quantities, viz., his passions and appetites and all his lowest affinities are even increased. His thoughts, too, run as rapidly as they ever did, only they run low; his imaginations live, only they live in the

I

stye of his passions. It is not, then, annihilation that we see
in him. Nothing is really annihilated but the celestial possibilities. And so it is with every soul that refuses God and
religion. A living creature remains,—a mind, a memory, a
heart of passion, fears, irritability, will,—all these remain; nothing is gone but the angel life that stood with them, and bound
them all to God. What remains, remains; and, for aught that
we can see, must remain; and there is the fatal, inevitable fact.
How hopeless! God forbid that any of us may ever know what
it means!

Finally, how clear it is that the earliest time in religion is the
best time. If there be any of my hearers that have lived many
years, and have consciously not begun to live unto God, they
have much to think of in a subject like this. How well do they
know that God is further off than He was, and their spiritual
apprehensions less distinct. They have felt the sentence—
"Take therefore the talent from him"—passing upon them
in its power for many years. And how much further will you
go in this neglect of God before the extirpation begun is fatally
complete? My friends, there is not an hour to lose. Only with
the greatest difficulty will you be able, now, to gather up yourself and open your closing gates to the entrance of God and His
salvation.

Here, too, is the peculiar blessing and the hopeful advantage
of youth. The talents which older men lose out, by their
worldly practice and neglect of God, are fresh in them and free.
Hence their common readiness to apprehend God and the
things of religion. It is not because they are green, or unripe,
as many think, but because they have a side of talent not yet
eaten out by sinful practice; because God is mirrored so clearly
in the depths of their nature, and breathed so freely into the
recesses of their open life. Hence their ready sensibility, their
quick perception, their ability to feel out, in experiment, what
reason cannot master,—God, Christ, the inspiring grace, the
heavenly peace, eternal life. Hence, also, the fact that so great
a share of those who believe, embrace Christ in their youth.
And this, my young friends, is the day therefore of privilege to
you. Oh, that you could see the bright eminence of your condition. The holy talent now is yours. In a few selfish years it
will be shortening, and, before you know it, will be quite taken

away. This best, highest, most glorious talent of your nature God is now calling you to save. Make, then, no delay in this first matter of life, the choice of God. Give Him up thy talent, whole and fresh, to be increased by early devotion and a life-long fidelity in His service. Call it the dew of thy youth, understanding well that, when thy sun is fairly up, it will, like dew, be gone.

XI.

UNCONSCIOUS INFLUENCE.

JOHN xx. 8—"*Then went in also that other disciple.*"

IN this slight touch or turn of history is opened to us, if we scan it closely, one of the most serious and fruitful chapters of Christian doctrine. Thus it is that men are ever touching unconsciously the springs of motion in each other; thus it is that one man, without thought or intention, or even a consciousness of the fact, is ever leading some other after him. Little does Peter think, as he comes up where his doubting brother is looking into the sepulchre, and goes straight in, after his peculiar manner, that he is drawing in his brother apostle after him. As little does John think, when he loses his misgivings, and goes into the sepulchre after Peter, that he is following his brother. And just so, unawares to himself, is every man, the whole race through, laying hold of his fellow-man, to lead him where otherwise he would not go. We overrun the boundaries of our personality—we flow together. A Peter leads a John, a John goes after a Peter, both of them unconscious of any influence exerted or received. And thus our life and conduct are ever propagating themselves, by a law of social contagion, throughout the circles and times in which we live.

There are, then, you will perceive, two sorts of influence belonging to man—that which is active or voluntary, and that which is unconscious; that which we exert purposely, or in the endeavour to sway another, as by teaching, by argument, by persuasion, by threatenings, by offers and promises, and that which flows out from us, unawares to ourselves, the same which Peter had over John when he led him into the sepulchre. The importance of our efforts to do good, that is, of our voluntary influence, and the sacred obligation we are under to exert ourselves in this way, are often and seriously insisted on. It is thus that Christianity has become, in the present age, a principle of so much greater activity than it has been for many centuries before ; and we fervently hope that it will yet become far more active than it now is, nor cease to multiply its industry till it is seen by all mankind to embody the beneficence and the living energy of Christ himself.

But there needs to be produced at the same time, and partly for this object, a more thorough appreciation of the relative importance of that kind of influence, or beneficence, which is insensibly exerted. The tremendous weight and efficacy of this, compared with the other, and the sacred responsibility laid upon us in regard to this, are felt in no such degree or proportion as they should be ; and the consequent loss we suffer in character, as well as that which the Church suffers in beauty and strength, is incalculable. The more stress, too, needs to be laid on this subject of insensible influence, because it is insensible ; because it is out of mind, and, when we seek to trace it, beyond a full discovery.

If the doubt occur to any of you, in the announcement of this subject, whether we are properly responsible for an influence which we exert insensibly, we are not, I reply, except so far as this influence flows directly from our character and conduct. And this it does, even much more uniformly than our active influence. In the latter, we may fail of our end by a want of wisdom or skill, in which case we are still as meritorious, in God's sight, as if we succeeded. So, again, we may really succeed, and do great good by our active endeavours, from motives altogether base and hypocritical, in which case we are as evil, in God's sight, as if we had failed. But the influences we exert unconsciously will almost never disagree with our real character. They are honest influences, following our character as the shadow follows the sun. And, therefore, we are much more certainly responsible for them and their effects on the world. They go streaming from us in all directions, though in channels that we do not see, poisoning or healing around the roots of society, and among the hidden wells of character. If good ourselves, they are good ; if bad, they are bad. And, since they reflect so exactly our character, it is impossible to doubt our responsibility for their effects on the world. We must answer not only for what we do with a purpose, but for the influence we exert insensibly. To give you any just impressions of the breadth and seriousness of such a reckoning, I know to be impossible. No mind can trace it. But it will be something gained if I am able to awaken only a suspicion of the vast extent and power of those influences, which are ever flowing out unbidden upon society, from your life and character.

In the prosecution of my design, let me ask of you, first of all, to expel the common prejudice that there can be nothing of consequence in unconscious influences, because they make no report, and fall on the world unobserved. Histories and biographies make little account of the power men exert insensibly over each other. They tell how men have led armies, established empires, enacted laws, gained causes, sung, reasoned, and taught—always occupied in setting forth what they do with a purpose. But what they do without a purpose, the streams of influence that flow out from their persons unbidden on the world, they cannot trace or compute, and seldom even mention. So also the public laws make men responsible only for what they do with a positive purpose, and take no account of the mischiefs or benefits that are communicated by their noxious or healthful example. The same is true in the discipline of families, churches, and schools ; they make no account of the things we do, except we will them. What we do insensibly passes for nothing, because no human government can trace such influences with sufficient certainty to make their authors responsible.

But you must not conclude that influences of this kind are insignificant, because they are unnoticed and noiseless. How is it in the natural world? Behind the mere show, the outward noise and stir of the world, nature always conceals her hand of control, and the laws by which she rules. Who ever saw with the eye, for example, or heard with the ear, the exertions of that tremendous astronomic force, which every moment holds the compact of the physical universe together? The lightning is, in fact, but a mere fire-fly spark in comparison ; but, because it glares on the clouds, and thunders so terribly in the ear, and rives the tree or the rock where it falls, many will be ready to think that it is a vastly more potent agent than gravity.

The Bible calls the good man's life a light, and it is the nature of light to flow out spontaneously in all directions, and fill the world unconsciously with its beams. So the Christian shines,

light giving

it would say, not so much because he will, as because he is a luminous object. Not that the active influence of Christians is made of no account in the figure, but only that this symbol of light has its propriety in the fact that their unconscious influence is the chief influence, and has the precedence in its power over the world. And yet, there are many who will be ready to think that light is a very tame and feeble instrument, because it is noiseless. An earthquake, for example, is to them a much more vigorous and effective agency. Hear how it comes thundering through the solid foundations of nature! It rocks a whole continent. The noblest works of man—cities, monuments, and temples—are in a moment levelled to the ground, or swallowed down the opening gulfs of fire. Little do they think that the light of every morning, the soft, genial, and silent light, is an agent many times more powerful. But let the light of the morning cease and return no more, let the hour of morning come, and bring with it no dawn; the outcries of a horror-stricken world fill the air, and make, as it were, the darkness audible. The beasts go wild and frantic at the loss of the sun. The vegetable growths turn pale and die. A chill creeps on, and frosty winds begin to howl across the freezing earth. Colder, and yet colder, is the night. The vital blood, at length, of all creatures, stops congealed. Down goes the frost toward the earth's centre. The heart of the sea is frozen; nay, the earthquakes are themselves frozen in under their fiery caverns. The very globe itself, too, and all the fellow planets that have lost their sun, are to become mere balls of ice, swinging silent in the darkness. Such is the light, which revisits us in the silence of the morning. It makes no shock or scar. It would not wake an infant in his cradle. And yet it perpetually new creates the world, rescuing it, each morning as a prey from night and chaos. So the Christian is a light, even "the light of the world;" and we must not think that, because he shines insensibly or silently, as a mere luminous object, he is, therefore, powerless. The greatest powers are ever those which lie back of the little stirs and commotions of nature; and I verily believe that the insensible influences of good men are as much more potent than what I have called their voluntary or active, as the great silent powers of nature are of greater consequence than her little disturbances and tumults. The law of human influence is deeper than many suspect, and they lose sight of it altogether. The outward endeavours made by good men or bad to sway others, they call their influence; whereas it is, in fact, but a fraction, and, in most cases, but a very small fraction, of the good or evil that flows out of their lives. Nay, I will even go further. How many persons do you meet, the insensible influence of whose manners and character is so decided as often to thwart their voluntary influence; so that, whatever they attempt to do in the way of controlling others, they are sure to carry the exact opposite of what they intend. And it will generally be found that, where men undertake by argument or persuasion to exert a power, in the face of qualities that make them odious or detestable, or only not entitled to respect, their insensible influence will be too strong for them. The total effect of the life is, then, of a kind directly opposite to the voluntary endeavour; which, of course, does not add so much as a fraction to it.

I call your attention, next, to the twofold powers of effect and expression by which man connects with his fellow-man. If we distinguish man as a creature of language, and thus qualified to communicate himself to others, there are in him two sets or kinds of language, one which is voluntary in the use, and one that is involuntary; that of speech in the literal sense, and that expression of the eye, the face, the look, the gait, the motion, the tone or cadence, which is sometimes called the natural language of the sentiments. This natural language, too, is greatly enlarged by the conduct of life, that which, in business and society, reveals the principles and spirit of men. Speech, or voluntary language, is a door to the soul, that we may open or shut at will; the other is a door that stands open evermore, and reveals to others constantly, and often very clearly, the tempers, tastes, and motives of their hearts. Within, as we may represent, is character, charging the common reservoir of influence, and through these twofold gates of the soul, pouring itself out on the world. Out of one it flows at choice, and whensoever we purpose to do good or evil to men. Out of the other it flows each moment, as light from the sun, and propagates itself in all beholders.

Then if we go over to others, that is, to the subjects of influence, we find every man endowed with two inlets of impression; the ear and the understanding for the reception of speech, and the sympathetic powers, the sensibilities or affections, for tinder to those sparks of emotion revealed by looks, tones, manners, and general conduct. And these sympathetic powers, though not immediately rational, are yet inlets, open on all sides, to the understanding and character. They have a certain wonderful capacity to receive impressions, and catch the meaning of signs, and propagate in us whatsoever falls into their passive moulds, from others. The impressions they receive do not come through verbal propositions, and are never received into verbal propositions, it may be, in the mind, and therefore many think nothing of them. But precisely on this account are they the more powerful, because it is as if one heart were thus going directly into another, and carrying in its feelings with it. Beholding, as in a glass, the feelings of our neighbour, we are changed into the same image by the assimilating power of sensibility and fellow-feeling. Many have gone so far, and not without show at least of reason, as to maintain that the look or expression, and even the very features of children, are often changed by exclusive intercourse with nurses and attendants. Furthermore, if we carefully consider, we shall find it scarcely possible to doubt, that simply to look on bad and malignant faces, or those whose expressions have become infected by vice, to be with them and become familiarised to them, is enough permanently to affect the character of persons of mature age. I do not say that it must of necessity subvert their character, for the evil looked upon may never be loved or welcomed in practice ; but it is something to have had these bad images in the soul, giving out their expressions there, and diffusing their odour among the thoughts, as long as we live. How dangerous a thing is it, for example, for a man to become accustomed to sights of cruelty ? What man, valuing the honour of his soul, would not shrink from yielding himself to such an influence ? No more is it a thing of indifference to become accustomed to look on the manners, and receive the bad expression of any kind of sin.

The door of involuntary communication, I have said, is always open. Of course we are communicating ourselves in this way to others at every moment of our intercourse or presence with them. But how very seldom, in comparison, do we undertake by means of speech to influence others! Even the best Christian, one who most improves his opportunities to do good, attempts but seldom to sway another by voluntary influence, whereas he is all the while shining as a luminous object unawares, and communicating of his heart to the world.

But there is yet another view of this double line of communication which man has with his fellow-men, which is more general, and displays the import of the truth yet more convincingly. It is by one of these modes of communication that we are constituted members of voluntary society, and by the other, parts of a general mass, or members of involuntary society. You are all, in a certain view, individuals, and separate, as persons, from each other; you are also, in a certain other view, parts of a common body, as truly as the parts of a stone. Thus, if you ask how it is that you and all men came, without your consent, to exist in society, to be within its power, to be under its laws, the answer is, that while you are a man, you are also a fractional element of a larger and more comprehensive being, called society—be it the family, the church, the state. In a certain department of your nature, it is open; its sympathies and feelings are open. On this open side you all adhere together, as parts of a larger nature, in which there is a common circulation of want, impulse, and law. Being thus made common to each other voluntarily, you become one mass, one consolidated social body, animated by one life. And observe how far this involuntary communication and sympathy between the members of a state or family is sovereign over their character. It always results in what we call the national or family spirit; for there is a spirit peculiar to every state and family in the world. Sometimes, too, this national or family spirit takes a religious or an irreligious character, and appears almost to absorb the religious self-government of individuals. What was the national spirit of France, for example, at a certain time, but a spirit of infidelity? What is the religious spirit of Spain at this moment, but a spirit of bigotry, quite as wide of Christianity and destructive to character as the spirit of falsehood? What is the family spirit in many a house, but the spirit of gain, or pleasure, or appetite, in which everything that is warm, dignified, genial, and good in religion, is visibly absent? Sometimes you will almost fancy that you see the shapes of money in the eyes of the children. So it is that we are led on by nations, as it were, to a good or bad immortality. Far down in the secret foundations of life and society, there lie concealed great laws and channels of influence, which make the race common to each other in all the main departments or divisions of the social mass—laws which often escape our notice altogether, but which are to society as gravity to the general system of God's works.

But these are general considerations, and more fit, perhaps, to give you a rational conception of the modes of influence and their relative power, than to verify that conception, or establish its truth. I now proceed to add, therefore, some miscellaneous proofs of a more particular nature.

And I mention, first of all, the instinct of imitation in children. We begin our mortal experience, not with acts grounded in judgment or reason, or with ideas received through language, but by simple imitation, and, under the guidance of this, we lay our foundations. The child looks and listens, and whatsoever tone of feeling or manner of conduct is displayed around him, sinks into his plastic, passive soul, and becomes a mould of his being ever after. The very handling of the nursery is significant, and the petulance, the passion, the gentleness, the tranquillity indicated by it, are all reproduced in the child. His soul is a purely receptive nature, and that, for a considerable period, without choice or selection. A little further on, he begins voluntarily to copy everything he sees. Voice, manner, gait, everything which the eye sees, the mimic instinct delights to act over. And thus we have a whole generation of future men receiving from us their very beginnings, and the deepest impulses of their life and immortality. They watch us every moment, in the family, before the hearth, and at the table; and when we are meaning them no good or evil, when we are conscious of exerting no influence over them, they are drawing from us impressions and moulds of habit, which, if wrong, no heavenly discipline can wholly remove; or, if right, no bad associations utterly dissipate. Now it may be doubted, I think, whether, in all the active influence of our lives, we do as much to shape the destiny of our fellow-men, as we do in this single article of unconscious influence over children.

Still further on, respect for others takes the place of imitation. We naturally desire the approbation or good opinion of others. You see the strength of this feeling in the article of fashion. How few persons have the nerve to resist a fashion! We have fashions, too, in literature, and in worship, and in moral and religious doctrine, almost equally powerful. How many will violate the best rules of society, because it is the practice of their circle! How many reject Christ because of friends or acquaintance, who have no suspicion of the influence they exert, and will not have, till the last day shews them what they have done! Every good man has thus a power in his person, more mighty than his words and arguments, and which others feel when he little suspects it. Every bad man, too, has a fund of poison in his character, which is tainting those around him, when it is not in his thoughts to do them an injury. He is read and understood. His sensual tastes and habits, his unbelieving spirit, his suppressed leer at religion, have all a power, and take hold of the hearts of others, whether he will have it so or not.

Again, how well understood is it, that the most active feelings and impulses of mankind are contagious. How quick enthusiasm of any sort is to kindle, and how rapidly it catches from one to another, till a nation blazes in the flame! In the case of the Crusades, you have an example where the personal enthusiasm of one man put all the states of Europe in motion. Fanaticism is almost equally contagious. Fear and superstition always infect the mind of the circle in which they are manifested. The spirit of war generally becomes an epidemic of madness, when once it has got possession of a few minds. The spirit of party is propagated in a similar manner. How any slight operation in the market may spread like a fire, if successful, till trade runs wild in a general infatuation, is well known. Now, in all these examples, the effect is produced, not by active endeavour to carry influence, but mostly by that insensible propagation which follows when a flame of any kind is once kindled.

Is it also true, you may ask, that the religious spirit propagates itself or tends to propagate itself in the same way? I see no reason to question that it does. Nor does anything in the doctrine of spiritual influences, when rightly understood, forbid the supposition. For spiritual influences are never separated from the laws of thought in the individual and the laws of feeling and influence in society. If, too, every disciple is to be an " epistle known and read of all men," what shall we expect, but that all men will be somehow affected by the reading? Or, if he is to be a light in the world, what shall we look for, but that others, seeing his good works, shall glorify God on his account? How often is it seen, too, as a fact of observation, that one, or a few good men, kindle at length a holy fire in the community in which they live, and become the leaven of a general reformation! Such men give a more vivid proof in their persons of the reality of religious faith, than any words or arguments could yield. They are active; they endeavour, of course, to exert a good voluntary influence; but still their chief power lies in their holiness, and the sense they produce in others of their close relation to God.

It now remains to exhibit the very important fact, that where the direct or active influence of men is supposed to be great, even this is due, in a principal degree, to that insensible influence by which their arguments, reproofs, and persuasions are secretly invigorated. It is not mere words which turn men; it is the heart mounting uncalled into the expression of the features; it is the eye illuminated by reason—the look beaming with goodness; it is the tone of the voice, that instrument of the soul, which changes quality with such amazing facility, and gives out, in the soft, the tender, the tremulous, the firm, every shade of emotion and character. And so much is there in this, that the moral stature and character of the man that speaks are likely to be well represented in his manner. If he is a stranger, his way will inspire confidence and attract good will. His virtues will be seen, as it were, gathering round him to minister words and forms of thought, and their voices will be heard in the fall of his cadences. And the same is true of bad men, or men who have nothing in their character corresponding to what they attempt to do. If without heart or interest you attempt to move another, the involuntary man tells what you are doing in a hundred ways at once. A hypocrite, endeavouring to exert a good influence, only tries to convey by words what the lying look, and the faithless affectation, or dry exaggeration of his manner, perpetually resist. We have it for a fashion to attribute great or even prodigious results to the voluntary efforts and labours of men. Whatever they effect is commonly referred to nothing but the immediate power of what they do. Let us take an example like that of Paul and analyse it. Paul was a man of great fervour and enthusiasm. He combined withal more of what is lofty and morally com-

manding in his character than most of the very distinguished
men of the world.   Having this for his natural character, and
his natural character exalted and made luminous by Christian
faith, and the manifest indwelling of God, he had, of course, an
almost superhuman sway over others.   Doubtless he was intelligent, strong in argument, eloquent, active to the utmost of his
powers, but still he moved the world more by what he was than
by what he did.   The grandeur and spiritual splendour of his
character were ever adding to his active efforts an element of
silent power, which was the real and chief cause of their efficacy.
He convinced, subdued, inspired, and led, because of the half-
divine authority which appeared in his conduct and his glowing
spirit. He fought the good fight, because he kept the faith, and
filled his powerful nature with influences drawn from higher
worlds.

And here I must conduct you to a yet higher example, even
that of the Son of God, the Light of the world. Men dislike to
be swayed by direct, voluntary influence.   They are jealous of
such control; and are, therefore, best approached by conduct,
and feeling, and the authority of simple worth, which seem to
make no purposed onset. If goodness appears, they welcome
its celestial smile; if heaven descends to encircle them, they
yield to its sweetness; if truth appears in the life, they honour
it with a secret homage; if personal majesty and glory appear,
they bow with reverence, and acknowledge with shame their
own vileness. Now, it is on this side of human nature that
Christ visits us, preparing just that kind of influence which
the Spirit of truth may wield with the most persuasive and
subduing effect.   It is the grandeur of His character which
constitutes the chief power of His ministry, not His miracles
or teachings apart from His character. Miracles were useful
at the time to arrest attention, and His doctrine is useful
at all times as the highest revelation of truth possible in
speech; but the greatest truth of the gospel, notwithstanding,
is Christ himself—a human body become the organ of the
Divine nature, and revealing, under the conditions of an earthly
life, the glory of God! The Scripture writers have much to
say, in this connexion, of the image of God; and an image,
you know, is that which simply represents, not that which acts,
or reasons, or persuades. Now it is this image of God which

makes the centre, the sun itself, of the gospel. The journeyings, teachings, miracles, and sufferings of Christ, all had their use in bringing out this image, or, what is the same, in making conspicuous the character and feelings of God, both toward sinners and toward sin. And here is the power of Christ—it is what of God's beauty, love, truth, and justice shines through Him. It is the influence which flows unconsciously and spontaneously out of Christ, as the Friend of man, the Light of the world, the Glory of the Father, made visible. And some have gone so far as to conjecture that God made the human person originally, with a view to its becoming the organ or vehicle by which He might reveal His communicable attributes to other worlds. Christ, they believe, came to inhabit this organ that He might execute a purpose so sublime. The human purpose is constituted, they say, to be a mirror of God; and God, being imaged in that mirror, as in Christ, is held up to the view of this and other worlds. It certainly is to the view of this; and if the Divine nature can use this organ so effectively to express itself unto us, if it can bring itself, through the looks, tones, motions, and conduct of a human person, more close to our sympathies than by any other means, how can we think that an organ so communicative, inhabited by us, is not always breathing our spirit and transferring our image insensibly to others?

I have protracted the argument on this subject beyond what I could have wished; but I cannot dismiss it without suggesting a few thoughts necessary to its complete practical effect.

One very obvious and serious inference from it, and the first which I will name, is, that it is impossible to live in this world and escape responsibility. It is not they alone, as you have seen, who are trying purposely to convert or corrupt others, who exert an influence; you cannot live without exerting influence. The doors of your soul are open on others, and theirs on you. You inhabit a house which is well-nigh transparent; and what you are within, you are ever shewing yourself to be without, by signs that have no ambiguous expression. If you had the seeds of a pestilence in your body, you would not have a more active contagion than you have in your tempers, tastes, and principles.

Simply to be in this world, whatever you are, is to exert an influence—an influence, too, compared with which mere language and persuasion are feeble. You say that you mean well; at least you think that you mean to injure no one. Do you injure no one? Is your example harmless? Is it ever on the side of God and duty? You cannot reasonably doubt that others are continually receiving impressions from your character. As little can you doubt that you must answer for these impressions. If the influence you exert is unconsciously exerted, then it is only the most sincere, the truest expression of your character. And for what can you be held responsible, if not for this? Do not deceive yourselves in the thought that you are, at least, doing no injury, and are, therefore, living without responsibility; first make it sure that you are not every hour infusing moral death insensibly into your children, wives, husbands, friends, and acquaintances. By a mere look or glance, not unlikely, you are conveying the influence that shall turn the scale of some one's immortality. Dismiss, therefore, the thought that you are living without responsibility; that is impossible. Better is it frankly to admit the truth; and if you will risk the influence of a character unsanctified by duty and religion, prepare to meet your reckoning manfully, and receive the just recompence of reward.

The true philosophy or method of doing good is also here explained. It is, first of all and principally, to be good—to have a character that will of itself communicate good. There must and will be active effort where there is goodness of principle; but the latter we should hold to be the principle thing, the root and life of all. Whether it is a mistake more sad or more ridiculous, to make mere stir synonymous with doing good, we need not inquire; enough, to be sure that one who has taken up such a notion of doing good, is for that reason a nuisance to the church. The Christian is called a light, not lightning. In order to act with effect on others, he must walk in the Spirit, and thus become the image of goodness; he must be so akin to God, and so filled with His dispositions, that he shall seem to surround himself with a hallowed atmosphere. It is folly to endeavour to make ourselves shine before we are luminous. If the sun without his beams should talk to the planets, and argue with them till the final day, it would not make them shine; there must be light in the sun itself, and then they will shine, of course. And this, my brethren, is what God intends for you all. It is the great idea of His gospel, and the work of His Spirit, to make you lights in the world. His greatest joy is to give you character, to beautify your example, to exalt your principles, and make you each the depository of His own almighty grace. But in order to this, something is necessary on your part—a full surrender of your mind to duty and to God, and a perpetual desire of this spiritual intimacy; having this, having a participation thus of the goodness of God, you will as naturally communicate good as the sun communicates his beams.

Our doctrine of unconscious and undesigning influence shews how it is, also, that the preaching of Christ is often so unfruitful, and especially in times of spiritual coldness. It is not because truth ceases to be truth, nor, of necessity, because it is preached in a less vivid manner, but because there are so many influences preaching against the preacher. He is one—the people are many; his attempt to convince and persuade is a voluntary influence. Their lives, on the other hand, and especially the lives of those who profess what is better, are so many unconscious influences, ever streaming forth upon the people, and back and forth between each other. He preaches the truth, and they, with one consent, are preaching the truth down; and how can he prevail against so many, and by a kind of influence so unequal? When the people of God are glowing with spiritual devotion to Him and love to men the case is different. Then they are all preaching with the preacher, and making an atmosphere of warmth for his words to fall in; great is the company of them that publish the truth, and proportionally great its power. Shall I say more? Have you not already felt, my brethren, the application to which I would bring you? We do not exonerate ourselves; we do not claim to be nearer to God or holier than you; but, ah! you know not how easy it is to make a winter about us, or how cold it feels! Our endeavour is to preach the truth of Christ and His cross as clearly and as forcibly as we can. Sometimes it has a visible effect, and we are filled with joy; sometimes it has no effect, and then we struggle on as we must, but under great oppression. Have we none among you that

K

preach against us in your lives? If we shew you the light of God's truth, does it never fall on banks of ice, which, if the light shines through, the crystal masses are yet as cold as before? We do not accuse you—that we leave to God and to those who may rise up in the last day to testify against you. If they shall come out of your own families; if they are the children that wear your names, the husband or wife of your affections; if they declare that you, by your example, kept them away from Christ's truth and mercy—we may have accusations to meet of our own, and we leave you to acquit yourselves as best you may. I only warn you here of the guilt which our Lord Jesus Christ will impute to them that hinder His gospel.

X

OBLIGATION A PRIVILEGE.

PSALM cxix. 54—"*Thy statutes have been my songs in the house of my pilgrimage.*"

WHEN the eastern traveller takes shelter from the scorching heat of noon, or halts for the night in some inn or caravansary, which is for the time the house of his pilgrimage, he takes the sackbut or the lyre and soothes his rest with a song—a song, it may be, of war, romance, or love. But the poet of Israel finds his theme, we perceive, in the statutes of Jehovah : "Thy statutes have been my songs in the house of my pilgrimage." These have been my pastime, with these I have refreshed my resting hours by the way, and cheered myself onward through the wearisome journey and across the scorching deserts of life. Not songs of old tradition, not ballads of war, or wine, or love, have supported me, but I have sung of God's commandments, and these have been the solace of my weary hours, the comfort of my rest. This 119th Psalm, which is, in every verse, an ode or hymn in praise of God's law, sufficiently illustrates his meaning.

Multitudes of men, it is evident as it need be, have a very different conception of this matter. Divine law, divine obligation, responsibility in any form, authority under any conditions, they feel to be a real annoyance to life. They want their own will and way. Why must they be hampered by these constant restrictions? Why must they be shortened in their pleasures, crippled in their ambition, held back from all their strongest impulses—just those by which they might otherwise shew their vigour, and make a brave and manly figure of their life. But, instead of being allowed any such generous freedom, they are tethered, they fancy, tamed, subjected to continual scruples of fear and twinges of conviction, confused, weakened, let down in their confidence, and all the best comfort of their life is taken

away.   Could they only be rid of this annoyance, life would be
a comparatively easy and fair experience.

In this controversy you have taken up with the Psalmist; he
is very plainly right, and you as plainly wrong, as I shall now
undertake to shew; and as you, considering that God's law is
upon you, and can by no means be escaped, ought most gladly
to hear and discover.   His doctrine, removing the poetry of the
form, is this—

That obligation to God is our privilege.

Some of you will fancy, it may be, at the outset, that the pilgrimage he speaks of is made by the statutes; that the restrictions of obligations are so hard and close as to cut off, in fact,
all the true pleasures of life, and reduce it to a pilgrimage in its
dryness.   But this pilgrimage is made by no sense of restriction.
Every man, even the most licentious and reckless, is a pilgrim;
the atheist is a pilgrim; such are only a more unhappy class of
pilgrims, a reluctant class, who are driven across the deserts,
cheerfully traversed by others, and by the fountains where
others quench their thirst.   There is a perfect harmony between
obligation to God and all the sources of pleasure and happiness
God has provided, so that there is no real collision between the
statutes over us and the conditions round us.   It is only false
pleasures that are denied us, those that would brutalise the mind,
or mar the health of the body, or somehow violate the happiness
of fellow-beings round us.   Consider the long run of life, and
take in all the interests of it, and you will find that what we call
obligation to God, not only does not infringe upon your pleasures, but actually commands you on, to the greatest and highest
enjoyments of which you are capable.

There is another objection or false impression that needs to be
noticed—viz., that the very enforcements of penalty and terror
added to God's law, to compel an acceptance of it, or obedience
to it, are a kind of concession that it is not a privilege, but a
restriction or severity rather, which cannot otherwise be carried.
Is it, then, a fair inference that human laws are severe and hard
restrictions, and no true privilege or blessing, because they are
duly enforced by additions of penalty?   It is only to malefactors and felons that they are so; and for these only, considered

as being enforced by terrors, they are made. They are restrictions to the lawless and disobedient, never to the good. On the contrary, a right-minded, loyal people, will value their laws, and cherish them as the safeguard even of their liberty. Just so, also, the righteous man will have God's statutes for his songs in all the course of his pilgrimage.

Dismissing now these common impressions, let us go on to inquire a little more definitely how it would be with us, if we existed under no terms of obligation ; for, if we are to settle it fairly, whether obligation is a privilege or not, this manifestly is the mode in which the question should be stated. The true alternative between obligation and no obligation supposes, on the negative side, that we are not even to have the sense of obligation, or of moral distinctions; for the sense of obligation is the same thing as being obliged, or put in responsibility.

In such a case, our external condition must obviously be as different as possible from what it is now.

In the first place, there could, of course, be no such thing as criminal law for the defence of property, reputation, and life; because the moral distinctions, in which criminal law is grounded, are all wanting. The laws against theft and murder, for example, suppose the fact that these are understood already, and blamed as being wrongs—violations, that is, of moral obligation. And there is no conceivable way of defining these crimes, and bringing them to judgment, except by reference to notions or distinctions already admitted. Murder, for example, cannot be defined as a mere killing, or in any external way; for no external sign will hold without exception. Hence the law is obliged to define it as a killing with malice aforethought—to go into the heart. that is, and distinguish it there, as being done with a consciously criminal intent. The defences of civil society, therefore, must all be wanting where there is no recognised obligation to God. We are so far reduced to the condition of the quadruped races. Having, as they, no moral and religious ideas, we cannot legislate. Civil society is, in fact, impossible ; and all that is genial and peaceful under the benign protection of the state, is a good no longer attainable. If a man's property is plundered, he knows it only as a loss, not as a crime. If his children are murdered, or sold into slavery, he may be angry, as a bear robbed of her whelps, but he has no conception of a wrong in what he suffers. There is nothing left us in these low possibilities, but to herd, as animals do, and take from each other what we must; to gore, and tear, and devour; to fly, to hide, to quiver with terror—the weak before the strong, and so live on as we best can; for to invent a criminal law without even the notion of a crime, and to phrase it in language that any tribunal could interpret, when the idea of crime has not yet arrived, is manifestly impossible.

Again, what we call society, as far as there is any element of dignity or blessing in it, depends on these moral obligations. Without these it would be intercourse without friendship, truth, charity, or mercy. All that is warm, and trustful, and dear in society, rests in the keeping of these moral bonds. Extinguish moral ideas and laws, and these lovely virtues also die; for their life is upheld by the sense of duty and right. Where there is no law, there is no sin or guilt; as little is there any virtue. Of course, there is nothing to praise or confide in. Truth is not conceived. Friendship and love are things of convenience, determinable also by convenience. Chastity, without the moral idea, is a name as honourable as hunger, and as worthy to be kept. Purity and truth are accidents. Domestic faith and the tender affections that ennoble and bless the homes are as reliable as the other caprices of unregulated impulse and passion. Without moral obligations, therefore, binding us to God, society is discontinued. Nothing that deserves the name is possible. Life, in fact, is wrong without a sense of wrong; society, a proximity of distrust and fear; and the passions, unrestrained by duty, a hell of general torment, without any sense of blame to explain it.

But these are matters external to which I refer just to call up some faint conception of the immense revolution it makes in our human existence only to remove this one element of obligation. Let us enter now the spiritual nature itself, and see how much is there depending on this great privilege of obligation to God.

This claim of God's authority, this bond of duty laid upon us, is virtually the throne of God erected in the soul. It is sovereign, of course, unaccommodating therefore, and may be felt as a sore annoyance. When violated, it will scorch the bosom ever with pangs of remorse, that are the most fiery and implacable of all mental sufferings. But of this there is no need; all such pains are avoidable by due obedience. And then obligation to God becomes the spring instead of the most dignified, fullest, healthiest joys anywhere attainable. The self-approving consciousness—the consciousness of good—what can raise one to a loftier pitch of confidence and blessing? It is with these obligations to God just as it is with the physical laws. These latter, violated by neglect, excess, or obstinacy, are our most relentless enemies and persecutors; respected and deferred to, they become our most faithful friends and helpers. Did any one ever judge, on this account, that they are only hindrances and restraints on our happiness which were better to be discontinued? Loosen, then, the grand attractions, and let the huge bulks of heaven fly as they will. Make the stones soluble at times, and the waters combustible without any change of conditions; let congelation be sometimes by fire, and lique-faction by frost; let the waterfall sometimes mount upward into the air, and the smoke plunge downward on the ground. Abolish all the stable restrictions of law and let nature loose to go such way or after such gait as she pleases, and by that time we shall find that her uses are gone, and that all our magni-ficent liberty in them is taken away. The powers, which before consented to serve us, have become our enemies, and we are lost in a hell of physical anarchy that suffers none of the uses of life. Just so it would be, if we could exterminate and strip out of our way these constraints of obligation to God. We should find that even the release we covet is, in fact, the bitterest and sorest frustration of our desired liberty.

Thus how much, for example, does it signify, as regards your comfort, that this one matter, a matter so profoundly central too in your experiences and views of life, is fixed. Opinions, sentiments, hopes, fears, popularities, and to these also you may add all the honours and gifts of fortune, are in a fluxile, shifting state. There is no fixed element in any one of them. You live in them as you do in the weather. Even the courses of your mind, and the shifting phases you pass are a kind of internal weather that never settles, or becomes fixed. But in the sacred

fact of obligation you touch the immutable and lay hold, as it
were, of the eternities. At the very centre of your being there
is a fixed element, and that of a kind or degree essentially sovereign. And in that fact everything pertaining to your existence
is changed. You are no more afloat or a-sea in the endless
phases and variabilities just referred to, but a very large class
of your judgments and views of life and acknowledged principles are immovably settled. A standard is set up in your
thought by which a great part of your questions are determined,
and about which your otherwise random thoughts may settle
into order and law. Few men ever conceive what they owe to
obligation here, as the mere bond of order and mental conserva-
tion. Doubtless, obligation violated is the minister of pain,
but to be without obligation is a pain more bitter and distract-
ing; for it is much to know that you have a compass in the
ship even if you do not use it. Sent forth into life to choose
everything by mere interest and will, to be played with always
by your passions and your fancies, and to frame your judgments
apart from any fixed point or standard of judgment, life would
soon become a distressful puzzle to you which you could not
bear. You would make and unmake till you lost all stability
and all confidence in your own thoughts. Your confusion
itself would be insupportable. You would even go mad
in the struggle; you would cry aloud and lift your dismal
prayer to accident, in fault of any other divinity, for something fixed. Give me fate—give me something established—
though it be a continent of fire ! I cannot live in these bottom-
less sands !

How good and sublime a gift, in this view, is the gift of law.
It comes down smiling from the skies and enters into souls, as
the beginning and throne of wisdom. Or, using a different
figure, we may say that man comes into being bringing his law
with him—a law as definite and stable as that of the firmament
—one that shall go with him, when consentingly accepted, and
mark out the path of his pilgrimage, binding all his otherwise
random exercises of desire, fancy, and free will, to an orbit of
goodness and truth. Everything within him now is under a
determinating rule. His soul is held in a harmonious balance
of powers, like the heavenly worlds. Reason, feeling, passion,
fancy, all work in together under the great conserving law of

obligation to God, and the soul is kept in recollection, as a self-understanding nature. Who can think of man, wedded in this manner to the stability and eternity of God, without uniting a sense even of grandeur and sublimity with the bond of obligation by which he is thus set fast and centralised in the immutable.

Consider, again, the truly fraternal relation between our obligations to God and what we call our liberty. Instead of restraining our liberty, they only shew us, in fact, how to use our liberty, and how to air it, if I may so speak, in great and heroic actions. How insipid and foolish a thing were life, if there were nothing laid upon us to do! What is it, on the other hand, but the zest and glory of life, that something good and great, something really worthy to be done, is laid upon us. It is not self-indulgence allowed, but victory achieved, that can make a fit happiness for man. Therefore we are set down here amid changes, perils, wrongs, and miseries, where, to save ourselves and serve our kind, all manner of great works are to be done. Besides, we practically admit the arrangement, much oftener than we think. Tell any young man, for example, who is just converted to Christ, of some great sacrifice he is called to make—as in preaching Christ to men, or going to preach Him to the heathen—and that call, set forth as a sacrifice of all things, will work upon him more powerfully, by a hundred times, than it would if you undertook to soften it by shewing what respect he would gain, how comfortable he would be, and how much easier in this than in any other calling of life. We do not want any such caresses in the name of duty. To let go self-indulgence and try something stronger is a call that draws us always when our heart is up for duty; nay, even nature loves heroic impulse, and oftentimes prefers the difficult.

It is well, therefore, all the better, that we are put upon the doing of what is not always agreeable to the flesh. And when God lays upon us the duties of self-command and self-sacrifice, when He calls us to act and to suffer heroically, how could He more effectually dignify or ennoble our liberty? Now we have our object and our errand, and we know that we can meet our losses, come as they will. Before every man, and in all his duties, there is something like a victory to be gained; and he can say, as the soldier of duty,—" Strike me, my enemy, beat upon me, O ye hail! Mine it is to fulfil God's statutes, and therein I make you my servants."

Obligation to God also imparts zest to life, by giving to our actions a higher import, and, when they are right, a more consciously elevated spirit. The most serene, the most truly godlike enjoyment open to man, is that which he receives in the testimony that he pleases God, and the moral self-approbation of his own mind. When he regards his life as having a moral quality, over and above what may be called its secular and economic import ; as having to do with the holy and true and good, and as being, in that highest view, a worthy and upright life ; then he feels a joy, which, if it be human, partakes also of the divine. It is a kind of joy, too, that connects in his mind with thoughts of his own personal perfection, and this makes it even a sublime thing to live. In the mere prudential life of man as an earthly creature, in his cares, doings, plans, and pleasures, there is no respect to any results of quality in the person, but only to what he may get, or suffer, or be, in this life. The idea of personal perfection enters only with that of obligation to God. There dawns the thought of a divine quality —the moral, the good, the holy ; and his soul rises out of a life in the dust, to look about for those angelic prospects which are suited to the perfect glory of a perfect mind. Now, too, enters the great thought of eternity. Obligation is a word that opens eternity ; for the idea itself is immutable, and therefore it must needs suggest and prove an immutable state. Now you become to yourself quite another and different creature, a denizen of eternity. Breathing, digestion, growth, a fine show, and a titled name—none of these have much to do with the real import of life. You are living on the verge of great perils, meditating perfection after the style of God, and in your every thought of duty coupling the thought also of immutable good and glory. If you are a politician, a tradesman, a man of toil, or of letters, you are yet in none of these a mere life-time creature, but, in all, you are doing battle for eternity, and receiving the discipline of an angel. Ennobled by such a thought, how is the soul armed against evil, made superior to passion, and assisted to act a worthy part in life's scenes. Now you find a power in th very sublimity of your trial. You surmount your narrow infirmities, you exercise yourself easily in great virtues, you rise into a lofty and glorious serenity of spirit, all because the inspiring presence of eternity fills your life.

In this article of obligation to God, you are set also in immediate relation to God himself ; and, in a relation so high, everything in you and about you changes its import. The world is no more a mere physical frame—it exists rather as a theatre of religion. God is in it everywhere, training His creatures unto Himself. He is clearly seen by the things that are made. The objects of science take a moral import. Human history becomes divine history, the history of Providence. The soul's King is here on every side looking in upon it, encouraging to duty, and smiling upon what is rightly done. The intellect pierces through the shell of the senses, and discerns everywhere God. The reason is encircled by mysteries vast and holy. Imagination soars into her own appropriate realm of spirit and divinity, and all the faculties we have are bathed in joy and transfigured in the Creator's light. Set thus in a personal relation to God, everything changes its aspect and its meaning.

How different thus, one from the other, is the world of Voltaire and the world of Milton. They look, if you please, upon the same sun, and consider the light together. They walk the same shore of the same ocean, they meditate on its vastness, and listen to the chorus of its waters. They feel the gentleness of the dew, and the majesty of the storm. They ask what is the meaning of man's history, what is birth, life, death ; but how different all are, the things they look upon and the thoughts they cherish. One discovers only the clay world and its material beauties, flashes into shallow brilliancy, and, weaving a song of surfaces, empties himself of all that he has felt or seen. But the other, back of all, and through all visible things, has seen spirit and divinity. God is there, giving out Himself to His children, and all the furniture of life, its objects, scenes, and relations, take a religious meaning. A radiant glow and warmth pervade the world. The meanings are inexhaustible. Nothing is wearisome, or dull, or mean ; for nothing can be that is dignified by God's presence, and ordered by His care, to serve a religious use.

It is also a great fact, as regards a due impression of obligation to God, and of what is conferred in it, that it raises and tones the spiritual emotions of obedient souls into a key of sublimity, which is the completeness of their joy. For ye are complete in Him, says our apostle, well knowing that it is not what we are in ourselves that makes our completeness, but that our measure of being is full only when we come unto God as an object, and unite ourselves to the good and great emotions of God. This brings all high affinities and affections into play; for, without God as an object for the soul to admire, love, and worship, it were only an incomplete nature, an instrument of music without a medium of sound. True, the cowardly spirit of guilt finds no such happiness in being related to God, and would even shun the thought of any such relation. Therefore some will even argue against religious obligation, because it introduces fear, and fear, they say, is a base and uncomfortable passion. Rather say that the guilt is base, by which God is offended, and confidence changed to fear. Neither forget that one thing is baser for the guilty even than fear, and that is not to fear. Besides, it is a part of the blessing and greatness of obligation that life is thus made critical, and that obedience is thus intensified in its joy by great and fearful emotions. The more critical, therefore, life is, without shaking our courage, the closer are we to sublimity of feeling; for in all sublimity there is an element of fear. And so the greatness of God, the infinitude of His nature, the majesty of His Word and will, the purity, justice, and severe perfection of His character—all these bring a sense of fear to the mind, and precisely on this account, God, as an object, will raise every good mind to a perpetual sublimity of feeling, and in that manner fill out the measure of its possible joy; for joy is never full, save when the soul quivers with awe, and the beatitude itself rises to a pitch of fearfulness. And thus it is that obligation to God is precisely that which is needed to make our good complete; for this only sets our mind before an object that can sufficiently move it. Before Him, all the deep and powerful emotions that lie in the vicinity of fear are waked into life; every cord of feeling is pitched to its highest key or capacity, and the soul quivers eternally in the sacred awe of God and His commandments; thrilled as by the sound of many waters, or the roll of some anthem that stirs the framework of the worlds.

On this subject, too, experimental proofs may be cited, such as ought to leave no doubt and even no defect of impression.

OBLIGATION A PRIVILEGE. 143

Would that I could refer you each to his own experience; which I cannot, because, by the supposition, I am speaking to those that have had no such experience. And yet there have been many who, without any specially religious habit, have discovered still this truth, in its regulative and otherwise beneficent influence on their life. A few years before his death, the great statesman of New England, having a large party of friends dining with him at Marshfield, was called on by one of the party, as they became seated at the table, to specify what one thing he had met with in his life which had done most for him, or contributed most effectually to the success of his personal history. After a moment, he replied, "The most fruitful and elevating influence I have ever seemed to meet has been my impression of obligation to God." Precisely in what manner the benefit was supposed to accrue I am not informed; probably, however, as an influence that raised the pitch of his mind, gave balance and clearness to his judgments, and set him on a moral footing in his ideas and principles, such as certified his consciousness as a speaker, and added insight and energy to his words. Whatever may have been the particular benefits of which he spoke, the scene, as described by one present, was one most impressive in its dignity. He dropped the knife, as if turned to some better hospitality, and went on for many minutes in a discourse on his theme, unfolding it with wonderful beauty and freshness. The guests were taken by surprise, and sat listening with intense wonder at the exposition he was making, and still more at the subdued, yet lifted, manner, by which his feeling was attested—agreeing generally, as they fell into little groups afterward, that he probably never spoke with a finer eloquence.

But there are higher and holier witnesses, and a great cloud of them, whose testimony ought to be more convincing. Thus, if you will but open the Word of God's truth and listen to the songs that break out there, under God's statutes; if you will behold the good of past ages bending over God's law, as the spring of their sweetest enjoyments, crying each, "Oh, how love I Thy law!" if you will observe, too, what enlargement and freedom of soul they find in their obedience, and how they look upon the mere natural life of the flesh as bondage in comparison; if you will see how they disarm all their trials and dangers

by this same obedience; how they come away to God from the
scorching sands of their pilgrimage, as to the shadow of a great
rock, and refresh their fainting spirits by singing the statutes
of the Lord; if you will see what a character of courage, and
patience, and self-sacrifice they receive; how all great sentiments, such as carry their own dignity and blessing with them,
spring up in the rugged trials of duty and obedience to God;
then, last of all, if you will dare to break over the confines of
mortality, ascending to look on, as spectator, in that world of
the glorified, where the law of God makes full illustration of its
import in the high experiences it nourishes, and the benign
society it organises, you will, by that time get, I am sure, an
impression of the bliss, and greatness, and glory of obligation
to God, such as will profoundly instruct you. What seems to
you now to be a most unwelcome constraint, or even an annoyance to your peace, you will thus find reason, after all, to believe
is only the best and dearest privilege vouchsafed you.

Arresting my argument here, to what, in conclusion, shall I
more fitly draw you than to that which is, in truth, the point
established, viz., the fact that it is only religion, the great bond
of love and duty to God, that makes our existence valuable or
even tolerable. Without this, to live were only to graze. We
could not guess why we exist, or care to exist longer. If responsibility to God is felt as a constraint, if it makes you
uneasy and restive, better this than to find no real import in
anything. If you chafe, it is still against the throne of order, and
there is some sense of meaning in that. If God's will is heavy
on you, the protection it extends is not. If the circle of your
motion is restricted, it is only that the goodness of Jehovah is
drawing itself more closely round you. If you tremble, it is
not because of the cold. If still you sigh over the emptiness of
your experience, it might be even more empty; for you do, at
least, know that everything in life is now become great and
momentous. You cannot make it seem either futile or insignificant. If you are only a transgressor, still the liveliest
thoughts and the most thrilling truths that ever visit your
mind are such as come from the throne of duty. Religion !
religion !—it is the light of the world, the sun of its warmth,
the zest of all its works. Without this, the beauties of the

world are but splendid gewgaws, the stars of heaven glittering orbs of ice, and, what is yet far worse and colder, the trials of existence profitless and unadulterated miseries.

How convincing, how appalling a proof then is it, of some dire disorder and depravation in mankind, that when obligation to God is the spring of all that is dearest, noblest in thought, and most exalted in experience, we are yet compelled to urge it on them by so many entreaties, and even to force it on their fears by God's threatened penalties. What does it mean, this strange, suicidal aversion to God's statutes; that which ought to be our song, endurable only as we are held to it by terrors and penalties of fire? Nay, worse, if possible, you shall even hear, not seldom, the men that say they love God's statutes, and who therefore ought to be singing on their way, complaining of their dearth and dryness, and the necessary vanity of their experience. Let these latter see that the vanity they complain of is the cheat of their own self-devotion, and the littleness of their own empty heart. Let them pray God to enlarge their heart, and then they will run the way of God's commandments with true lightness and freedom. All this moping ends when the fire of duty kindles. As to the other and larger class, who are living, confessedly, in no terms of obligation to God, let them see, first of all, what they gain by it; how the load of life's burden chafes them; how they are crushed, crippled, wearied, confounded, when they try to get their songs out of this world and the dust itself of their pilgrimage; then go to God, and set their life on the footing of religion, or duty to God, which if they do, it shall be all gladness and peace; for the rhythm of all God's works and worlds chimes with His eternal law of duty.

Nothing is more certain or clear than that human souls are made for law, and so for the abode of God. Without law therefore, without God, they must even freeze and die. Hence, even Christ himself must needs establish and sanctify the law; for the deliverance and liberty He comes to bring are still to be sought only in obedience. Henceforth duty is the brother of liberty, and both rejoice in the common motherhood of law. And just here, my friends, is the secret of a great part of your misery and of the darkness that envelops your life. Without obligation you have no light, save what little may prick through your eyelids. Only he that keeps God's commandments walks in the light. The moment you can make a very simple discovery, viz., that obligation to God is your privilege and is not imposed as a burden, your experience will teach you many things—that duty is liberty, that repentance is a release from sorrow, that sacrifice is gain, that humility is dignity, that the truth from which you hide is a healing element that bathes your disordered life, and that even the penalties and terrors of God are the artillery only of protection to His realm.

Such and no other is the glad ministry of religion. Say not, when we come to you tendering its gifts, as we do to-day, that you are not ready, that you are not sufficiently racked by remorse and guilty conviction, that you have spent, as yet, no sorrowing days or sleepless nights,—what can these do for you? God wants none of these; He only wants you to accept Him as your privilege. When He calls you to repentance and new obedience, this is what He means; that you quit your madness, cease to gore yourself by your sins, come to your right mind, and accept, as a privilege, His good, eternal law. Giving thus your life to duty, let it, from this time forth, suffuse alike your trials and enjoyments with its own pure gladness, and let the self-approving dignity and greatness of a right mind be gilded—visibly and consciously gilded—by the smile of God. And, as the good and great society of the blessed is to be settled in this glorious harmony of law, and the statutes of the Lord are to be the song of their consolidated joy and rest, sing them also here; and in all life's changes—in the dark days and the bright, in sorrow and patience and wrong, in successes and hopes and consummated labours—everywhere adhere to this, and have it as the strength of your days, that your obligations to God are the best and highest privilege He gives you.

XI.

HAPPINESS AND JOY.

JOHN xv. 11—"*These things have I spoken unto you, that my joy might remain in you, and that your joy might be full.*"

CHRIST enters the world bringing joy : "Good tidings of great joy," cry the angels, "which shall be to all people." So now He leaves it, bestowing His gospel as a gift of joy : "These things have I spoken unto you, that my joy might remain in you, and that your joy might be full." This testament of His joy He also renews in His parting prayer : "And now come I to thee ; and these things I speak in the world, that they might have my joy fulfilled in themselves." "Man of sorrows" though we call Him, still He counts Himself the man of joy.

Would that I could bring you into His meaning when He thus speaks, and assist you to realise the unspeakable import which it has to Him. It is an impression deeply rooted in the minds of men, that the Christian life is a life of constraint, hardship, loss, penance, and comparative suffering ; Christ, you perceive, has no such conception of it, and no such conception is true. Contrary to this, I shall undertake to shew *that it is a life of true joy, the profoundest and only real joy attainable,—not a merely future joy, to be received hereafter, as the reward of a painful and sad life here, but a present, living, and completely full joy, unfolded in the soul of every man whose fidelity and constancy permit him to receive it.*

To clear this truth and shew it forth in the proper light of evidence, it is necessary, first of all, to exhibit a mistake which clouds the judgments, almost or quite universally, of those who are not in the secret of the Christian joy as revealed to a religious experience. It is the mistake of not distinguishing between happiness and joy, or of supposing them to be really one and the same thing. It is the mistake, indeed, not merely of their judgment, but of their practice ; for they all go after happiness without so much as a thought, more commonly of anything higher or better. Happiness they assume, and in their practice say, is the real joy of existence, beyond which and different from which there is, in kind, no other.

Now there is even a distinction of kind between the two, a distinction beautifully represented in the words themselves. Thus happiness, according to the original use of the term, is that which *happens*, or comes to one by a *hap ;* that is, by an outward befalling, or favourable condition. Some good is conceived, out of the soul, which comes to it as a happy visitation, stirring in the receiver a pleasant excitement. It is what money yields, or will buy—dress, equipage, fashion, luxuries of the table ; or it is settlement in life—independence, love, applause, admiration, honour, glory, or the more conventional and public benefits of rank, political standing, victory, power. All these stir a delight in the soul, which is not of the soul, or its quality, but from without. Hence they are looked upon as happening to the soul, and, in that sense, create happiness. We have another word from the Latin, which very nearly corresponds with this from the Saxon—viz., *fortune.* For whatever befell the soul, or came to it bringing it pleasure, was considered to be its good chance, and was called fortunate. I suppose, indeed, that there is no language in the world that does not contain this idea, just because all mankind are after benefits that will stir pleasure in the soul, without regard to its quality —after happiness, after fortune.

But joy differs from this, as being of the soul itself, originating in its quality. And this appears in the original form of the word, which, instead of suggesting a *hap*, literally denotes a *leap* or *spring.* Here again, also, the Latin had *exult*, which literally means a *leaping forth.* The radical idea, then, of joy is this—that the soul is in such order and beautiful harmony, has such springs of life opened in its own blessed virtues, that it pours forth a sovereign joy from within. The motion is outward and not toward as we conceive it to be in happiness. It is not the bliss of condition, but of character. There is in this a well-spring of triumphant, sovereign good, and the soul is able thus to pour out rivers of joy into the deserts of outward experience. It has a light in its own luminous centre, where God is, that gilds the darkest nights of external adversity—a

music charming all the stormy discords of outward injury and
pain into beats of rhythm and melodies of peace.

I ought, perhaps, to say that the original distinction between
these two words, thus sharply defined, is not always regarded.
I have traced the distinction only for the convenience of my
present subject, and not because the words are always used, or
must be, in this manner. In their secondary uses words are
often applied more loosely ; and so it has fallen out with these,
which are used by the common class of writers indiscriminately
one for the other. Still it will be seen that one of our English
poets, Mr Coleridge, distinguished always for the exactness of
his language, uses them both in immediate connexion, so as to
preserve their exact distinction, without any apparent design to
do so or consciousness of the fact. Addressing a noble Christian lady, he gives his conception of joy as an all-transforming,
all-victorious power in virtuous souls in terms like these—

> " O pure of heart ! thou need'st not ask of me
> What this strong music of the soul may be !
> What, and wherein it doth exist—
> This light, this glory, this fair luminous mist,
> This beautiful and beauty-making power.
>   Joy, virtuous lady ! Joy that ne'er was given
> Save to the pure, and in their purest hour—
> Life and life's effluence, cloud at once and shower ;
> Joy, lady, is the spirit and the power
> That wedding nature gives to us in dower,
>   A new earth and new heaven.
> We in ourselves rejoice ! "

Immediately after, without any thought of drawing the contrast, he speaks of his own folly with regret, because he was
caught by the temptations of fortune and now endures the
bitter penalty—

> " Fancy made me dreams of happiness ;
> For hope grew round me, like the twining vine,
> And fruits, and foliage, *not my own, seem'd mine*."

The picture he draws of himself is the picture, alas ! of the
general folly of mankind. Their "fancy makes them dreams of
happiness," promising to bless them in what may be gathered
"round" them in "fruits and foliage not their own ;" that is,
not of themselves, but external. All good, they fancy, is in

condition, not in character.   They think of happiness, go after happiness, and have, alas, how generally ! no thought of joy.

And yet we have many and various symbols of joy about us, from which we might well enough take the hint, as it would seem, of some possible felicity that is freer and higher in quality than the mere pleasures of fortune or condition.   The sportive children, too full of physical life to be able even to restrain their activity; the birds of the morning pouring out their music simply because it is in them, ought to suggest the possibility of some free, manly joy that is nobler than happiness.   Precisely this, too, we have been permitted, thank God, to look upon, in the examples of goodness, and to hear in the report of history ; for history is holding up her holy examples ever before us, shewing us the saints of God singing out their joy together in caves and dens of the earth at dead of night, shewing, too, the souls of her martyrs issuing, with a shout, from the fires that crisp their bodies.

Again, it is necessary, in order to a right conception of the meaning of Christian joy, as now defined, that we discover how to dispose of certain facts, or incidents, which commonly produce a contrary impression.

Thus, when the Saviour bequeaths His joy to us, and prays to have it fulfilled in us, it will naturally be remembered that He lives a persecuted and abused life, that He passes through an agony to His death, and dies in a manner most of all ignominious and afflictive.   Where, then, is the joy of which He speaks, or which He prays to have bestowed upon us ?   Are burdens, toils, sorrows, persecutions, crucifixions, joys ?

To this I answer that they may, in one view, be such, and in His case actually were.   He was a truly afflicted being, a man of sorrows in the matter of happiness; that is, in the outward condition, or befalling of His earthly state; still He had ever within a joy, a centre of rest, a consciousness of purity and harmony, a spring of good, an internal fulness which was perfectly sufficient.   And, indeed, we may call it one of the highest points of sublimity in His life, that He reveals the essentially victorious power of joy in the Divine nature itself; for God, in the contradictions of sinners, in the wrongs, disorders, ungrateful returns, and disgusting miseries of His sinful subjects, suffers a degree of abhorrence and pain that may properly be called so much of unhappiness; and He would even be an unhappy Being were it not that the love, and patience, and redeeming tenderness He pours into their bosom, are to Him a welling up eternally of conscious joy; joy the more sublime, because of its inherent and victorious excellence. And exactly so He represents Himself in the incarnate person of Christ. In His parable of the shepherd calling in his neighbours to rejoice with him over the sheep he has found, He opens the secret consciousness of joy He feels Himself as being that shepherd. His manner, too, was sometimes that of exultation even, as when the evangelist, noticing His deep, inward joy of heart, says, "In that hour Jesus rejoiced in spirit." And then, how much does it signify when, coming to the close of His career, and just about to finish it by a suffering death, He says, glancing backward in thought over all He has experienced, "My joy;" bequeathing it to His disciples as the dearest legacy He can give, the best, last wish He is able to express! What, then, does it signify of real privation or loss to become His follower!

But it requires, you will say, the admission of serious and, indeed, of painful thought in us to begin such a life; the solemn review of our character, the discovery of our sin, the sense of our shame and bondage, and our miserably lost condition under it; sorrow, repentance, self-renunciation, the loss of all things. The whole prospect, in short, which is opened, in coming to Christ, is painfully forbidding. The gospel even requires of us, in so many words, to cut off right hands, and pluck out right eyes, and deny and crucify ourselves, and be poor in spirit, and pass through life under a cross. Where, then, is the place for joy? How can the Christian life be called a life of joy?

It is not, I answer, in these things, taken simply by themselves. But receive an illustration: consider, a moment, what labours, cares, self-denials, restrictions of freedom, limitations of present pleasure, all men have to suffer in the way of what is called success; what application the scholar must undergo to win the distinctions of genius, what dangers and privations the hero must encounter to command the honours of victory. Are all these made unhappy because of the losses they are obliged to make? Are they not rather raised in feeling on this very account? If they all gained their precise point, or standing of success, by mere fortune, as by a ticket in some lottery, would the sacrifices and labours thus avoided be a clear saving or addition to their happiness? Contrary to this, it would render their successes almost or quite barren of satisfaction.

But how is this? There are so many hard burdens and painful losses, or sacrifices, and yet they subtract nothing, we say, but rather add to the real amount of enjoyment, in the successes gained by endurance and industry! There appears to be something bordering on contradiction here, how shall we solve it?

The solution is easy, viz., that the sacrifice made is a sacrifice of happiness, a sacrifice of ease, pleasure, comfort of condition; and the gain made is a gain of something more ennobling and more consciously akin to greatness, a gain that partakes, as far as any outward success can, the nature of joy. The man of industry and enterprise, the scholar, the statesman, the hero, says within himself these are not gifts of fortune to me, they are my conquests; tokens of my patience, economy, application, fortitude, integrity. In them his soul is elevated from within. He has a higher consciousness, and a felicity of course, that partakes, in some remote degree, of the sublime nature of joy. It is not condition, or things about him, making him happy, but it is the fire kindling within, the soul awaking to joy as a creative and victorious energy; and, in this view, it is a faint realisation, on the footing of a mere worldly life, of the immense superiority of joy to happiness. And it will be found, accordingly, as a matter of fact, that men, even worldly men, despise and nauseate mere happiness, if we hold the word to its strictest and most proper meaning. Using it more loosely, they fancy, and will say, that they are after happiness. Still the instinct of a higher life is in them, and they really despise what they do not conquer. None but the tamest and most abject will sit down to be nursed by fortune. All that have any real manhood we see cutting their way through severities and toils that promise achievement or a sense of victory. In such a truth, meeting your eyes on every hand, you may see how it is possible for the repentances, sacrifices, self-denials, and labours of the Christian life, to issue in joy. If Christ requires you literally to renounce all happiness, all good of condition, nothing is more clear than the possibility that even this may issue in a most complete and sovereign joy.

Or take an illustration somewhat different of the nature of these Christian struggles and sacrifices. A great and noble spirit, some archangel or prince of the sky, who is highest in his mould of all the forms of created being, has somehow come under a conscious respect, we will suppose, to condition ; fallen out of joy and become a lover of fortune or happiness. He finds that he is looking for good only in objects round him, and in things that imply no dignity of soul or merit of quality in him ; shows and equipages, liveries, social rank, things that please his appetite or his lusts. He finds that he is living for these, and really makes nothing of any higher good ; living as if there were no fountains of good to be opened within ; or as if, being only a vegetable, there could be nothing for him better than just to feel what the rain, and sun, and soil of outward condition give him to feel. He blushes at the discovery, and drops his head. And, as he begins to weep, a thought of fire strikes out from his immortality, and he says, " No ; it shall not be. God made me, not to be under and subject to things about me, or to ask my happiness at their hands. Rather was it for me to be above all creatures, as I was before them in order ; having my joy in the greatness of my spirit, and the victorious freedom and fulness of my life. Oh, I hear the call of my God ! I will arise and be what He commands me to be. These felicities of fortune shall tempt me and humble me no more. I cast them off, I renounce them for ever ! "

In the execution, then, of such a purpose, you see him go to his work. That he may clear himself of the dominion of things, he gives up all his outward splendours of state and show, makes a loss of all his resources and even comforts, and, finding his soul still looking covertly after the goods she has lost, he goes to frequent voluntary fasting, that he may clear himself yet more effectually from his bondage. He is not yet free. He finds the pampered spirit of self-indulgence still asking for ease, and indisposing him to victory. Then he asks for labour, seeks out something to be done, asks it of his God to give him some hard service, nay, a warfare, if He will, that his soul may fight herself clear.

Now, the question I have to ask is this, When you look upon the sacrifices and struggles of this great being, his losses, repentances, self-mortifications, works and warfares, does it seem

to you that he is growing miserable under them? Do you not
see how his consciousness rises in elevation, as he clears himself
of his humiliating bondage; how his soul finds springs of joy
opening in herself, as the good of condition falls off and
perishes; how every loss disencumbers him; how every toil,
and fasting, and fight, as it clears him more of the notion or
thought of happiness, lifts him into a joy as much more ennobled as it is more sovereign? Nay, you can hardly look on,
as you see him fight his holy purpose through, without being
kindled and exalted in feeling yourself by the sublimity of his
warfare.

But, exactly this is the true conception of the sacrifices
required in the Christian life. They are all required to
emancipate the soul and raise it above its servile dependence
on condition. They are losses of mere happiness, and for just
that reason they are preparations of joy.

Having disposed in this manner of what may seem to be
facts opposed or adverse to the supposition that Christian
sacrifice and piety support a victorious joy, I will now undertake to shew the positive reality itself.

And here we notice, first of all, the fact that, in a life of
selfishness and sin, there is a well-spring of misery which is
now taken away. No matter what, or however fortunate, the
external condition of an unbelieving, evil mind, there is yet a
disturbance, a bitterness, a sorrow within, too strong to be
mastered by any outward felicity. The whole internal nature
is in a state of discord. The understanding, conscience, will,
affections, appetites, imaginations, make a battle-field of the
breast, and the unhappy subject is rasped, irritated, bittered,
filled with fear, shamed by self-reproaches, stung by guilty convictions, gnawed by remorse, jealous, envious, hateful, lustful,
discontented, fretful, living always under a sky in which some
kind of storm is raging. And this discord is the misery, the
hell of sin. Oh, if men had only some contrary experience of
the heavenly peace, how great this misery would seem! And
yet they know it not; they even dare to imagine sometimes
that they are happy, just because their experience has brought
no contrasts to reveal the torment they suffer. Still they break
out notwithstanding now and then with impatience, and vent
their uneasiness in complaints that shew how poorly they get

on. They even testify in words that life is a burden. It is a burden, a much heavier and more galling burden than they know—and will be, even though they have all gifts of fortune, all honours and applauses crowded upon them—to make them happy. How much, then, does it signify, that Christ takes away this burden, restores this discord. For Christ is the embodied harmony of God, and he that receives Him settles into harmony with Him. "My peace I give unto you," are the Saviour's words; and this peace of Christ is the equanimity, dignity, firmness, serenity, which made His outwardly-afflicted life appear to flow in a calmness so nearly sublime. Bring any most fortunate of worldly minds into this peace, and the mere negative power of it, in quelling the soul's discords, would even seem to be a kind of translation. Just to exterminate the evil of the mind, and clear the sovereign hell which sin creates in it, would suffice to make a seeming paradise.

Besides, there is a fact more positive—the soul is such a nature that, no sooner is it set in peace with itself than it becomes an instrument in tune, a living instrument, discoursing heavenly music in its thoughts, and chanting melodies of bliss, even in its dreams. We may even say, apart from all declamation, for such is its nature, that when a soul is in this harmony, no fires of calamity, no pains of outward torment can for one moment break the sovereign spell of its joy. It will turn the fires to freshening gales, and the pains to sweet instigations of love and blessing.

Thus much we say, looking only at the soul's nature, its necessary distraction under the power of evil, its necessary blessedness in the harmony of rectitude. But we must ascend to a plain that is higher, and consider, more directly, what pertains to its religious nature. Little conception have we of its joy, or capacities of joy, till we see it established in God. The Christian soul is one that has come unto God, and rested in the peace of God. It dares to call Him Father, without any sense of daring. It is in such confidence toward Him that it even partakes His confidence in Himself. It is strong with His strength, having all its faculties in a glorious play of energy. It endures hardness with facility. It turns adversity into peace, for it sees a friendly hand ministering only good in what it suffers. In dark times it is never anxious, for God is its trust;

and God will suffer no harm to befall it. Having the testimony within that it pleases God, it approves itself in the holy smile of God that consciously rests upon it. Divinely guided, walking in the Spirit, it is raised by a kind of inspiration. It sees God, and knows Him, by an immediate and ever-present knowledge; according even to the promise, "Blessed are the pure in heart, for they shall see God." It is consciously ennobled, in this manner, by the proximity of God—expanded in volume, raised in greatness, thrilled by the eternal sublimities of God's deep nature and counsel. To a mind thus tempered, fortune can add little, and as little take away. Nothing can reach, or, at least, break down a soul established in this lofty consciousness. It partakes a divine nature, it is become a kind of divine creature, and the clouds that overcast the sky of other men sail under it. The hail that beats other men to the ground, the reproaches, execrations, conspiracies, and lies, under which other men are cowed, cannot hail upward, and therefore cannot reach the height of this divine confidence. "Blessed are ye, when men shall revile you, and persecute you, and shall say all manner of evil against you falsely, for my sake. Rejoice, and be exceeding glad." Such is the joy Christ bequeathed to His followers; such the good tidings of great joy that He brought into the world.

There is also, in the Christian type of character as related to God a peculiarity which needs, in this connexion, to be mentioned by itself. It is a character rooted in the divine love, and in that view is a sovereign bliss welling up from within; able thus to triumph and sing, independent of all circumstances and condition. A human soul can love everybody in despite of every hindrance, and by that love can bring everybody into its enjoyment. No power is strong enough to forbid this act of love, none therefore strong enough to conquer the joy of love; for whoever is loved, even though it be an enemy, is and must be enjoyed. Besides, it is a peculiarity of love that it takes possession of its neighbour's riches and successes, and makes them its own. Loving him, it loves all that he has for his sake, whether he be friend or enemy; enjoys his comforts, looks on his prospects, and all the beauties of his gardens and fields, with a pleasure as real as if they were legally its own. Love, in fact, overleaps all titles of law, and becomes a kind of universal owner; appropriates all wealth, and beauty, and blessing to itself, and enters into the full enjoyment. It understands the declaration well, "For all things are yours." Having such resources of joy in its own nature, the word that signifies *love*, in the original of the New Testament, is radically one with that which signifies *joy*. According to the family registers of that language, they are twins of the same birth. Love is joy, and all true joy is love—they cannot be separated. And Christ is an exhibition to us of this fact in His own person, a revelation of God's eternal joy, as being a revelation of God's eternal love; coming down thus to utter in our ears this glorious call, as a voice sounding out from God's eternity, "Enter ye into the joy of your Lord." He finds us hunting after condition; the low and questionable felicity of happiness. He says, "Behold my poverty, look on my burden of contempt, take the guage of my labours, note the insults and wrongs of my enemies, watch with me in my agony, follow me to my cross. This, O mortal! this, worshipper of happiness! is my joy. I give it to remain in you, that your joy, as mine, might be full. Enter into this love as God made you to love; love with me your enemies, labour and pray with me for their recovery to God, make my cause your cause, take up my cross and follow me, and then, in the loss of all things, you shall know that love is the sovereignty of good, the highest throne of sufficiency to which any being, created or uncreated, can ascend. Coming up into love, you clear all dependence of condition, you ascend into the very joy of God, and this is my joy. This I have taught you; this I now bequeath to your race."

Now it is precisely in this love, and nowhere else, that the followers of Christ have actually found so great joy. This is their light, the day-star dawning in their hearts, the renewing of their inward man, their joy of faith, the believing that makes them rejoice with joy unspeakable and full of glory. By this they become exceeding joyful in all their tribulations. They are raised above the world and conquer it, in the loss they make of it—dying, and still able to live; chastened, but not killed; sorrowful, yet always rejoicing; poor, yet making many rich; having nothing, yet possessing all things. Their heart is enlarged in the Divine love, and is become, in that manner, a fountain of essential, eternal, indestructible, and sovereign joy. They realise, in a word, the very testament of Christ; His joy is in them, and their joy is full.

Mark, now, some of the inspiring and quickening thoughts that crowd upon us in the subject reviewed. And—

1. Joy is for all men. It does not depend on circumstance or condition; if it did, it could only be for the few. It is not the fruit of good luck, or of fortune, or even of outward success, which all men cannot have. It is of the soul, or the soul's character; it is the wealth of the soul's own being, when it is filled with the spirit of Jesus, which is the spirit of eternal love. If you want, therefore, to know who of mankind can have the gift of joy, you have only to ask who of them have souls; for every soul is made to be a well-spring of eternal blessedness, and will be, if only it permits the waters of the eternal love to rise within. It can have right thoughts and true, and be set in everlasting harmony with itself. It can love, and so, without going about to find what shall bless it, it has all the material of blessing in itself; resources in its own immortal nature, as a creature dwelling in the light of God, which cannot fail, or be exhausted. All men are for joy, and joy for all.

2. It is equally evident that the reason why they do not have it is that they do not seek it where it is—in the receiving of Christ and the spirit of His life. They go after it in things without, not in character within; they have all faith in fortune, none in character. So they build palaces, and accumulate splendours about them, and keep a desert within. And then, since the desert within cannot be made to rejoice in the gewgaws and vanities without, they sigh, thy are very melancholy, the world is a hard world, vanity of vanities, all is vanity. Let them cease this whimpering about the vanities and come to Christ; let them receive His joy, and there is an end to the hunger. "'Take my yoke upon you, and learn of me: and ye shall find rest to your souls.' There is nothing hard in what I require. When I call you to renounce all, and take up your cross and follow me, I only seek to withdraw you from the chase after happiness, that I may fill you with joy. My yoke is easy, therefore, and my burden is light." Ah! how many have found it to be exactly so! What surprise have they felt in the dawning of this Christian joy! They seemed about to lose everything, and found themselves, instead, possessing all things.

3. It is here seen to be important that we hold some rational

and worthy conception of the heavenly felicity. How easy it is
for the Christian, who has tasted the true joy of Christ, to let
go the idea of joy and slide into the pursuit only of happiness,
or the good of condition. Worldly minds are in this vein
always; they more generally do not even conceive anything
different, and the whole gravitation therefore of the world,
both in its pursuits and opinions, is in this direction. Heaven
itself is thought of as a place, a condition, a kind of paradise
external, which has power to make everybody happy. The
question of universal salvation turns on just this point, inquiring
whether all souls will be got into the happy place, not whether
they will all break into eternity as carrying the eternal joy
with them. Stated in that manner, the question is even too
absurd for debate. I very much fear, too, that those teachers
who propose religion to us as a problem only of happiness, calling us to Christ that we may get the rewards of happiness,
the highest happiness, degrade our conceptions, and let us
down below the truth. When we speak of joy, we do not
speak of something we are after, but of something that will
come to us, when we are after God and duty. It is a prize un-
bought, and is freest, purest in its flow, when it comes unsought.
No getting into heaven, as a place, will compass it. You must
carry it with you, else it is not there. You must have it in
you, as the music of a well-ordered soul, the fire of a holy purpose, the welling up, out of the central depths, of eternal springs
that hide their waters there. It is the rest of confidence, the
blessedness of internal light and outflowing benevolence—the
highest form of life and spiritual majesty. Being the birth of
character, it has eternity in it. Rising from within, it is sovereign over all circumstance and hindrance. It is the joy of the
Lord in the soul of man, because it is joy like His, and because
it is from Him, participated by the secret life of goodness.

And this, my friends, is the glory of the heavenly state. If
you have been thinking of heaven only as a happy place, looking for it as the reward of some dull, lifeless service, arguing it
for all men, as the place where God will shew His goodness, by
making blessed loathsome and base souls, cheat yourselves no
more by this folly. Consider only whether heaven be in you
now. For heaven, as we have seen, is nothing but the joy of a
perfectly harmonised being, filled with God and His love. The

charter of it is—He that overcometh shall inherit.   It is the
victorious energy of righteousness for ever established in the
soul.   And this in us, pure and supreme, fulfils the glorious
bequest of Christ our Lord, "that my joy might remain in you,
and that your joy may be full."   It remains—it is full.

XII

THE TRUE PROBLEM OF CHRISTIAN EXPERIENCE.

REVELATION ii. 4—"*Nevertheless I have somewhat against thee, because thou hast left thy first love.*"

THERE are some texts of Scripture that suffer a much harder lot than any of the martyrs, because their martyrdom is perpetual ; and this, I think, is one of the number. Two classes appear to concur in destroying its dignity—viz., the class who deem it a matter of cant to make anything of conversion, and the class who make religion itself a matter of cant, by seeing nothing in it but conversion.

My object, however, is not so much to balance these opposites, or even to recover the passage of Scripture that is lost between them ; but it is to clear the way of all Christian experience, by shewing what it does and how it proceeds. There are many disciples of our time, who, like the Ephesian disciples, are to be warmly commended for their intended fidelity, and are yet greatly troubled and depressed by what appears to be a real loss of ground in their piety. Christ knows their works, approves their patience, commends their withdrawing always from them that are evil ; testifies for them that they have withstood false teachers, with a wary and circumspect fidelity, made sacrifices, laboured, and not fainted ; and yet they are compelled to sigh over a certain subsidence of that pure sensibility and that high inspiration, in which their discipleship began. The clearness of that hour is blurred, the fresh joy interspaced with dryness. Omissions of duty are discovered which they did not mean ; they do not enjoy the sacrifices they make as they once did, and make them often in a legal, self-constrained manner. Rallying themselves to new struggles, as they frequently do, to retrieve their losses, they simply hurry on their own will, and therefore thrust themselves out of faith only the more rapidly. The danger is, at this

Ephesian point of depression, that not knowing what their change of phase really signifies, or under what conditions a real progress in holy character is to be made, they will finally surrender, as to a doom of retrogradation too strong to be resisted. I design, if possible, to bring them help, calling their attention directly to these two points :—

I. *The relation of the first love, or the beginning of the Christian discipleship, to the subsequent life.*

II. *The relation of the subsequent life, including its apparent losses, to the beginning.*

What we call conversion is not a change distinctly traceable in the experience of all disciples, though it is and must be a realised fact in all. There are many that grew up out of their infancy, or childhood, in the grace of Christ, and remember no time when they began to love Him. Even such, however, will commonly remember a time, when their love to God and divine things became a fact so fresh, so newly conscious, as to raise a doubt whether it was not then for the first time kindled. In other cases there is no doubt of a beginning—a real, conscious, definitely-remembered beginning — a new turning to God, a fresh-born Christian love. The conversion to Christ is marked as distinctly as that of the Ephesian Church, when coming over to Christ, from their previous idolatry. The love is consciously first love, a new revelation of God in the soul, a restored consciousness of God, a birth of joy and glorified song in the horizon of the soul's life, like that which burst into our sky when Jesus was born into the world. All things were new— Christ was new, the Word a new light, worship a new gift, the world a new realm of beauty, shining in the brightness of its Author : even the man himself was new to himself. Sin was gone, and fear also was gone with it. To love was his all, and he loved everything. The day dawned in joy, and the thoughts of the night were songs in his heart. Then how tender, how teachable ! in his conscience how true, in his works how dutiful ! It was the divine childhood, as it were, of his faith, and the beauty of childhood was in it. This was his first love, and if all do not remember any precise experience of the kind, they do, at least, remember what so far resembled this as to leave no important distinction.

I. What, now, is the import of such a state, what its relation to the subsequent life and character?

It is not, I answer, what they assume, who conceive it to be only a new thought taken up by the subject himself, which he may as naturally drop the next moment, or may go on to cultivate till it is perfected in a character. It is more, a character begun, a divine fact accomplished, in which the subject is started on a new career of regenerated liberty in good. I answer again that it is not any such thing as they assume it to be, who take it as a completed gift, which only needs to be held fast. It is less, far less than this. To God it is one of His beginnings, which He will carry on to perfection; to the subject himself it is the dawn of his paradise, an experience that will stand behind him as an image of the glory to be revealed before, an ideal set up, in his beatitude, of that state in which his soul is to be perfected and to find its rest. In one view, indeed, it is a kind of perfect state—a state resembling innocence. It is free, it is full of God, it is for the time without care. New born, as it were, the spirit of a babe is in it. The consciousness of sin is, for a time, almost or quite suspended,—sin is washed away, the heart is clean. The eye is single, as a child's eye. The spirit is tender, as a child's spirit,—so ingenuous, so pure in its intentions, so simple in its love, that it even wears the grace of a heavenly childhood.

In this flowering state of beauty the soul discovers, and even has in its feeling the sense of perfection, and is thus awakened from within to the great ideal, in which its bliss is to be consummated. The perfection conceived, too, and set up as the mark of attainment, is something more than a form of grace to be hereafter realised. It is now realised, as far as it can be— the very citizenship of the soul is changed; it has gone over into a new world, and is entered there into new relations. But it has not made acquaintance there; it scarcely knows how it came in, or how to stay, and the whole problem of the life-struggle is to become established in what has before been initiated.

M

There is a certain analogy between this state, paradisiacally beautiful, pure, and clean, and that external paradise in which our human history began. What could be more lovely and blessed, what, in a certain formal sense, more perfect than the upright, innocent, all-harmonious childhood of the first human pair. But it was beauty without strength, the ingenuous goodness of beings unacquainted with evil. A single breath of temptation is enough to sweep it all away. The only way to establish it is to lose it and regain it. Paradise lost and regained is not a conception only of the poet, but it is the grand world-problem of probation itself. No state of virtue is complete, however total the virtue, save as it is won by a conflict with evil, and fortified by the struggles of a resolute and even bitter experience. Somewhat in the same way, it is necessary that a Christian should fight out the conquest of his paradise, in order to be really established in it. There is no absolute necessity that he should lose it, nor any such qualified necessity as there was that the first man should fall from his integrity; for he is, by the supposition, one who has learned already the bitterness of evil, by a life thus far steeped in the gall of it. He has been outside of his paradise, to look on it from thence, as Adam had not. He has only not been inside long enough thoroughly to understand the place. He will commonly never be established in it, therefore, till he knows it more experimentally, and gets wonted in it. And yet there are a few, as I verily believe, who never go outside again, from the moment of their first entering, but stay within, unfolding all their life long, as flowers, in their paradise,—trustful, ductile, faithful, and therefore unfaltering in their steadfastness.

Still the probability that any one will continue in the clearness and freshness of his first love to God, suffering no apparent loss, falling into no disturbance or state of self-accusing doubt, is not great. And where the love is really not lost it will commonly need to be conquered again, over and over, and wrought into the soul by a protracted and resolute warfare. The germ that was planted as impulse must be nourished by discipline. What was initiated as feeling must be matured by holy application, till it becomes one of the soul's own habits.

A mere glance at the new-born state of love discovers how incomplete and unreliable it is. Regarded in the mere form of feeling, it is all beauty and life. A halo of innocence rests upon it, and it seems a fresh made creature, reeking in the dews of its first morning. But how strange a creature is it to itself—waking to the discovery of its existence, bewildered by the mystery of existence. An angel, as it were, in feeling, it is yet a child in self-understanding. The sacred and pure feeling you may plainly see is environed by all manner of defects, weaknesses, and half-conquered mischiefs, just ready to roll back upon it and stifle its life. The really sublime feeling of rest and confidence into which it has come, you will see is backed, a little way off, by causes of unrest, insufficiency, anxiousness, and fear. Questions numberless, scruples, fluctuating moods, bad thoughts, unmanageable doubts, emotions spent that cannot be restored by the will, novelty passing by, and the excitements of novelty vanishing with it—there is a whole army of secret invaders close at hand, and you may figure them all as peering in upon the soul from their places of ambush ready to make their assault. And, what is worst of all, the confidence it has in the Spirit of God, and which, evenly held, would bear it triumphantly through, is itself unpractised, and is probably underlaid by a suppressed feeling of panic, lest He should some time take His leave capriciously. It certainly would not be strange, if the disciple, beset by so many defects, and so little ripe in his experience, should seem for a while to lose ground, even while strenuously careful to maintain his fidelity. And then Christ will have somewhat against him. He will not judge him harshly, and charge it against him as a crime that has no mitigations; it will only be a fatal impeachment of his discipleship, when he finally surrenders the struggle, and relapses into a prayerless and worldly life.

The significance, then, of the first love, as related to the subsequent life, is twofold. In the first place, it is the birth of a new, supernatural, and divine consciousness in the soul, in which it is raised to another plane, and begins to live as from a new point. And secondly, it is so much of a reality, or fact realised, that it initiates, in the subject, experimentally, a conception of that rest, that fulness, and peace, and joyous purity, in which it will be the bliss and greatness of his eternity to be established. In both respects, it is the beginning of the end; and yet, to carry the beginning over to the end, and give it there its due fulfilment, requires a large and varied trial of experience. The office and operation of this trial it now remains to exhibit as proposed.

II. In a consideration of the subsequent life, as related to the beginning, or first love. The real object of the subsequent life, as a struggle of experience, is to produce in wisdom what is there begotten as a feeling, or a new love ; and thus to make a fixed state of that which was initiated only as a love. It is to convert a heavenly impulse into a heavenly habit. It is to raise the Christian childhood into a Christian manhood—to make the first love a second or completed love ; or, what is the same, to fulfil the first love, and give it a pervading fulness in the soul ; such that the whole man, as a thinking, self-knowing, acting, choosing, tempted, and temptible creature, shall coalesce with it, and be for ever rested, immovably grounded in it.

The paradise of first love is a germ,. we may conceive, in the soul's feeling of the paradise to be fulfilled in its wisdom. And when the heavenly in feeling becomes the heavenly in choice, thought, judgment, and habit, so that the whole nature consents and rests in it as a known state, then it is fulfilled or completed. Then is the ideal, awakened by the first love, become a fact or attainment. See now briefly in what manner the experimental life works this fulfilment.

At first the disciple knows, we shall see, very little of himself, and still less how to carry himself so as to meet the new state of divine consciousness into which he is born. You may look upon him as literally a new, supernatural man, and just as a child has to learn the use of his own body in handling, tasting, heaving, climbing, falling, running, so the new man learns, in the struggles of practical life, his own new nature, how to work his thoughts, rule his passions, feed his wants, settle his choices, and clear his affections. Thus at last his whole nature becomes limber and quick to his love, so that the life he had in feeling, he can operate, express, fortify, and feed. At first nothing co-operates in settled harmony with his new life, but if he is faithful, he will learn how to make everything in him work with it, and assist the edifying of his soul in love.

A great point with him is the learning how to maintain his new supernatural relation of sonship and vital access to God.

Conscious of any loss or apparent separation, he is likely, at first, to throw himself out of God's peace only the more completely by the panic he indulges, and the violent throes he makes to re-establish himself. The feeling in which he is raised to a participation of God cannot instruct him how to maintain that participation or to keep an open state of access. How to work his will, his inward suggestions and outward duties—how to shape his life and order his prayers, so as to set himself always before God and command a ready approach, he knows as yet only by the guidance of his feeling. But the struggle of experience brings him into a growing acquaintance both with God, and himself as related to God, removing in this manner his awkwardness, so that he is able to reject all false methods and all raw experiments, and address himself to God skilfully, as a friend will address a friend. He knows exactly how he must stand before God to be one with Him and abide in Him. He comes into the secret of God easily, and, as it were, naturally, and receives the manifestation of God as one who lives in the adoption of a son.

In the same way, or by the same course of experience, he conceives more and more perfectly what is the true idea of character. At first, character is to him a mere feeling or impulse —a frame. Next, perhaps, it becomes a life of work and self-denial. Next a principle—nothing but a matter of principle. Next he conceives that it is something outwardly beautiful—a beautiful life. After a while, he discovers that he has been trying to mould what is spiritual by his mere natural taste, and forgotten the first love as the animating life and divine principle of beauty. And so he draws himself on, by degrees, through all the varied phases of loss and self-criticism, to a more full and rounded conception of character, returning at last to that which lay in his first love. So that character is, at last, conceived as a life whose action, choice, thought, and expression, are all animated and shaped by the Spirit of holiness and divine beauty which was first breathed into his feeling. Nothing is so difficult to settle as the conception of a perfect character—nothing at the same time so necessary. And every faithful Christian will be conscious of a constantly progressive change in his conception of what he is to be.

A very great point to be gained, by the struggle of experi-

ence, is to learn when one has a right to the state of confidence
and rest. At first the disciple measures himself wholly by his
feeling. If feeling changes, as it will and must at times, then
he condemns himself, and condemning himself perhaps without
reason, he breaks his confidence toward God and stifles his
peace. Then he is ready to die to get back his confidence, but
not knowing how he lost it, he knows not where to find it. He
had been at his business, and as that occupied his attention, it
took off also somewhat of his feeling : charging this to the
account of sin, and not to any want of experience in turning
the mind so as to keep or recover its emotions, he put his conscience against him where it ought to have been his helper, and
fell into the greater difficulty because he fell into mental confusion. Or perhaps he had played with his children, or he had
talked in society about things not religious, in order to accommodate the circle he was in : this touched the delicate feeling
of his soul ; and, as feeling does not reason or judge, the wound
was taken for admitted sin. On one occasion he did not give
heed to some insignificant or really absurd scruple. On another he declined some duty which really was no duty, and was
better not to be done. In short, he was continually condemning
and tormenting himself, and gratuitously forbidding himself all
confidence toward God. But finally, after battering down his
own confidence and stifling his love in this manner by self-dis-
couragement for many years, he is corrected by God's Spirit
and led into a discovery of himself and the world that is more
just, ceases to condemn himself in that which he alloweth, so
to allow himself in anything which he condemneth ; and now
behold what a morning it is for his love! His perturbed,
anxious state is gone. God's smile is always upon him. His
peace flows down upon him as a river from the throne. His
first love returns, henceforth to abide and never depart.
Everywhere it goes with him, into all the callings of industry
and business, into social pleasures and recreations, bathing his
soul as a divine element.

By a similar process he learns how to modulate and operate
his will. On one side his soul was in the Divine love. On the
other he had his will. But, how to work his will so as perfectly to suit his love, he at first did not know. He accordingly
took his love into the care of his will ; for assuredly he must

do all that is possible to keep it alive. He thus deranged all right order and health within by his violent superintendence, battered down the joy he wished to keep, and could not under-stand what he should do more; for, as yet, all he had done seemed to be killing his love. He had not learned that love flows down only from God, who is its object, and cannot be manufactured within ourselves. But he discovers finally that it was first kindled by losing, for the time, his will. Under-standing now that he is to lose his will in God's will, and abandon himself wholly to God, to rest in Him and receive of His fulness; finding, too, that will is only a form of self-seeking, he makes a total loss of will, self, and all his sufficiency; where-upon the first love floods his nature again, and bathes him like a sea without a shore. And yet it will not be strange if he finds, within a year, that, as he once overacted his will in self-conduct, so now he is underacting it in quietism; that his love grows thin for want of energy, and, returning to his will again, he takes it up in God; dares to have plans and ends, and to be a person; wrestles with God and prevails with Him; and so becomes, at last, a prince, acknowledged and crowned before him.

His thinking power undergoes a similar discipline. At first, he doubted much, doubted whether he had a right to doubt, and whether he did doubt, and yet more how to get rid of his doubts. The clatter of his old, disordered, thinking nature began, ere long, to drown his love by the perpetual noise it made; old associations led in trains of evil suggestions, which, like armies of wrath, overran and desolated his soul. He at-tacked every one of them in turn, and that kept him thinking of the base things he wanted to forget. He discovers, at length, that all he can do is to fill his capacity with something better; his mind with truth, his heart with God and faith, his hands with duty, and all with the holy enthusiasm of Christian hope; and then, since there is no room left for idle fancies and vain imaginations to enter, he is free, the torments of evil suggestion are shut away. The courses and currents of the soul are now cleared, and his thoughts, like couriers sent up through the empyrean, will return, bringing visions of God and divine beauty to waken the pure, first love and kindle its joyful flames.

At first he had a very perplexing war with his motives. He feared that his motive was selfish, and then he feared that his fear was selfish. He dug at himself so intently, to detect his selfishness, as to create the selfishness he feared. The complications of his heart were infinite, and he became confused in his attempt to untwist them. He blamed his love to God because he loved Him for His goodness, and then tried to love Him more without any thought of His goodness. He was so curious, in fact, to know his motives that he knew nothing of them; and finally stifled his love in the effort to understand it, and act the critic over it. At length, after months or years, it may be, of desolation, he discovers, as he had never done before, that he was a child in his first love, and had a child's simplicity. And now he has learned simplicity by his trial! Falling now into that first simplicity, there to abide, because he knows it, the first love blooms again—blooms as a flower, let us hope, that is never to wither. His motive is pure because it is simple; and his eye, being single toward God, his whole body is full of light.

Thus far it is supposed, in all the illustrations given, that the new love kindled by the Spirit has to maintain itself, in company with great personal defects in the subject. These defects are a constant tendency in him to defections that correspond. Whenever he yields to them, he suffers a loss which is, in that case a guilty or blameable loss. But he will sometimes be reduced, or let down, simply because, or principally because, he has too little skill or insight to avoid it. And this reduction will sometimes go so far as to be a kind of subsidence out of the supernatural into the natural state. He is confused and lost, and his very love appears to be quite dead. God is hidden, as it were, behind a veil, and cannot be found. Duties kept up, as by the Ephesians, without liberty, yield no fruit of peace or blessing. And now, since it is not in the nature of a soul to stand empty, and fight off evil, with no power left but a vacuum, it will not be strange if he lets in the world, grows light, covetous, ambitious, and has only a name to live. All this, in one view, is but the working of his defects. Doubtless he is blameable, in a degree, though not as he would be if he had no such defects to contend with. Christ has somewhat against him, looks on him as one made subject to vanity not willingly, or willingly in part, and waits to restore him. His very losses, too, will be a lesson of experience really invaluable. He has learned his defects by his failures, and the day is not far distant when the dryness of his present experience will create in his heart an irrepressible longing for the recovery of the ground he has lost. For there is yet, slumbering in his memory, the dim ideal of a first love to Christ. Around that ideal are gathered many distasteful recollections and associations; but there is a faint, sweet light of beauty in the centre. And now as, in turn, the world itself palls, that faint spot of light remembered as the dawn of love to Christ, will grow radiant and beam as a sun upon him. As a prodigal he will return; as a prodigal returning, be met a great way off, and welcomed by his forgiving and rejoicing Father. Now he is in his love as one instructed. His defects are corrected by his failures, and, by a common paradox of experience, supplemented by his losses; and so he is prepared to stand fast in his love. Sometimes a very dull and carnal, or capricious nature will go through this kind of bad experience more than once, and then will appear to be saved only so as by fire. But, more commonly, the time past of one such misery will suffice.

You perceive, in this review, how everything in the subsequent life of the disciple is designed of God to fulfil the first love. A great part of the struggle which we call experience, appears to operate exactly the other way; to confuse and stifle the first fire of the Spirit. Still the process of God is contrived to bring us round, at last, to the simple state which we embraced, in feeling, and help us to embrace it in wisdom. Then the first love fills the whole nature, and the divine beauty of the child is perfected in the divine beauty of a vigorous and victorious manhood. The beginning is the beginning of the end —the end the child and fruit of the beginning.

I am well aware that some will be dissatisfied with a view of the Christian life that appears to anticipate so many turns and phases, and so much of loosing experience. They will think it better to take a keynote that is lower, and start upon a level that can be maintained. Thus, if we say nothing of a conversion, or the high experience involved in that term, and commence a course of devout observances and church formalities;

or if, taking a different method, we set ourselves to a careful
and diligent self-culture, praying and worshipping as a part of
the process, and for the sake of the effect, noting our defects,
chastening our passions, cherishing our religious tastes and
sentiments ; then, in one or other of these methods, we may go
steadily on, it will be imagined, clear of all fluctuations, maintain-
ing an even, respectable, and dignified piety.   Yes, undoubtedly
we may, and that for the very reason that we have no first love
to lose, no fervours to be abated, and, in fact, no divine birth or
experience at all.   The piety commended is, in either case, a
kind of stalagmite piety, built up from below, with the disadvantage of no drippings from above; a really cavernous forma-
tion, upon which the true light of day never shone.   In some
cases, the soul may pass over in this manner imperceptibly, into
some faint experience of God that is genuine; but the dignity
it boasts is the dignity of a consistent poverty and ignorance of
God, and nothing is more easy to be maintained.   On the other
hand, the very reason why there are so many phases, or seeming
lapses, in Christian experience, is not because it is false, but
oftener because it is genuine; because God has really dawned
upon the soul's faith, and kindled a fire supernatural in its love.
Hence, to settle it into this high relation, as a properly known
relation, is often a work of much time and difficulty.   The problem is neither more nor less than to learn the way of God, and
come into practical acquaintance with Him.   And how can this
be done without a large experience of defeat and disasters endlessly varied.   How can a being so weak and ignorant, knowing,
at first, almost nothing of the high relations into which he has
come, learn to walk evenly with God, save as he is instructed
by many waverings, reactions, irregularities, and throes of losing
experience.   Grazing in the pasture-ground of a mere human
culture, we might shew more plausibly; but now we move irreg-
ularly, just because we are in a level where the experience of
nature does not instruct us.   We lose ground, fall out of place,
subside and waver, just because we are after something transcendent, something above us; climbing up unto God, to rest
our eternity in Him—a being whom, as yet, we do not sufficiently know, and whom to know is life eternal.   Therefore we
best like that kind of life which appears least plausible in present show, well understanding that, if nothing more were in

hand than simply to maintain a level march, on the footing of
mere nature, there is no feeblest Christian, or even no Christian,
who could not do it triumphantly.

The fact, then, of a truly first love, the grand Christian fact of
a spiritual conversion or regeneration, is no way obscured by
the losing experiences that so often follow. On the contrary,
its evidence is rather augmented by these irregularities and
seeming defections. And, if it be more than nothing, then it is,
of all mortal experiences, the chief ; a change mysterious, tremendous, luminous, joyful, fearful, everything which a first contact of acquaintance with God can make it.

Where the transition to this state of divine consciousness,
from a merely self-conscious life under sin, is inartificially made,
and distorted by no mixtures of tumult from the subject's own
eagerness, it is, in the birth, a kind of celestial state, like that
of the glorified,—clear, clean, peaceful and full, wanting nothing
but what, for the time, it does not know it wants—the settled
confidence, the practically-instructed wisdom, the established
and tried character of the glorified. And yet all the better is
it, imparadised in this glory, this first love, this regenerative
life, this inward lifting of the soul's order, that a prize so transcendent is still, in a sense, to be won or fought out and gained
as a victory. For life has now a meaning, and its work is
great—as great, in fact, in the humblest walks and affairs as in
the highest. And the more difficulties one has to encounter
within and without, the more significant and the higher in inspiration his life will be. The very troubles that others look on
with pity, as if he had taken up a kind of piety more perilous
and burdensome than was necessary, will be his fields of victory ;
and his course of life will be just as much happier as it is more
consciously heroic. He has something great to live for, nay,
something worthy even to die for, if he must,—that which
makes it glorious to live, and not less glorious to die.

This war, too, is one, my brethren, as I verily believe, that, in
all that is bitterest and most painful, may be effectually carried
and ended without waiting for the end of your life. The bitterness and painfulness are, in fact, nowhere, except in the losing
or apparently losing experiences of which I have been speaking,

and these may assuredly be surmounted. There is a standing above all sense of loss, a peace of God that cannot be shaken, a first love made second and final, into which you may come soon, if you are faithful, and in which you may abide. The doctrine of Wesley and his followers may be exaggerated, or partially misconceived ; I think it is. They appear to hold that there is a kind of second conversion, higher than the first, which they imagine is complete sanctification. But it is, if I am right, neither more nor less than the point of the first love reached again, with the advantage of much wisdom or self-understanding brought back with it. The disciple is, for that reason, stronger, wider in volume, more able to abide or stand fast. But, if he is not strong enough, he will very certainly take another circuit, and perhaps another. Enough that there is hope,—that there is a state of profound liberty, assurance, and peace, which you may attain to, and in which you may abide. Indeed, the original love itself was but a foretaste in feeling of that which you may achieve in wisdom ; and you are to set that mark in your eye, expecting to emerge again, or to climb patiently up into a state of purity and fellowship closely resembling that.

If, then, you have now become entangled, discouraged, darkened,—if you seem to have quite given over,—blame yourself, not in your infirmity, but only in your sin. See, if possible, exactly what and where your blame is, and let your repentances and confessions exactly cover it. Probably you did not fall consentingly, but you seem to have been thrown by your own distracted, half-illuminated mind. You struggled hard, and with so great self-exertion, not unlikely, that you fell out of faith, and were even floored by your struggles themselves. You fanned the love so violently, that you rather blew out than kindled the flame. The harder you lifted, the deeper in mire you sank. At last, you gave over with a sigh, and fell back as one quite spent. And now, it may be that you even look upon the whole subject of spiritual religion with a kind of dread. It wears a painful and distasteful look. And yet there is one bright spot in the retrospect — viz., the gentle, ingenuous, heavenly feeling, the peace, the cleanness, the fulness of heart, the liberty in God and His love, the luminous, inward glory ;

and, if you could see nothing else but this, how attractive the remembered blessedness would be! the more attractive for the emptiness you have since experienced, and the general distaste of the world which so often afflicts you. Nay, with all the disrespect you may possibly put on this former experience, it is precisely this, and the opening of your higher nature in it, that makes a great part of the distaste you now suffer toward the world. What a call, then, have you in this joy remembered! And God indorses it, offering to seal all this upon you, and more. He blames you not for anything unavoidable; He only blames you for your letting go of Him, and your final surrender of the struggle. This He waits to forgive. He will do more, He will even make what is blameable in your sad loss and defection turn to your account. Can you ask encouragement to a new effort better than this? Come back, then, O thou prodigal, to thy Father! Quit thy sad folly and emptiness, thy reproaches of soul, thy diseased longings, and thy restless sighs. Return again to thy God, and give thyself to Him, in a final and last sacrifice. Ask the restored revelation. Conquer again, as Christ will help you, the original love, in that to abide and rest.

XIII

THE LOST PURITY RESTORED

1 JOHN iii. 3—" *And every man that hath this hope in him puri-fieth himself, even as He is pure.*"

THIS hope, as the apostle is speaking, is a hope to be with Christ ; and as Christ is, in highest verity, the manifestation of God, who is infinite purity, it is a hope to be concomitant with purity, the purity of Christ, and of God, which again is but a hope of being entered into, and perfectly answerable to, the purity of God. And then it follows, yet again, that every man that hath this hope in him will be purifying himself here on earth even according to the purity of Christ, with whom he hopes to be.

Accordingly, the subject raised for our consideration is *purity of soul as the aim of spiritual redemption, and the legitimate issue of Christian experience.* Let us see,

I. If we can form a fit conception of what purity is. If we refer to examples, it is the character of angels and of God—the simplicity, the unstained excellence, the undimmed radiance, the spotless beauty. Or it is God, as represented here on earth, in the sinless and perfect life of Christ ; His superiority to sense, and passion, and the opinions of the world, His simple devotion to truth, His unambitious goodness, His holy, harmless, unde-filed life, as being with, yet separate from, sinners.

If we go to analogy, purity is, in character, what transparency is in the crystal. It is water flowing, unmixed and clear, from the mountain spring. Or it is the white of snow. Or it is the clear open heaven, through which the sparkling stars appear, hidden by no mist of obstruction. Or it is the pure light itself in which they shine. A pure character is that, in mind, and feeling, and spirit of life, which all these clear, untarnished symbols of nature, image, in their lower and merely sensible sphere, to our outward eye.

Or, if we describe purity by reference to contrasts, then it is a character opposite to all sin, and so to most of what we see in the corrupted character of mankind. It is innocent, just as man is not. It is incorrupt, as opposed to passion, self-seeking, foul imaginations, base desires, enslaved affections, a bad conscience, and turbid currents of thought. It is the innocence of infancy without the stain—that innocence matured into the spotless, positive, and eternally-established holiness of a responsible manhood. It is man lifted up out of the mire of sin, washed as a spirit into the clean white love and righteousness of his Redeemer, and so purged of himself as to be man, without anything of the sordid and defiled character of a sinner.

Or we may set forth the idea of purity under a reference to the modes of causes. In the natural world, as, for example, in the heavens, causes act in a manner that is unconfused and regular. All things proceed according to their law. Hence the purity of the firmament. In the world of causes, it is the scientific ideal of purity that events transpire normally, according to the constitutive order and original law of the creation. But as soon as a soul transgresses, it breaks out of order, and its whole internal working becomes mixed, confused, tumultuous, corrupt. Abiding in God, all its internal motions would proceed in the simple, harmonious, orderly progress of the firmament, and it would be a pure soul. Plunging into sin, it breaks order, and falls into mixtures of causes in all its actions. The passions are loose upon the reason, the will overturns the conscience, the desires become unruly, the thoughts are, some of them, suggested by the natural law of the mind, and some are thrust in by the disorders of vitiated feeling, corrupt imagination, disordered memory, and morbid impulse. In short, the soul is in a mixture of causes, and so out of all purity. The man is corrupted, as we say, and the word *corrupt* means *broken together*, dissolved into mixture and confusion—which is the opposite of purity.

Or finally, we may describe purity absolutely, as it is when viewed in its own positive quality. And here it is chastity of soul, that state of the spiritual nature in which it is seen to have no contacts or affinities, but such as fall within the circle of unforbidden joy and uncorrupted pleasure. It is unsensual, superior to the dominion of passion, living in the pleasures of the mind and of goodness, devoted in its virgin love to the converse of truth only, and inaccessible to evil. Absolute purity is untemptible, as in God. Adam therefore was never in absolute purity. His purity was more negative than positive. He was innocent, he had not sinned; but for want of an established positive purity, he was ready to be tempted and open to temptation. But if he is now among the glorified, he is in absolute purity, because he is untemptible. Real chastity is that which cannot know temptation, and this is what we mean by absolute purity. It puts the soul as truly asunder and apart from the reach of evil suggestion as God himself is in the glorious chastity of His holiness.

In all these methods, we make so many distinct approaches to the true idea of spiritual purity. Distant as the character is from anything we know, in this sad world of defilement and corrupted life, still it is the aim and purpose of Christian redemption, as I now proceed,

II. To shew, to raise us up into the state of complete purity before God. The call of the Word is, "Come now, and let us reason together, saith the Lord : though your sins be as scarlet, they shall be as white as snow; though they be red like crimson, they shall be as wool." And it is curious to observe, when we read the Scripture, what an apparatus of cleansing God appears to have set in array for the purification of souls; sprinklings, washings, baptisms of water, and, what are more searching and more terribly energetic purifiers, baptisms of fire; fierce meltings also as of silver in the refiner's crucible; purifyings of the flesh and purgings of the conscience; lustrations of blood, even of Christ's own blood; washings of the Word, and washings of regeneration by the Holy Ghost. It would seem, on looking at the manifold array of cleansing elements, applications, gifts, and sacraments, as if God had undertaken it as the great object and crowning mercy of His reign, to effect a solemn purgation of the world. We seem, as we read, to see Him summoning up all angels and ministers of His will and instruments of His power, and sending them out in commission to cleanse the sin of the world, or even to wash the defiled planet itself into purity.

Or, if we observe more directly what is said concerning the particular object of Christ's mission as a work of redemption, it is plainly declared that He gave Himself for the Church, "That he might sanctify and cleanse it with the washing of water by the word, that he might present it to himself a glorious church, not having spot, or wrinkle, or any such thing; but that it should be holy and without blemish." And then again the disciple himself who has embraced the Lord, in that which is the chief mercy and last end of His mission, will purify himself, it is declared, even as Christ is pure; that is, if I rightly understand the language of the text, he will be engaged to purify himself, endeavouring after purity, such as Christ himself reveals. It is not intended, I suppose, to affirm that every disciple, in the Christian hope, has actually become as pure as Christ, but only that this is his end or mark.

But a question rises here of great practical significance, viz., whether, by a due improvement of the means offered in Christ, or by any possible faith in Him, it is given us to attain to a state which can fitly be called purity, or which is to itself a state consciously pure.

To this I answer both "Yes," and "No." There may be a Christian purity that is related to the soul as investiture, or as a condition superinduced, which is not of it, or in it, as pertaining to its own quality or to the cast of its own habit. Christ, in other words, may be so completely put on that the whole consciousness may be of Him, and all the motions of sins give way to the dominating efficacy of His harmonious and perfect mind; when, at the same time, the subject viewed in himself, or in the contents and modes of causes in his own personality, is disordered, broken, mixed, chaotic, and widely distant still from real purity. The point may be illustrated by a supposition. Let a man, habitually narrow and mean in his dispositions, fall into the society of a great and powerful nature in some one distinguished for the magnanimity of his impulses. Let this nobler being be accepted as his friend, trusted in, loved, admired, so as virtually to infold and subordinate the mean person, as long as he is with him, to his own spirit. This, at least, we can imagine, whether any such example ever occurred or not. Now it will be seen that, as long as this nobler nature is side by side with the other, it becomes a kind of investiture,

N

clothes it, as it were, with its own impulses, and even puts it in the sense of magnanimity. Consciously now the mean man is all magnanimous, for his mean thoughts are, by the supposition, drunk up and lost in the abysses of the nobler nature he clings to. He is magnanimous by investiture; that is, by the occupancy of another, who clothes him with his own character. But if you ask what he is in his own personal habit, cast, or quality, he is little different possibly from what he was before. He has had the consciousness waked up in him of a generous life and feeling, which is indeed a great boon to his meagre nature, and if he could be kept for long years in the mould of this superinduced character, he would be gradually assimilated to it. But if the better nature were to be soon withdrawn by a separation, he would fall back into the native meanness of his own proper person, and be what he was with only slight modifications.

Now Christ, in His glorious and Divine purity, is that better nature, which has power, if we believe in Him with a total, all-subjecting faith, to invest us with a complete consciousness of purity—to bring every thought into captivity to His own incorruptible order and chastity. He is such a cause upon us, when so received, that all our mixed modes of causes will be subjected to the interior chime of His own all-perfect harmony. Our consciousness even is cast in the moulds of His, for He is so effectually put on, that He dominates in the whole movement of our experience. This, at least, is conceivable as being the permitted or possible triumph of faith, while, at the same time, regarding what we are in ourselves, and apart from this Divine investiture, we are very far from any such purity. Still, the case is varied here from that which we just now supposed, in the fact that the assimilation of the subject-party will be more rapid and certain because of the agency of the Spirit concurring with the power of Christ, and also in the fact that the union established by faith is more interior and more indissoluble. He may, therefore, have the Spirit to work in him and the power of Christ to rest upon him in such measure as to be kept in the conscious chastity of Christ's own love, year by year, and be wrought into a continually approaching assimilation to it.

The answer thus given to the question raised, agrees at all points, it will be seen, with the Scripture, and particularly with what is taught by our apostle in close connexion with my text. On one side of it he writes, "If we say that we have no sin, we deceive ourselves, and the truth is not in us ;" for, however deep we are in our union with Christ, or however completely we are invested in His purity, we are not in ourselves restored, in the same degree, to the character of it. We are in a kind of anticipative purity, which is becoming personal to us and a fixed habit; we are living to be pure, as Christ is ; but, regarded as apart from Him, the work is only initiated—we still have sin, we are broken, disordered, and corrupt. For, as long as we abide in Christ, our action is from Him, not from our own corrupt and broken nature ; exactly as the apostle writes, on the other side of the text, or immediately after—"Whosoever abideth in Him sinneth not." He lives in a consciousness, that is, which is not sustained by his own mere humanly personal character, but by the sense of another, and the righteousness that is of God by faith upon Him.

The result, consequently, is, that being thus held up by the attachment to him of Christ's affinities, he is growing like Him —pure as He is pure. The diseased qualities gendered in him heretofore are being gradually purged away. His passions are being tamed to order and refined to God's pure dominion. His imaginations settle into the truth, and grow healthy and clear. The fashion of this world is not only broken, as it was in the first moment of God's discovery to his heart, but the memories of it fade, the diseased longings are healed, so that all his old affinities, in this direction, will at last be extirpated. All the mixed causes involved in sin or spiritual impurity will fall into chime, and all the foul currents of evil suggestion be cleared to a transparent flow. The mind will grow regular and simple in its action, ceasing to be vexed, as it was, by noxious mixtures of fear, selfishness, doubt, and temptation. And so all the inbred corruptions of its bad state—that is, those which remain over as effects of sin, after sin as a voluntary life is forsaken—will be gradually purged away.

To illustrate how far it is possible for this purifying work to go on in the present life, I will simply say that the very currents of thought, as it is propagated in the mind, may become so purified that, when the will does not interfere, and the mind is allowed, for an hour, to run in its own way, without hindrance,

one thing suggesting another, as in reverie, there may yet be no
evil, wicked, or foul suggestion thrust into it.   Or in the state
of sleep, where the will never interferes, but the thoughts rush
on by a law of their own, the mixed causes of corruption may
be so far cleared away, and the soul restored to such simplicity
and pureness, that the dreams will be only dreams of love and
beauty; peaceful, and clear, and happy; somewhat as we may
imagine the waking thoughts of angels to be.   There have been
Christians who have testified to this heavenly sereneness of
thought, out of their own experience.   And precisely this is
what Paul refers to when he speaks of bringing into captivity
every thought to the obedience of Christ.   When the mixed
causes are taken captive in the soul, and Christ is the law of
the whole action, then, in the same degree, simplicity and
purity return.

Still the body is dead because of sin.   Disease, corruption, so
far at least remain, and therefore it doth not yet appear what we
shall be.   Perfect, absolute purity it is hardly supposable may
be realised here.   Enough to know that there need be no limit
to the process while life remains, and that, when life ends, it
may be gloriously approximated to the state of completeness.

Or, perhaps, some one of my audience may just here raise a
doubt from the other side—whether absolute purity can ever
be restored.   Can the soul's chastity, once lost, ever be recovered?   Having once sinned, can it ever become pure, in the
absolute and perfect sense, as if it had not?   Let no such
doubt be harboured.   We must not be too much under the
power of social impressions.   If society pronounces on the irredeemable loss of fallen chastity, society has no mercy, and pride
as well as truth enters into its relentless judgments.   Be this
as it may, God has undertaken to redeem the fall of sin and
restore the soul to purity as a condition of absolute holiness.
Browned by sin, mottled by the stains of a corrupted life, He
has undertaken still to give it the whiteness of snow.   True, He
cannot undo what has been done.   The sin is committed, the
corruption has followed.   Therefore, if there were any prudish-
ness in angelic minds, they might well enough refuse for ever
to own us as beings intact by sin.   And yet God can raise us
to a purity that is higher even than the purity of an intact
virtue.   He can make us untemptibly pure—pure even as Christ

is pure, which Adam certainly was not. What we call purity in him, prior to his sin, is beautiful and lovely—a pure white lily blooming in the creation's morning—but it is frail also and temptible, and, before the noon is up, it hangs upon a broken stem, dishonoured and torn. God can raise us up, if not to the same, yet to a much higher, and stronger, and more absolute chastity—the participation, viz. of His own unchangeable holiness.

Having this view of Christ and His gospel as the plan of God for restoring men to a complete spiritual purity, seeing that He invites us to this, gives us means and aids to realise this, and yields to them that truly desire it a hope so high as this, I proceed—

III. To inquire in what manner we may promote our advancement toward the state of purity, and finally have it in complete realisation.

And, first of all, we must set our heart upon it. We must learn to conceive the beauty, and glory, and the essential beatitude of a pure state. We must see the degradation, realise the bitterness, confusion, disorder, instability, and conflict of a mixed state, where all the causes of internal action are thrown out of God's original law. We must learn to conceive, on the other hand—and what can be more difficult—the dignity, the beauty, the infinitely peaceful and truly divine elevation of a pure soul. Nothing is more distant from us, in our unreflective, headlong state of carnality and self-devotion, than to conceive purity. It is high like God, and we cannot attain unto it. And therefore our desire after it cannot be duly inflamed or kindled, as it must be if we are ever to obtain it. Labour, then, with all closest, most persistent application, to conceive purity ; what it would be to you if your soul were in it ; the consciousness of it ; the essential peace ; the elevation above all passion and unregulated impulse ; the singleness and simplicity of it ; the glowing shapes and glorified visions of a pure imagination ; the oneness of your soul with God ; the conscious participation of what is highest in God—His untemptible chastity in goodness and truth. Work at this idea of purity, turn it round and round in your contemplations, reach after it, pray yourself into it, and have it thus as the highest conceivable good, the real

good you seek—to be pure. Let it be your life to envy God's
purity, if I may so speak, for if there be any holy, and blessed,
and fruitful kind of envy it is this. Have it as the accepted
aim and effort of your life to be assimilated thus in purity to
God, for when such a desire becomes practically fixed in you
the way will certainly be found. The way to purity is difficult
of discovery only to those who practically do not care to find it.

One of your early discoveries will be, that the way to attain
to purity of soul is not to forsake the world and retire from it.
This was the error that originally carried men and women into
remote deserts and caves, and finally built up monasteries and
instituted vows of single life or celibacy. It was to get away
from the world and have nothing to think of but God, and so
to present the soul as a chaste virgin to Christ. It was called
the state of spiritual chastity, and the souls thus taken out of
the world were supposed to be specially pure and incorrupt, or
in a certain way to be. It was as if the Church had prayed,
directly against Christ's word, to be taken out of the world.
And then what a horrible imposture did this unchristian gospel
of purity prove itself ere long to be! No, the only real and truly
Christian way of purity is to live in the open world and not be
of it, and keep the soul unspotted from it. There are no fires
that will melt out our drossy and corrupt particles like God's
refining fires of duty and trial, living, as He sends us to live, in
the open field of the world's sins and sorrows—its plausibilities
and lies—its persecutions, animosities, and fears—its eager
delights and bitter wants.

St Francis de Sales had been able, in his knowledge of the
cloistered men and the cloistered life, to see how necessary it
is for the soul to be aired in the outward exposures of the
world; and, if we do not stop to question the facts of his illustrations, no one has spoken of this necessity with greater force
and beauty of conception. " Many persons believe," he says,
"that as no beast dares taste the seed of the herb Palma
Christi, so no man ought to aspire to the palm of Christian
piety as long as he lives in the bustle of temporal affairs.
Now, to such I shall prove that, as the mother-pearl fish lives
in the sea without receiving a drop of salt water, and as, toward
the Chelidonian Islands, springs of fresh water may be found
in the midst of the sea, and as the fire-fly passes through the

flames without burning its wings, so a vigorous and resolute soul may live in the world without being infected with any of its humours, may discover sweet springs of piety amidst its salt waters, and fly among the flames of earthly concupiscence without burning the wings of the holy desires of a devout life." It was only forbidden him to say, what is not forbidden me, that here *alone*, in these common exposures of work and contacts of duty, is true Christian purity itself successfully cultivated. Alas, for the man who is obliged to be shut up to himself, as in the convent life, to face his own lusts, disorders, and passions, and strangle them in direct conflict, with nothing else to do or to occupy the soul.

Having this determined—that he who will purify himself, as Christ is pure, must live in the world—then one thing more is needed—viz., that we live in Christ, and seek to be as closely and intimately one with Him as possible. And this includes more things than the time will suffer me to name.

First, a willingness wholly to cease from the old man, as corrupt, in order that a completely new man from Christ may be formed in you; for, if you will halve the sacrifice, and retain what portion is safe or convenient of the old life of nature, it is no such thing as purity that you propose—nothing but a baptizing of mixture and defilement. I call it a new man that you want, after the Scripture method, because the character is the man more truly than anything else, and there is no purity but to be completely new. Therefore the old must as completely die; which it will not, if we secretly nourish and cling to it.

Secondly, the life must be determined implicitly by the faith of Christ. "Purifying their hearts by faith," says an apostle, well understanding that faith in Christ, as the true sacrifice and grace, is the only power that can "purge the conscience from dead works to serve the living God" in purity. It is faith only that can truly appropriate Christ as a Saviour, able to save to the uttermost, and faithful to cleanse us from all unrighteousness. Then again, which is more, if possible, it is faith alone that enables one to embrace Christ as a power, and live in the society of His person; for it is thus, pre-eminently, that a soul may become purified. It is Christ beheld, with face unveiled, reflecting God's own beauty and

love upon us, as in a glass, that changes us from glory to glory.
If by faith we go with Christ—if we bear His cross in duty
after Him—if we hang upon His words, wrestle with Him in
His agony, die with Him in His passion, rise with Him in His
resurrection; in a word, if we are perfectly insphered in His
society, so as to be of it, then we shall grow pure.   The assimilating power of Christ, when faithfully adhered to as the soul's
Divine brother, and lived with and lived upon, will infallibly
renovate, transform, and purify us.   The result is just as certain as our oneness or society with Him.   We shall grow pure
because He is.   The glorious power of His character and life
will so invest our nature, that we shall be in it and live it.
It is only they that talk much of faith, meaning by it the faith
of notions and opinions, and not the faith of Jesus as a personal revelation—these only it is who cannot be purified by
their faith.   Sometimes they even have it as their merit, judging from their confessions, that they are growing more and
more corrupt.   Having that faith to which Jesus is personally
revealed, you can be conscious of a growing purity of soul;
and I know not any other way.   God forbid that you should
think of making purity for yourself, or by any operation on
yourself!   It must flow into you from above; it must be the
new man that is created in Christ Jesus—created by your
faith, as receiving of Him and of His fulness, grace for grace.
And, oh, the dignity, the conscious blessedness of a life of faith,
when it knows in itself, or distinctly sees the Divine purity
forming its own chaste image of love and truth within—beholds the fine linen, clean and white, which is the righteousness of the saints, investing the soul as a robe of life from
God!   In such a life, there is consciously something going on
which answers to the great errand of life, and gives it the seal
of blessing.

Again, passing over many other particulars, I will simply draw
your minds a little closer to the text by observing, as included
in the general idea of living in Christ, a looking forward to Him
in His exalted state, and a habitual converse with Him there.
He that hath this hope in him, says the text—understanding
that the hope of being with Christ, and seeing Him as He is,
does of itself draw the soul toward His purity.   I say not that
we are to be looking away to heaven, as being disgusted with

the world; much less to be praising heaven's adorable purity in high words of contrast, as if to excuse or atone for the lack of all purity here. I only say that we are to be much in the meditation of Christ as glorified, surrounded with the glorified; to let our mind be hallowed by its pure converse and the themes in which it dwells; to live in the anticipation of what is most pure in the universe, as being what we most love and long for in the universe; and so we are to be raised by our longings, and purified with Christ by the hopes we rest upon His person. This hope, this reaching upward of soul to Christ, is exactly what Paul means, when he speaks of living a life that is hid with Christ in God. When a soul is there infolded, hid with Christ in the recesses of God's pure majesty, oh, what airs of health breathe upon it and through it! how vital does it become, and how rapidly do the mixed causes of sin settle into the transparent flow of order and peace!

It only remains just to name—

IV. Some of the signs by which our growth in purity may be known. This I will do in the briefest manner possible, and conclude.

Fastidiousness, then, I will first of all caution you, is not any evidence of purity, but the contrary. A fastidious character is one that shews, by excess of delicacy, a real defect and loss of it. It is too delicate to be practical, simply because it is practically indelicate and corrupt. Hence, in religion, it is a great principle that, to the pure all things are pure. When any disciple, therefore, calls it purity to be shocked or repelled by the Scripture names of sins, or the practical works of mercy needed in a world of shame and defilement, he reveals therein a bad imagination and a mind that is itself defiled. No, the true signs of purity are these:—

That we abide in the conscious light of God, while living in a world of defilement, and know Him as a presence manifested in the soul. "Blessed are the pure in heart, for they shall see God." Purity sees God.

A good conscience signifies the same; for the conscience, like the eye, is troubled by any speck of defilement and wrong that falls into it.

A growing sensibility to sin signifies the same; for, if the conscience grows peaceful and clear, it will also grow tender and delicate.

If you are more able to be singular and think less of the opinions of men, not in a scornful way, but in love, that again shews that the world's law is loosing its power over you, and your devotion to God is growing more single and true.

Do you find that passion is submitting itself to the gentle reign of God within you, losing its heat and fierceness, and becoming tamed under the sweet dominion of Christian love? That again is the growth of purity.

The discovery that your imagination ceases to revel in images of wrong, revenge, and lust, becoming at once more quiet and more clear, conceiving God and Christ and unseen worlds of purity with greater distinctness and sublimity, and roving, as by a divine instinct, among the eternal verities and transcendent glories of a perfect state, asking there to be employed and nowhere else with so great zest—this also shews that a high and sacred affinity for what is pure is growing stronger and more clear within you.

So, again, if your feeling reaches after heaven, and your longings are thitherward, if you love and long for it because chiefly of its purity; loosened from this world not by your wearinesses and disgusts, which all men suffer, but by the positive affinities of your heart for what is best and purest above—this also is a powerful token of growing purification.

Do you also find that your thoughts, when freest and most unrestrained, are yet growing simple, orderly, right, and true, interrupted less and less frequently by bad or wicked suggestion?—then you have in this a most convincing and conclusive proof, that you are being delivered from the mixtures and defilements of a corrupted nature.

Or, again, it is a yet more simple sign, and one that includes, in a manner, all others, if you find that you are deeper and deeper in the love of Christ. For, if Christ spreads Himself over your being, and you begin to know nothing else and want nothing else; if you love Him for His character, as the only perfect, and cleave to His sinless life, as the holiest, and loveliest, and grandest miracle of the earth; if words begin to faint when you speak of Him, and all that can be said or thought looks cheap and low, compared with what He is; then it is most certain that you are growing in purity; for the growing enlargement of your apprehensions of Christ is the result of a growing purity, and will be also the cause of a purity more perfect still.

And now, my brethren, I have many things to say, but I only ask whether you perceive, by signs like these, that you are growing pure? That you believe yourselves to be disciples we know—that is easy; but I ask you here seriously, before God, whether you find that your religion has any purifying power? Is it a baptism? Is it a finer's fire? Does it move you to cry, "Create in me a clean heart, O God?" True piety, brethren, is a power, and purity is the result; a result, as I have shewn you, that may be indefinitely realised even here on earth. Is it realised in you by the signs I have named? You hope in Christ that you shall be with Him, "and see Him as He is." Oh, it is well, the most elevating hope, the most inspiring and celestial thought, which ever fell into the soul of a mortal! I only ask if you see in your life, in the practical bent of your works, that this hope has verity enough in you to take hold of your springs of action, and bring you into a true endeavour after Christ's purity? What an opinion then will you be seen to have of the soul when you are living for its purity! And, then, what sublimity is there to your eye in that state of glory in which your soul practically dwelleth among its kindred spirits, pure as they, and all as Christ is pure. "These are they that have washed their robes and made them white in the blood of the Lamb."

But how little signifies this discourse of purity to very many of my hearers! I well understand the vacant, dreamy sound of such discourses before the conception of purity—and the sense of it gotten out of the want, and out of Christ the supply—is opened to the soul. What is there so great in purity? who, that is untouched by God's gracious quickening, cares enough for purity to give the word an earnest significance? It has, of course, no greatness to us, because the fact itself is a lost fact. We cannot think it, because it is really gone out of the mind's reach and knowledge. But, oh, when once the heart feels a touch of its divinity, then a yearning is wakened, then the greatest and sublimest thing for a mortal is the unmixed life! a soul established in the eternal chastity of truth and goodness!

O God! who of this people shall ever know what it is ? I cannot tell them ; Thou alone canst breathe into them, and set in
their living apprehension a truth so impossible for any mere
words to express !

This only I can testify, as God has given me words (and I
pray God to shew you their meaning,) that the heaven we are
sent here to prepare for, is a most pure world, open only to the
pure : "And there shall in no wise enter into it anything
that defileth, neither whatsoever worketh abomination, or
maketh a lie: but they which are written in the Lamb's book
of life."

XIV.

Luke xvi. 10—"*He that is faithful in that which is least is faithful also in much; and he that is unjust in the least is unjust also in much.*"

A READINESS to do some great thing is not peculiar to Naaman, the Syrian. There are many Christians who can never find a place large enough to do their duty. They must needs strain after great changes, and their works must utter themselves by a loud report. Any reform in society short of a revolution, any improvement in character less radical than that of conversion, is too faint a work, in their view, to be much valued. Nor is it merely ambition, but often it is a truly Christian zeal, guarded by no sufficient views of the less imposing matters of life, which betrays men into such impressions. If there be anything, in fact, wherein the views of God and the impressions of men are apt to be at total variance, it is in respect to the solemnity and importance of ordinary duties. The hurtfulness of mistake here, is, of course, very great. Trying always to do great things, to have extraordinary occasions every day, or to produce extraordinary changes, when small ones are quite as much needed, ends, of course, in defeat and dissipation. It produces a sort of religion in the gross, which is no religion in particular. My text leads me to speak,

Of the importance of living to God on common occasions, and in small things.

"He that is faithful in that which is least," says the Saviour, "is faithful also in much; and he that is unjust in the least is unjust also in much." This was a favourite sentiment with Him. In His sermon on the mount, it was thus expressed, "Whosoever therefore shall break one of these least commandments, and shall teach men so, he shall be called the least in the kingdom of heaven ; but whosoever shall do and teach them, the same shall be called great in the kingdom of heaven." And when He rebuked the Pharisees, in their tithing of mint, anise, and cummin, He was careful to speak very guardedly, "These things ought ye to have done, and not to leave the other undone." It will instruct us in prosecuting this subject,

1. To notice how little we know concerning the relative importance of events and duties. We use the terms *great* and *small* in speaking of actions, occasions, plans, and duties, only in reference to the mere outward look and first impression. Some of the most latent agents and mean-looking substances in nature are yet the most operative ; but yet, when we speak of natural objects, we call them great or small, not according to their operativeness, but according to size, count, report, or show. So it comes to pass, when we are classing actions, duties, or occasions, that we call a certain class great, and another small, when really the latter are manifold more important and influential than the former. We may suppose, for illustration, two transactions in business, as different in their nominal amount as a million of dollars and a single dollar. The former we call a large transaction, the latter a small one. But God might reverse these terms. He would have no such thought as the counting of dollars. He would look, first of all, at the principle involved in the two cases. And here He would discover, not unlikely, that the nominally small one, owing to the nature of the transaction, or to the humble condition of the parties, or to their peculiar temper and disposition, took a deeper hold of their being, and did more to settle or unsettle great and everlasting principle, than the other. Next, perhaps, He would look at the consequences of the two transactions as developed in the great future ; and here He would perhaps discover that the one which seems to us the smaller, is the hinge of vastly greater consequences than the other. If the dollars had been sands of dust, they would not have had less weight in the Divine judgment.

We are generally ignorant of the real significance of events, which we think we understand. Almost every person can recollect one or more instances, where the whole after-current of his life was turned by some single word, or some incident so trivial as scarcely to fix his notice at the time. On the other hand, many great crises of danger, many high and stirring occasions, in which, at the time, his total being was absorbed, have passed by, leaving no trace of effect on his permanent interests, and have wellnigh vanished from his memory. The conversation of the stage-coach is often preparing results which the solemn assembly and the most imposing and eloquent rites will fail to produce. What countryman, knowing the dairyman's daughter, could have suspected that she was living to a mightier purpose and result than almost any person in the Church of God, however eminent? The outward of occasions and duties is, in fact, almost no index of their importance; and our judgments concerning what is great and small are without any certain validity. These terms, as we use them, are, in fact, only words of outward description, not words of definite measurement.

2. It is to be observed that, even as the world judges, small things constitute almost the whole of life. The great days of the year, for example, are few, and when they come they seldom bring anything great to us. And the matter of all common days is made up of little things, or ordinary and stale transactions. Scarcely once in a year does anything really remarkable befall us. If I were to begin and give an inventory of the things you do in any single day, your muscular motions, each of which is accomplished by a separate act of will, the objects you see, the words you utter, the contrivances you frame, your thoughts, passions, gratifications, and trials, many of you would not be able to hear it recited with sobriety. But three hundred and sixty-five such days make up a year, and a year is a twentieth, fiftieth, or seventieth part of your life. And thus, with the exception of some few striking passages, or great and critical occasions, perhaps not more than five or six in all, your life is made up of common, and, as men are wont to judge, unimportant things. But yet, at the end, you have done an amazing work, and fixed an amazing result. You stand at the bar of God, and look back on a life made up of small things—but yet a life, how momentous for good or evil!

3. It very much exalts, as well as sanctions, the view I am advancing, that God is so observant of small things. He upholds the sparrow's wing, clothes the lily with His own beautifying hand, and numbers the hairs of His children. He holds the balancings of the clouds. He maketh the small drops of rain.

It astonishes all thought to observe the minuteness of God's government, and of the natural and common processes which He carries on from day to day. His dominions are spread out, system beyond system, system above system, filling all height and latitude, but He is never lost in the vast or magnificent. He descends to an infinite detail, and builds a little universe in the smallest things. He carries on a process of growth in every tree, and flower, and living thing; accomplishes in each an internal organisation, and works the functions of an internal laboratory, too delicate all for eye or instrument to trace. He articulates the members and impels the instincts of every living mote that shines in the sunbeam. As when we ascend toward the distant and the vast, so when we descend toward the minute, we see His attention acuminated, and His skill concentrated on His object; and the last discernible particle dies out of our sight with the same Divine glory on it as on the last orb that glimmers in the skirt of the universe. God is as careful to finish the mote as the planet, both because it consists only with His perfection to finish everything, and because the perfection of His greatest structures is the result of perfection in their smallest parts or particles. On this patience of detail rests all the glory and order of the created universe, spiritual and material. God could thunder the year round; He could shake the ribs of the world with perpetual earthquakes; He could blaze on the air, and brush the affrighted mountains each day with His comets. But if He could not feed the grass with His dew, and breathe into the little lungs of His insect family— if He could not expend His care on small things, and descend to an interest in their perfection, His works would be only crude and disjointed machines, compounded of mistakes and malformations, without beauty and order, and fitted to no perfect end.

The works of Christ are, if possible, a still brighter illustration of the same truth. Notwithstanding the vast stretch and compass of the work of redemption, it is a work of the most humble detail in its style of execution. The Saviour could have preached a sermon on the mount every morning. Each night He could have stilled the sea, before His astonished disciples, and shewn the conscious waves lulling into peace under His feet. He could have transfigured Himself before Pilate and the astonished multitudes of the temple. He could have made visible ascensions in the noon of every day, and revealed His form standing in the sun, like the angel of the Apocalypse. But this was not His mind. The incidents of which His work is principally made up are, humanly speaking, very humble and unpretending. The most faithful pastor in the world was never able, in any degree, to approach the Saviour, in the lowliness of His manner and His attention to humble things. His teachings were in retired places, and His illustrations drawn from ordinary affairs. If the finger of faith touched Him in the crowd, He knew the touch and distinguished also the faith. He reproved the ambitious housewifery of an humble woman. After He had healed a poor being, blind from his birth—a work transcending all but Divine power—He returned and sought him out, as the most humble Sabbath-school teacher might have done; and when He had found him, cast out and persecuted by men, He taught him privately the highest secrets of His Messiahship. When the world around hung darkened in sympathy with His cross, and the earth was shaking with inward amazement, He Himself was remembering His mother, and discharging the filial cares of a good son. And when He burst the bars of death, its first and final conqueror, He folded the linen clothes and the napkin, and laid them in order apart, shewing that in the greatest things, He had a set purpose also concerning the smallest. And thus, when perfectly scanned, the work of Christ's redemption, like the created universe, is seen to be a vast orb of glory, wrought up out of finished particles. Now a life of great and prodigious exploits would have been comparatively an easy thing for Him, but to cover Himself with beauty and glory in small things, to fill and adorn every little human occasion, so as to make it divine—this was a work of skill which no mind or hand was equal to but that which shaped the atoms of the world. Such everywhere is God. He nowhere overlooks or despises small things.

4. It is a fact of history and of observation, that all efficient men, while they have been men of comprehension, have also been men of detail. I wish it were possible to produce as high an example of this twofold character among the servants of God and benevolence in these times, as we have in that fiery prodigy of war and conquest, who, in the beginning of the pre-

o

sent century, desolated Europe. Napoleon was the most effective man in modern times—some will say of all times.   The
secret of his character was, that while his plans were more vast,
more various, and, of course, more difficult than those of other
men, he had the talent, at the same time, to fill them up with
perfect promptness and precision, in every particular of execution.   His vast and daring plans would have been visionary in
any other man ; but with him every vision flew out of his brain
a chariot of iron, because it was filled up, in all the particulars
of execution, to be a solid and compact framework in every
part.   His armies were together only one great engine of desolation, of which he was the head or brain. Numbers, spaces, times,
were all distinct in his eye.   The wheeling of every legion, however remote, was mentally present to him.   The tramp of every
foot sounded in his ear.   The numbers were always supplied,
the spaces passed over, the times met, and so the work was
done.   The nearest moral approximation I know of was Paul
the apostle.   Paul had great principles, great plans, and a great
enthusiasm.   He had the art, at the same time, to bring his
great principles into a powerful application to his own conduct,
and to all the common affairs of all the disciples in his churches.
He detected every want, understood every character ; set his
guards against those whom he distrusted ; kept all his work
turning in a motion of discipline ; prompted to every duty.
You will find his epistles distinguished by great principles ; and,
at the same time, by a various and circumstantial attention to
all the common affairs of life ; and in that you have the secret
of his efficiency.   There must be detail in every great work.   It
is an element of effectiveness, which no reach of plan, no enthusiasm of purpose, can dispense with.   Thus, if a man conceives the idea of becoming eminent in learning, but cannot toil
through the million of little drudgeries necessary to carry him
on, his learning will be soon told.   Or, if a man undertakes to
become rich, but despises the small and gradual advances by
which wealth is ordinarily accumulated, his expectations will,
of course, be the sum of his riches. Accurate and careful detail,
the minding of common occasions and small things, combined
with general scope and vigour, is the secret of all the efficiency
and success in the world.   God has so ordered things, that
great and sudden leaps are seldom observable.   Every advance·

in the general must be made by advances in particular. The trees and the corn do not leap out suddenly into maturity, but they climb upward by little and little, and after the minutest possible increment. The orbs of heaven, too, accomplish their circles not by one or two extraordinary starts or springs, but by travelling on through paces and roods of the sky. It is thus, and only thus, that any disciple will become efficient in the service of his Master. He cannot do his works of usefulness by the prodigious stir and commotion of a few extraordinary occasions. Laying down great plans, he must accomplish them by great industry, by minute attentions, by saving small advances, by working out his way as God shall assist him.

5. It is to be observed that there is more of real piety in adorning one small than one great occasion. This may seem paradoxical, but what I intend will be seen by one or two illustrations. I have spoken of the minuteness of God's works. When I regard the eternal God as engaged in polishing an atom, or elaborating the functions of a mote invisible to the eye, what evidence do I there receive of His desire to perfect His works? No gross and mighty world, however plausibly shaped, would yield a hundredth part the intensity of evidence. An illustration from human things will present a closer parallel. It is perfectly well understood, or if not, it should be, that almost any husband would leap into the sea or rush into a burning edifice to rescue a perishing wife. But to anticipate the convenience or happiness of a wife in some small matter, the neglect of which would be unobserved, is a more eloquent proof of tenderness. This shews a mindful fondness which wants occasions in which to express itself. And the smaller the occasion seized upon, the more intensely affectionate is the attention paid. Piety toward God may be well tested or measured in the same way. Peter found no difficulty in drawing his sword and fighting for his Master, even at the hazard of his life. though but an hour or less afterward he forsook Him and denied Him. His valour on that great and exciting occasion was no proof of his piety. But when the gentle Mary came, with her box of ointment, and poured it on the Saviour's head —an act which satisfied no want, met no exigency, and was of no use, except as a gratuitous and studied proof of her attachment to Jesus—He marks it as an eminent example of piety;

saying, "Verily I say unto you, Wheresoever this gospel shall
be preached in the whole world, there shall also this, that this
woman hath done, be told for a memorial of her."

My brethren, this piety which is faithful in that which is
least is really a more difficult piety than that which triumphs
and glares on high occasions. Our judgments are apt to be
dazzled by a vain admiration of the more public attempts and
the more imposing manifestations of occasional zeal. It requires
less piety, I verily believe, to be a martyr for Christ than it
does to love a powerless enemy ; or to look upon the success of
a rival without envy; or even to maintain a perfect and guileless
integrity in the common transactions of life. Precisely this, in
fact, is the lesson which history teaches. How many, alas! of
those who have died in the manner of martyrdom, manifestly
sought that distinction, and brought it on themselves by instigation of a mere fanatical ambition! Such facts seem designed
to shew us that the common spheres of life and business, the
small matters of the street, the shop, the hearth, and the table,
are more genial to true piety, than any artificial extraordinary
scenes of a more imposing description. Excitement, ambition,
a thousand questionable causes, may elevate us occasionally
to great attempts ; but they will never lead us into the more
humble duties of constancy and godly industry ; or teach us to
adorn the unpretending spheres of life with a heavenly spirit.
We love to do great things ; our natural pride would be greatly
pleased if God had made the sky higher, the world larger, and
given us a more royal style of life and duty. But He understands us well. His purpose is to heal our infirmity; and with
this very intent, I am persuaded, He has ordained these humble
spheres of action, so that no ostentation, no great and striking
explosions of godliness shall tempt our heart. And in the same
way, His Word declares, that bestowing all one's goods to feed
the poor, or giving his body to be burned, and of consequence,
that great speeches and donations, that a mighty zeal for reform, that a prodigious jealousy for sound doctrine, without
something better—without charity—profiteth nothing. And
the picture of charity is humble enough—it "suffereth long, and
is kind; envieth not ; vaunteth not itself, is not puffed up, doth
not behave itself unseemly. seeketh not her own, is not easily

provoked, thinketh no evil; beareth all things, believeth all things, hopeth all things, endureth all things."

6. The importance of living to God in ordinary and small things is seen in the fact that character, which is the end of religion, is in its very nature a growth. Conversion is a great change—"old things are passed away; behold, all things are become new." This, however, is the language of a hope or confidence somewhat prophetic, exulting at the beginning in the realisation of future victory. The young disciple, certainly, is far enough from a consciousness of complete deliverance from sin. In that respect his work is but just begun. He is now in the blade; we shall see him next in the ear; and after that he will ripen to the full corn in the ear. His character, as a man and a Christian, is to accomplish its stature by growing. And all the offices of life, domestic, social, civil, useful, are contrived of God to be the soil, as Christ is the sun, of such a growth. All the cares, wants, labours, dangers, accidents, intercourses of life, are adjusted for the very purpose of exercising and ripening character. They are precisely adapted for this end by God's all-perfect wisdom. This, in fact, is the grand philosophy of the structure of all things. And, accordingly, there never has been a great and beautiful character which has not become so by filling well the ordinary and smaller offices appointed of God.

The wonderful fortunes of Joseph seem at first to have fallen suddenly upon him, and altogether by a miracle. But a closer attention to his history will shew you that he rose only by a gradual progress, and by the natural power of his virtues. The astonishing art he had of winning the confidence of others had, after all, no magic in it save the magic of goodness; and God assisted him only as He assists other good men. The growth of his fortunes was the shadow only of his growth in character. By his assiduity he made everything prosper; and by his good faith he won the confidence, first of Potiphar, then of the keeper of the prison, then of Pharaoh himself. And so he grew up, gently and silently, till the helm of the Egyptian kingdom was found in his hand.

Peter, too, after he had flourished so vauntingly with his sword, entered on a growing and faithful life. From an ignorant fisherman, he became a skilful writer, a finished Christian, and a teacher of faithful living in the common offices of life. He occupied his great apostleship in exhorting subjects to obey the ordinances of governors, for the Lord's sake; servants to be subject to their masters; wives to study such a carriage as would win their unbelieving husbands; and husbands to give honour to the wife, as being heirs together of the grace of life. But in a manner to comprehend everything good, he said— "Giving all diligence (this is the true notion of Christian excellence)—giving all diligence, add to your faith virtue; to virtue knowledge; to knowledge temperance; to temperance patience; to patience godliness; to godliness brotherly kindness, and to brotherly kindness charity." The impression is unavoidable, that he now regarded religion, not as a sword-fight, but as a growth of holy character, kept up by all diligence in the walks of life.

Every good example in the Word of God is an illustration of the same truth. To finish a character on a sudden, or by any but ordinary duties, carefully and piously done, by a mere religion of Sundays, and birthdays, and revivals, and contributions, and orthodoxies, and public reforms, is nowhere undertaken. They watered the plant in secret, trained it up at family altars, strengthened it in the exposures of business, till it became a beautiful and heavenly growth, and ready, with all its blooming fruit, to adorn the paradise of God.

It ought also to be noticed, under this head, that all the mischiefs which befall Christian character and destroy its growth, are such as lie in the ordinary humble duties of life. Christians do not fall back into declension or disgraceful apostasy on a sudden, or by the overcoming power of great and strange temptations. They are stolen away rather by little and little, and almost insensibly to themselves. They commonly fall into some lightness of carriage; some irritation of temper in their family or business; some neglect of duty to children, apprentices, or friends; some artfulness; some fault of integrity in business. These are the beginnings of evil. At length they grow a little more remiss. They begin to slight their secret duties. The world and its fashions become more powerful, and they yield a little further; till at length they are utterly fallen from the spirit and standing of Christians. And thus, you perceive that all the dangers which beset our piety, lie in the humble and ordinary matters of life. Here, then, is the place where religion must make her conquests. Here she must build her barriers and take her stand. And if it be a matter of consequence that the people of God should live constant and godly lives; that they should grow in the strength of their principles, and the beauty of their example; that the Church should clear herself of all reproach, and stand invested with honour in the sight of all mankind,—if this be important, so important is it that we live well in small things, and adorn the common incidents of life with a heavenly temper and practice. Religion must for ever be unstable, the people of Christ must fall into declension and disgrace, if it be not understood that here is the true field of the Christian life.

These illustrations of the importance of living to God in ordinary and common things might be carried to almost any extent; but I will arrest the subject here, and proceed to suggest some applications which may be useful.

1. Private Christians are here instructed in the true method of Christian progress and usefulness. It is a first truth with you all, I doubt not, brethren, that Divine aid and intercourse are your only strength and reliance. You know, too well, the infirmity of your best purposes and endeavours, to hope for anything but defeat, without the Spirit of God dwelling in you, and superintending your warfare. In what manner you may secure this Divine indwelling permanently is here made plain. It is not by attempts above your capacity, or by the invention of great and extraordinary occasions; but it is by living unto God daily. If you feel the necessity of making spiritual attainments, of growing in holiness; if you think as little of mere starts and explosions in religious zeal as they deserve, and as much of growths, habits, and purified affections, as God does, you will have a delightful work to prosecute in the midst of all your ordinary cares and employments, and you will have the inward witness of Divine communion ever vouchsafed you. The sins by which God's Spirit is ordinarily grieved are the sins of small things—laxities in keeping the temper, slight neglects of duty, lightness, sharpness of dealing. If it is your habit to walk with God in the humblest occupations of your days, it is very nearly certain that you will be filled with the Spirit always.

If it be a question with you how to overcome bad and perni-cious habits, the mode is here before you. The reason why those who are converted to Christ often make so poor a work of rec-tifying their old habits, is, that they lay down their work in the very places where it needs to be prosecuted most carefully, that is, in their common employments. They do not live to God in that which is least. They reserve their piety for those exercises, public and private, which are immediately religious, and so a wide door is left open in all the common duties of life for their old habits to break in and take them captive. As if it were enough, in shutting out a flood, to dike the higher points of the ground and leave the lower.

If the question be, in what manner you may grow in know-ledge and intellectual strength, the answer is readily given. You can do it by no means save that of pertinacious, untiring application. No one becomes a Christian who cannot, by the cultivation of thought, and by acquiring a well-discriminated knowledge of the Scriptures, make himself a gift of fourfold, and, perhaps, even an hundredfold value to the Church. This he can do by industry, by improving small opportunities, and, not least, by endeavouring to realise the principles and the beauty of Christ in all his daily conduct. In this point of view, reli-gion is cultivation itself, and that of the noblest kind. And never does it truly justify its nature, except when it is seen ele-vating the mind, the manners, the whole moral dignity of the subject.

Why is it that a certain class of men, who never thrust them-selves on public observation by any very signal acts, do yet attain to a very commanding influence, and leave a deep and lasting impression on the world? They are the men who thrive by constancy and by means of small advances, just as others do who thrive in wealth. They live to God in the com-mon doings of their daily life as well as in the more extra-ordinary transactions in which they mingle. In this way, they shew themselves to be actuated by good principle not from respect to the occasions where it may be manifested, but from respect to principle itself. And their carefulness to honour God in humble things is stronger proof to men of their uprightness than the most distinguished acts or sacrifices. Such persons operate principally by the weight of confidence and moral respect they acquire, which is the most legitimate and powerful action in the world. At first it is not felt, because it is noiseless, and is not thoroughly appreciated. It is action without pretence, without attack, and therefore, perhaps, without notice for a time. But by degrees the personal motives begin to be understood, and the beauty and moral dignity of the life are felt. No proclamation of an aim or purpose has, in the meantime, gone before the disciple to awaken suspicion or start opposition. The simple power of his goodness and uprightness flows out as an emanation on all around him. He shines like the sun, not because he purposes to shine, but because he is full of light. The bad man is rebuked, the good man strengthened by his example; everything evil and ungraceful is ashamed before him—everything right and lovely is made stronger and lovelier. And now, if he has the talent to undertake some great enterprise of reform or of benevolence, in the name of his Master, he has something already prepared in the good opinions of mankind, to soften or neutralise the pretence of such attempts, and give him favour in them. Or, if a Christian of this stamp has not the talents or standing necessary to lead in the more active forms of enterprise, he will yet accomplish a high and noble purpose in his life. The silent savour of his name may, perhaps, do more good after he is laid in his grave, than abler men do by the most active efforts.

I often hear mentioned, by the Christians of our city, the name of a certain godly man who has been dead many years; and he is always spoken of with so much respectfulness and affection, that I, a stranger of another generation, feel his power, and the sound of his name refreshes me. That man was one who lived to God in small things. I know this, not by any description which has thus set forth his character, but from the very respect and homage with which he is named. Virtually, he still lives among us, and the face of his goodness shines upon all our Christian labours. And is it not a delightful aspect of the Christian faith, that it opens so sure a prospect of doing good on all who are in humble condition, or whose talents are too feeble to act in the more public spheres of enterprise and duty? Such are called to act by their simple goodness more than others are; and who has not felt the possibility that such, when faithful, do actually discharge a calling, the

more exalted because of its unmixed nature? If there were
none of these unpretending but beautiful examples, blooming
in depression, sweetening affliction by their Christian patience,
adorning poverty by their high integrity, and dying in the
Christian heroism of faith — if, I say, there were no such
examples making their latent impressions in the public mind,
of the dignity and truth of the gospel, who shall prove that our
great men, who are supposed to accomplish so much by their
eloquence, their notable sacrifices and far-reaching plans, would
not utterly fail in them? However this may be, we have
reason enough, all of us, for living to God in every sphere of
life. "Blessed are they that keep judgment, and he that doeth
righteousness at all times."

2. Our subject enables us to offer some useful suggestions
concerning the manner in which churches may be made to
prosper.

First of all, brethren, you will have a care to maintain your
purity and your honour by the exercise of a sound discipline.
And here you will be faithful in that which is least. You will
not wait until a crisis comes, or a flagrant case arises, where the
hand of extermination is needed. That is often a very cruel
discipline rather than one of brotherly love. Nothing, of course,
should be done in a meddlesome spirit, for this would be more
mischievous than neglectful. But small things will yet be
watched, the first gentle declinings noted and faithfully but
kindly reproved. Your church should be like a family, not
waiting till the ruin of a member is complete and irremedi-
able, but acting preventively. This would be a healthy discipline, and it is the only sort, I am persuaded, on which God
will ever smile.

The same spirit of watchfulness and attention is necessary to
all the solid interests of your church. It is not enough that
you attempt to bless it occasionally by some act of generosity or
some fit of exertion. Your brethren, suffering from injustice
or evil report, must have your faithful sympathy; such as are
struggling with adversity must have your aid; when it is possible, the more humble and private exercises of your church
must be attended.

The impression cannot be too deeply fixed that a church must
grow chiefly by its industry and the personal growth of its

members. Some churches seem to feel that, if anything is to be done, some great operation must be started. They cannot even repent without concert and a general ado. Have you not the preaching of God's Word fifty-two Sabbaths in the year? Have you not also families, friendships, interchanges of business, meetings for prayer, brotherly vows, opportunities of private and public charity? Do not despise these common occasions— God has not planned the world badly. Christ did not want higher occasions than the Father gave Him. The grand maxim of His mission was, that the humblest spheres give the greatest weight and dignity to principles. He was the good carpenter saving the world! Rightly viewed, my brethren, there are no small occasions in this world as, in our haste, we too often think. Great principles—principles sacred even to God—are at stake in every moment of life. What we want, therefore, is not invention, but industry; not the advantages of new and extraordinary times, but the realising of our principles by adorning the doctrine of God our Saviour in all times.

One of the best securities for the growth and prosperity of a church is to be sought in a faithful exhibition of religion in families. Here is a law of increase which God has incorporated in His Church, and by which He designs to give it strength and encouragement. But why is it—I ask the question with grief and pain—why is it that so many children, so many apprentices and servants are seen to grow up, or to live many years in Christian families, without any regard or even respect for religion? It is because their parents, guardians, or masters have that sort of piety which can flourish only, like Peter's sword, on great occasions. Then, perhaps, they are exceedingly full of piety, and put forth many awkward efforts to do good in their families—enough, it may be, to give them a permanent disgust for religious things. But when the great occasion is past their work is done. A spirit of worldliness now rolls in again—a want of conscience begins to appear—a light and carnal conversation to shew itself. The preaching of the gospel is very critically and somewhat wittily canvassed on the Sabbath. The day itself, in the meantime, fares scarcely better than the preacher. It is shortened by degrees at both ends, and again by a newspaper or some trifling conversation in the middle. There is no instructive remark at the family prayers.

and perhaps no family instruction anywhere. There is no effort to point the rising family toward a better world, and apparently no living for such a world. Bad tempers are manifested in government and in business. Arts are practised below dignity, and wide of integrity. How is it possible that the children and youth of a family should not learn to despise such a religion? How different would be the result if there were a simple, unostentatious piety kept up with constancy, and the fear of God were seen to be a controlling principle in all the daily conduct and plans of life! I have heard of many striking cases of conversion which were produced, under God, by simply seeing the godly life of a Christian in his family, without a word of direct address, and in a time of general inattention to religious things. In such a family every child and inmate will certainly respect religion. And the Church, in fact, may count on receiving a constant and certain flow of increase from the bosom of such families.

I will not pursue this head further. But feel assured of this, brethren, that an every-day religion—one that loves the duties of our common walk, one that makes an honest man, one that accomplishes an intellectual and moral growth in the subject, one that works in all weather, and improves all opportunities— will best and most healthily promote the growth of a church and the power of the gospel. God prescribes our duty; and it were wrong not to believe that, if we undertake God's real work, He will furnish us to it, and give us pleasure in it. He will transfuse into us some portion of His own versatility; He will attract us into a nicer observation of His wisdom in our humble duties and concerns. We shall more admire the healthiness of that which grows up in God's natural spring-times, and ripens in the air of His common days. The ordinary will thus grow dignified and sacred in our sight; and without discarding all invention in respect to means and opportunities, we shall yet especially love the daily bread of a common grace in our common works and cares. And all the more that it was the taste of our blessed Master to make the ordinary glow with mercy and goodness. Him we are to follow. We are to work after no set fashion of high endeavour, but to walk with Him, performing as it were a ministry on foot, that we may stop at the humblest matters, and prove our fidelity there.

XV.

HEB. vii. 16—*" Who is made, not after the law of a carnal commandment, but after the power of an endless life."*

THIS word *after* is a word of correspondence, and implies two subjects brought in comparison. That Christ has the power of an endless life in His own person is certainly true ; but to say that He is made a priest after this power, subjective in Himself, is awkward even to a degree that violates the natural grammar of speech. The suggestion is different, viz., that the priesthood of Christ is graduated by the wants and measures of the human soul, as the priesthood of the law was not; that the endless life in which He comes, matches and measures the endless life in mankind whose fall He is to restore ; providing a salvation as strong as their sin, and as long or lasting as the run of their immortality. He is able thus to save unto the uttermost. Powers of endless life though we be, falling principalities, wandering stars shooting downward in the precipitation of evil, He is able to bring us off, re-establish our dismantled eternities, and set us in the peace and confidence of an eternal righteousness.

I propose to exhibit the work of Christ in this high relation, which will lead me to consider—

I. *The power of an endless life in man, what it is, and, as being under sin, requires.*

II. *What Christ, in His eternal priesthood, does to restore it.*

I. The power of an endless life, what it is, and requires.

The greatness of our immortality, as commonly handled, is one of the dullest subjects, partly because it finds apprehension asleep in us, and partly because the strained computations entered into, and the words piled up as magnifiers, in a way of impressing the sense of its eternal duration, carry no impression, start no sense of magnitude in us. Even if we raise no doubt or objection, they do little more than drum us to sleep in our own nothingness. We exist here only in the germ, and it is much as if the life-power in some seed, that, for example, of the great cedars of the west, were to begin a magnifying of its own importance to itself in the fact that it has so long a time to live; and, finally, because of the tiny figure it makes, and because the forces it contains are as yet unrealised, to settle inertly down upon the feeling that, after all, it is only a seed, a dull, insignificant speck of matter, wanting to be a little greater than it can. Instead, then, of attempting to magnify the soul by any formal computation on the score of time or duration, let us simply take up and follow the hint that is given us in this brief expression, the power of an endless life.

It is a power, a power of life, a power of endless life. The word translated *power* in the text, is the original of our word *dynamic*, denoting a certain impetus, momentum, or causative force, which is cumulative, growing stronger and more impelling as it goes. And this is the nature of life or vital force universally—it is a force cumulative as long as it continues. It enters into matter as a building, organising, lifting power, and knows not how to stop till death stops it. We use the word *grow* to describe its action, and it does not even know how to subsist without growth. In which growth it lays hold continually of new material, expands in volume, and fills a larger sphere of body with its power.

Now these innumerable lives, animal and vegetable, at work upon the world, creating and new-creating, and producing their immense transformations of matter, are all immaterial forces or powers; related, in that manner, to souls, which are only a highest class of powers. The human soul cannot be more efficiently described than by calling it the power of an endless life; and to it all these lower immaterialities, at work in matter, look up as mute prophets, testifying, by the magical sovereignty they wield in the processes and material transformations of growth, to the possible forces embodied in that highest, noblest form of life. And sometimes, since our spiritual nature, taken as a power of life, organises nothing material and external by which its action is made visible, God allows the inferior lives in given examples, especially of the tree species, to have a small eternity of growth, and lift their giant forms to the clouds, that we may stand lost in amazement before the majesty of that silent power that works in life, when many centuries only are given to be the lease of its activity. The work is slow, the cumulative process silent—viewed externally, nothing appears that we name force, and yet this living creature called a tree throbs internally in fulness of life, circulates its juices, swells in volume, towers in majesty; till finally it gives to the very word life a historic presence and sublimity. It begins with a mere seed or germ, a tiny speck so inert and frail that we might even laugh at the bare suggestion of power in such a look of nothingness; just as at our present point of dulness and weakness we can give no sound of meaning to anything said of our own spiritual greatness; and yet that seed, long centuries ago, when the tremendous babyhood of Mohammed was nursing at his mother's breast, sprouted apace, gathered to itself new circles of matter, year by year and age after age kept its pumps in play, sent up new supplies of food, piling length on length in the sky, conserving still and vitalising all; and now it stands entire in pillared majesty, mounting upward still, and tossing back the storms that break on its green pinnacles, a bulk immense, such as, being felled and hollowed, would even make a modern ship of war.

And yet these cumulative powers of vegetable life are only feeble types of that higher, fearfully vaster power, that pertains to the endless life of a soul—that power that, known or unknown, dwells in you and in me. What Abel now is, or Enoch, as an angel of God, in the volume of his endless life and the vast energies unfolded in his growth by the river of God, they may set you trying to guess, but can by no means help you adequately to conceive. The possible majesty to which any free intelligence of God may grow, in the endless increment of ages, is after all rather hinted than imaged in their merely vegetable grandeur.

Quickened by these analogies, let us pass directly to the soul or spiritual nature itself, as a power of endless growth or increment; for it is only in this way that we begin to conceive the real magnitude and majesty of the soul, and not by any mere computations based on its eternity or immortality.

What it means, in this higher and nobler sense, to be a power of life, we are very commonly restrained from observing by two or three considerations that require to be named. First, when looking after the measures of the soul, we very naturally lay hold of what first occurs to us, and begin to busy ourselves in the contemplation of its eternal duration. Whereas the eternal duration of the soul, at any given measure, if we look no further, is nothing but the eternal continuance of its mediocrity, or comparative littleness. Its eternal growth in volume and power is, in that manner, quite lost sight of, and the computation misses everything most impressive in its future significance and history. Secondly, the growth of the soul is a merely spiritual growth, indicated by no visible and material form that is expanded by it and with it, as in the growth of a tree, and therefore passes comparatively unnoticed by many, just because they cannot see it with their eyes. And then, again, thirdly, as the human body attains to its maturity; and, finally, in the decays of age, becomes an apparent limit to the spiritual powers and faculties, we drop into the impression that these have now passed their climacteric, and that we have actually seen the utmost volume it is in their nature ever to attain. We do not catch the significance of the fact that the soul outgrows the growth, and outlives the vigour of the body, which is not true in trees; revealing its majestic properties as a force independent and qualifiedly sovereign. Observing how long the soul-force goes on to expand after the body-force has reached its maximum, and, when disease and age have begun to shatter the frail house it inhabits, how long it braves these bodily decrepitudes, driving on, still on, like a strong engine in a poorly-timbered vessel, through seas not too heavy for it, but only for the crazy hulk it impels— observing this, and making due account of it, we should only be the more impressed with a sense of some inherent everlasting power of growth and progress in its endless life.

Stripping aside now all these impediments, let us pass directly into the soul's history, and catch, from what transpires in its first indications, the sign or promise of what it is to become. In its beginning it is a mere seed of possibility. All the infant faculties are folded up at first, and scarcely a sign of power is visible in it. But a doom of growth is in it, and the hidden momentum of an endless power is driving it on. And a falling body will not gather momentum in its fall more naturally and certainly than it will gather force in the necessary struggle of its endless life now begun. We may think little of the increase; it is a matter of course, and why should we take note of it? But if no increase or development appears, if the faculties all sleep as at the first, we take sad note of that, and draw, how reluctantly, the conclusion that our child is an idiot, and not a proper man! And what a chasm is there between the idiot and the man! one a being unprogressive, a being who is not a power; the other a careering force started on its way to eternity, a principle of might and majesty begun to be unfolded, and to be progressively unfolded for ever. Intelligence, reason, conscience, observation, choice, memory, enthusiasm, all the fires of his inborn eternity are kindling to a glow, and, looking on him as a force immortal, just beginning to reveal the symptoms of what he shall be, we call him man. Only a few years ago he lay in his cradle, a barely breathing principle of life, but in that life were gathered up, as in a germ or seed, all these godlike powers that are now so conspicuous in the volume of his personal growth. In a sense, all that is in him now was in him then, as the power of an endless life, and still the sublime progression of his power is only begun. He conquers now the sea and its storms. He climbs the heavens, and searches out the mysteries of the stars. He harnesses the lightning. He bids the rocks dissolve, and summons the secret atoms to give up their names and laws. He subdues the face of the world, and compels the forces of the waters and the fires to be his servants. He makes laws, hurls empires down upon empires in the fields of war, speaks words that cannot die, sings to distant realms and peoples across vast ages of time; in a word, he executes all that is included in history, shewing his tremendous energy in almost everything that stirs the silence, and changes the conditions of the world. Everything is transformed by him even up to the stars. Not all the winds, and storms, and earthquakes, and seas, and seasons of the world, have done so much to revolutionise the world as he, the power of an endless life, has done since the day he came forth upon it, and received, as he is most truly declared to have done, dominion over it.

And yet we have, in the power thus developed, nothing more than a mere hint or initial sign of what is to be the real stature

P

of his personality in the process of his everlasting development. We exist here only in the small, that God may have us
in a state of flexibility, and bend or fashion us, at the best
advantage, to the model of His own great life and character.
And most of us, therefore, have scarcely a conception of the
exceeding weight of glory to be comprehended in our existence. If we take, for example, the faculty of memory, how
very obvious is it that, as we pass eternally on, we shall have
more and more to remember, and finally shall have gathered
more into this great storehouse of the soul than is now contained in all the libraries of the world. And there is not one of
our faculties that has not, in its volume, a similar power of
expansion. Indeed, if it were not so, the memory would
finally overflow and drown all our other faculties, and the
spirits, instead of being powers, would virtually cease to be
anything more than registers of the past.

But we are not obliged to take our conclusion by inference.
We can see for ourselves that the associations of the mind,
which are a great part of its riches, must be increasing in
number and variety for ever, stimulating thought by multiply-
ing its suggestives, and beautifying thought by weaving into it
the colours of sentiment endlessly varied.

The imagination is gathering in its images and kindling its
eternal fires in the same manner. Having passed through many
trains of worlds, mixing with scenes, societies, orders of intelligence and powers of beatitude—just that which made the
apostle in Patmos into a poet by the visions of a single day—it
is impossible that every soul should not finally become filled
with a glorious and powerful imagery, and be waked to a
wonderfully creative energy.

By the supposition it is another incident of this power of endless life, that, passing down the eternal galleries of fact and
event, it must be for ever having new cognitions and accumulat-
ing new premises. By its own contacts it will, at some future
time, have touched even whole worlds and felt them through,
and made premises of all there is in them. It will know God
by experiences correspondently enlarged, and itself by a consciousness correspondently illuminated. Having gathered in,
at last, such worlds of premises, it is difficult for us now to conceive the vigour into which a soul may come, or the volume it

may exhibit, the wonderful depth and scope of its judgments, its rapidity and certainty, and the vastness of its generalisations. It passes over more and more, and that necessarily, from the condition of a creature gathering up premises, into the condition of God, creating out of premises; for if it is not actually set to the creation of worlds, its very thoughts will be a discoursing in world-problems and theories equally vast in their complications.

In the same manner, the executive energy of the will, the volume of the benevolent affections, and all the active powers, will be shewing, more and more impressively, what it is to be a power of endless life. They that have been swift in doing God's will and fulfilling His mighty errands, will acquire a marvellous address and energy in the use of their powers. They that have taken worlds into their love will have a love correspondently capacious, whereupon also it will be seen that their will is settled in firmness and raised in majesty according to the vastness of impulse there is in the love behind it. They that have great thoughts, too, will be able to manage great causes, and they that are lubricated eternally in the joys that feed their activity, will never tire. What force, then, must be finally developed in what now appears to be the tenuous and fickle impulse, and the merely frictional activity of a human soul.

On this subject the Scriptures indulge in no declamation, but only speak in hints, and start us off by questions, well understanding that the utmost they can do is to waken in us the sense of a future scale of being unimaginable, and beyond the compass of our definite thought. Here they drive us out in the almost cold mathematical question, " What shall it profit a man to gain the whole world and lose his own soul ? " Here they shew us, in John's vision, Moses and Elijah, as angels, suggesting our future classification among angels, which are sometimes called chariots of God, to indicate their excelling strength and swiftness in careering through His empire to do His will. Here they speak of powers unimaginable as regards the volume of their personality, calling them dominions, thrones, principalities, powers, and appear to set us on a footing with these dim majesties. Here they notify us that it doth not yet appear what we shall be. Here they call us sons of God. Here they bolt upon us, but "I said, Ye are gods;" as if meaning to waken us by a shock! In these and all ways possible, they contrive to start some better conception in us of ourselves, and of the immense significance of the soul; forbidding us always to be the dull mediocrities into which, under the stupor of our unbelief, we are commonly so ready to subside. Oh, if we could tear aside the veil, and see for but one hour what it signifies to be a soul in the power of an endless life, what a revelation would it be!

But there is yet another side or element of meaning suggested by this expression, which requires to be noted. It looks on the soul as a falling power, a bad force, rushing downward into ruinous and final disorder. If we call it a principality in its possible volume, it is a falling principality. It was this which made the mighty priesthood of the Lord necessary. For the moment we look in upon the soul's great movement as a power, and find sin entered there, we perceive that everything is in disorder. It is like a mighty engine in which some pivot or lever is broken, whirling, and crashing, and driving itself into a wreck. The disastrous effects of sin in a soul will be just according to the powers it contains, or embodies; for every force becomes a bad force, a misdirected and self-destructive force, a force which can never be restored, save by some other which is mightier and superior. What, in this view, can be more frightful than the disorders loosened in it by a state of sin.

And what shall we say of the result or end? Must the immortal nature still increase in volume without limit, and so in the volume of its miseries; or only in its miseries by the conscious depths of shame and weakness into which it is falling? On this subject I know not what to say. We do see that bad minds, in their evil life, gather force and expand in many, at least, of their capabilities, on to a certain point or limit. As far as to that point or limit, they appear to grow intense, powerful, and, as the world says, great. But they seem at last, and apart from the mere decay of years, to begin a diminishing process; they grow jealous, imperious, cruel, and so far weak. They become little, in the girding of their own stringent selfishness. They burn to a cinder in the heat of their own devilish passion. And so, beginning as heroes and demigods, they many of them taper off into awfully intense but still little men —intense at a mere point; which appears to be the conception of a fiend. Is it so that the bitterness of hell is finally created? Is it toward this pungent, acrid, awfully intensified, and talented littleness, that all souls under sin are gravitating? However this may be, we can see for ourselves that the disorders of sin, running loose in human souls, must be driving them downward into everlasting and complete ruin, the wreck of all that is mightiest and loftiest in their immortality. One of the sublimest and most fearful pictures ever given of this you will find in the first chapter to the Romans. It reads like some battle among the gods, where all that is great, and terrible, and wild in the confusion answers to the majesty of the powers engaged. And this is man, the power of an endless life, under sin. By what adequate power, in earth or in heaven, shall that sin be taken away? This brings me to consider—

II. What Christ, in His eternal priesthood, has done; or the fitness and practical necessity of it, as related to the stupendous exigency of our redemption.

The great impediment which the gospel of Christ encounters in our world, that which most fatally hinders its reception, or embrace, is that it is too great a work. It transcends our belief—it wears a look of extravagance. We are beings too insignificant and low to engage any such interest on the part of God, or justify any such expenditure. The preparations made, and the parts acted, are not in the proportions of reason, and the very terms of the great salvation have, to our dull ears, a declamatory sound. How can we really think that the eternal God has set these more than epic machineries at work for such a creature as man?

My principal object, therefore, in the contemplations raised by this topic, has been to start some conception of ourselves, in the power of an endless life, that is more adequate. Mere immortality, or everlasting continuance, when it is the continuance only of littleness or mediocrity, does not make a platform or occasion high enough for this great mystery of the gospel. It is only when we see in human souls, taken as germs of power, a future magnitude and majesty transcending all present measures, that we come into any fit conception at all of Christ's mis-

sion to the world. Entering the gospel at this point, and
regarding it as a work undertaken for the redemption of beings
scarcely imagined as yet—of dominions, principalities, powers—
spiritual intelligences so transcendent that we have, as yet, no
words to name them—everything done takes a look of proportion; it appears even to be needed, and we readily admit that
nothing less could suffice to restore the fallen powers, or stop
the tragic disorders loosened in them by their sin. How much
more if, instead of drawing thus upon our imagination, we
could definitely grasp the real import of our being, that which
hitherto is only indicated, never displayed, and have it as a
matter of positive and distinct apprehension. This power of
endless life, could we lay hold of it; could we truly feel its movement in us, and follow the internal presage to its mark; or could
we only grasp the bad force there is in it, and know it rushing
downward, in the terrible lava-flood of its disorders, how true
and rational, how magnificently divine would the great salvation of Christ appear, and in how great dread of ourselves
should we hasten to it for refuge!

Then it would shock us no more that visibly it is no mere
man that has arrived. Were he only a human teacher, reformer,
philosopher, coming in our human plane to lecture on our self-
improvement as men, in the measures of men, he would even
be less credible than now. Nothing meets our want, in fact,
but to see the boundaries of nature and time break way to let
in a Being and a power visibly not of this world. Let him be
the eternal Son of God and Word of the Father, descending
out of higher worlds to be incarnate in this. As we have lost
our measures, let us recover them, if possible, in the sense
restored of our everlasting brotherhood with Him. Let Him so
be made a priest for us, not after the law of a carnal commandment, but after the power of an endless life—"the brightness of
the Father's glory and the express image of his person"—"God
manifest in the flesh"—"God in Christ, reconciling the world
unto himself." All the better and more proportionate and probable is it, if He comes heralded by innumerable angels, bursting into the sky, to congratulate their fallen peers with songs of
deliverance—"Glory to God in the highest, on earth peace, and
good will toward men." Humbled to the flesh and its external
conditions, He will only the more certainly even Himself with

our want, if He dares to say, "Before Abraham was, I am;"
"all power is given unto me in heaven and in earth." Is He
faultless, so that no man convinceth Him of sin, revealing in
the humble guise of humanity the absolute beauty of God;
how could anything less or inferior meet our want? If He
dares to make the most astounding pretensions, all the better,
if only His pretensions are borne out by His life and actions.
Let Him heal the sick, feed the hungry, still the sea by His
word. Let His doctrine not be human—let it bear the stamp
of a higher mind, and be verified and sealed by the perfection
of His character. Let Him be transfigured, if He may, in the
sight of two worlds—of angels from the upper and of men from
this—that, beholding His excellent glory, no doubt may be left
of His transcendent quality.

No matter if the men that follow Him and love Him are,
just for the time, too slow to apprehend Him. How could
they see, with eyes holden, the divinity that is hid under such a
garb of poverty and patience? How could they seize on the possibility that this "man of sorrows" is revealing even the depths
of God's eternal love by these more than mortal burdens? If
the factitious distinctions of society pass for nothing with Him,
if He takes His lot among the outcast poor, how else could He
shew that it is not any tier of quality, but our great fallen
humanity, the power of an endless life, that engages Him. And
when, with a degree of unconcern that is itself sublime, He
says, "The prince of this world cometh, and hath nothing in
me," how else could He convey so fitly the impression that the
highest royalty and stateliest throne to Him is simple man
himself.

But the tragedy gathers to its last act, and fearful is to be the
close. Never did the powers of eternity, or endless life in souls,
reveal themselves so terribly before. But He came to break
their force, and how so certainly as to let it break itself across
His patience? By His miracles and reproofs, and quite as
much by the unknown mystery of greatness in His character,
the deepest depths of malice in immortal evil are now finally
stirred; the world's wild wrath is concentred on His person,
and His soul is, for the hour, under an eclipse of sorrow—"exceeding sorrowful, even unto death." But the agony is shortly
past. He says, "I am ready," and they take Him, Son of

God though He be, and Word of the Father, and Lord of glory, to a cross! They nail Him fast; and what a sign do they give, in that dire frenzy, of the immortal depth of their passion! The sun refuses to look on the sight, and the frame of nature shudders! He dies! "It is finished!" The body that was taken for endurance and patience has drunk up all the shafts of the world's malice, and now rests in the tomb.

No! there is more. Lo! He is not here, but is risen! He has burst the bars of death and become "the first-fruits of them that slept." In that sign behold His victory. Just that is done which signifies eternal redemption—the conquest and recovery of free minds, taken as powers dismantled by eternal evil. By this offering, once for all, the work is finished. What can evil do, or passion, after this, when its bitterest arrows, shot into the Divine patience, are by that patience so tenderly and sovereignly broken? Therefore now, to make the triumph evident, He ascends, a visible Conqueror, to the Father, there to stand as Priest for ever, sending forth His Spirit to seal, and testifying that He is able to save unto the uttermost all that come unto God by Him.

This, in brief historic outline, is the great salvation. And it is not too great. It stands in glorious proportion with the work to be done. Nothing else or less would suffice. It is a work supernatural transacted in the plane of nature; and what but such a work could restore the broken order of the soul under evil? It incarnates God in the world, and what but some such opening of the senses to God or of God to the senses, could reinstate Him in minds that have lost the consciousness of Him, and fallen off to live apart? What but this could enter Him again, as a power, into the world's life and history? We are astonished by the revelation of Divine feeling; the expense of the sacrifice wears a look of extravagance. If we are only the dull mediocrities we commonly take ourselves to be, it is quite incredible. But if God, seeing through our possibilities into our real eternities, comprehends in the view, all we are to be or become, as powers of endless life, is there not some probability that He discovers a good deal more in us than we do in ourselves; enough to justify all the concern He testifies, all the sacrifice He makes in the passion of His Son? And as God has accurately weighed the worlds, and even the atoms, accurately set them in their, distances and altitudes, has He not also, in this incarnate grace and passion, which offend so many by their excess, measured accurately the unknown depths and magnitudes of our eternity, the momentum of our fall, the tragic mystery of our disorder? And if we cannot comprehend ourselves, if we are even a mystery to ourselves, what should His salvation be but a mystery of godliness equally transcendent? If Christ were a philosopher, a human teacher, a human example, we might doubtless reason Him, and set Him in our present scales of proportion, but He would as certainly do nothing for us equal to our want.

Inasmuch as our understanding has not yet reached our measures, we plainly want a grace which only faith can receive; for it is the distinction of faith that it can receive a medication it cannot definitely trace, and admit into the consciousness what it cannot master in thought. Christ therefore comes not as a problem given to our reason, but as a salvation offered to our faith. His passion reaches a deeper point in us than we can definitely think, and his Eternal Spirit is a healing priesthood for us, in the lowest and profoundest roots of our great immortality, those which we have never seen ourselves. By our faith in Him, too, as a mystery, He comes into our guiltiness, at a point back of all speculative comprehension, restoring that peace of innocence which is speculatively impossible; for how, in mere speculation, can anything done for our sin annihilate the fact; and without that, how take our guilt away? Still it goes! We know, as we embrace Him, that it goes! He has reached a point in us, by His mysterious priesthood, deep enough even to take our guiltiness away, and establish us in a peace that is even as the peace of innocence!

So, if we speak of our passions, our internal disorders, the wild, confused, and even downward rush of our inthralled powers, He performs, in a mystery of love and the Spirit, what no teaching or example could. The manner we can trace by no effort of the understanding; we can only see that He is some how able to come into the very germ principle of our life, and be a central, regulating, new-creating force in our disordered growth itself. And if we speak of righteousness, it is ours when it is not ours; how can a being unrighteous be established in the sense of righteousness? Logically, or according to the sentence of our speculative reason, it is impossible. And yet, in Christ, we have it! We are consciously in it, as we are in Him, and all we can say is, that it is the righteousness of God, by faith, unto all and upon all them that believe.

But I must draw my subject to a close. It is a common impression with persons who hear, but do not accept the calls of Christ and His salvation, that they are required to be somewhat less in order to be Christian. They must be diminished in quantity, taken down, shortened, made feeble and little, and then, by the time they have let go their manhood, they will possibly come into the way of salvation. They hear it declared that, in becoming little children, humble, meek, poor in spirit; in ceasing from our will and reason; and in giving up ourselves, our eagerness, revenge, and passion—thus, and thus only, can we be accepted; but, instead of taking all these as so many figures antagonistic to our pride, our ambition, and the determined self-pleasing of our sin, they take them absolutely, as requiring a real surrender and loss of our proper manhood itself. Exactly contrary to this, the gospel requires them to be more than they are—greater, higher, nobler, stronger—all which they were made to be in the power of their endless life. These expressions, just referred to, have no other aim than simply to cut off weaknesses, break down infirmities, tear away boundaries, and let the soul out into liberty, and power, and greatness. What is weaker than pride, self-will, revenge, the puffing of conceit and rationality, the constringing littleness of all selfish passion? And in just these things it is that human souls are so fatally shrunk in all their conceptions of themselves; so that Christ encounters, in all men, this first and most insurmountable difficulty—to make them apprised of their real value to themselves. For no sooner do they wake to the sense of their great immortality than they are even oppressed by it. Everything else shrinks to nothingness, and they go to Him for life. And then, when they receive Him, it is even a bursting forth into magnitude. A new inspiration is upon them, all their powers are exalted, a wondrous, inconceivable energy is felt, and, having come into the sense of God, which is the element of all real greatness, they discover, as it were in amazement, what it is to be in the true capacity.

A similar mistake is connected with their impressions of faith. They are jealous of faith, as being only weakness. They blame the gospel, because it requires faith, as a condition of salvation. And yet, as I have here abundantly shewn, it requires faith just because it is a salvation large enough to meet the measures of the soul, as a power of endless life. And oh, if you could once get away, my friends, from that sense of mediocrity and nothingness to which you are shut up, under the stupor of your self-seeking and your sin, how easy would it be for you to believe! Nay, if but some faintest suspicion could steal into you of what your soul is, and the tremendous evils working in it, nothing but the mystery of Christ's death and passion would be sufficient for you. Now you are nothing to yourselves, and therefore Christ is too great, the mystery of His cross an offence. O thou Spirit of grace, visit these darkened minds, to whom Thy gospel is hid, and let the light of the knowledge of the glory of God, in the face of Jesus Christ, shine into them! Raise in them the piercing question, that tears the world away and displays the grimace of its follies, "What shall it profit a man to gain the whole world and lose his own soul?"

I should do you a wrong to close this subject without conducting your minds forward to those anticipations of the future which it so naturally suggests. You have all observed the remarkable interest which beings of other worlds are shewn, here and there in the Scripture, to feel in the transactions of this. These, like us, are powers of endless life, intelligences that have had a history parallel to our own. Some of them, doubtless, have existed myriads of ages, and consequently now are far on in the course of their development,—far enough on to have discerned what existence is, and the amount of power and dignity there is in it. Hence their interest in us, who as yet are only candidates in their view for a greatness yet to be revealed. And the interest they shew seems extravagant to us, just as the gospel itself is, and for the same reasons. They break into the sky, when Christ is born, chanting their "All-hail!" They visit the world on heavenly errands, and perform their unseen ministries to the heirs of salvation. They watch for our repentances, and there is joy among them before God when but one is gathered to their company in the faith of salvation. And the reason is, that they have learned so much about the proportions and measures of things which as yet are hidden from us. These angels that excel in strength—these ancient princes and hierarchs that have grown up in God's eternity and unfolded their mighty powers in whole ages of good, recognise in us compeers that are finally to be advanced as they are.

And here is the point where our true future dawns upon us. "It doth not yet appear what we shall be." We lie here in our nest, unfledged and weak, guessing dimly at our future, and scarce believing what even now appears. But the power is in us, and that power is to be finally revealed. And what a revelation will that be! Is it possible, you will ask in amazement, that you, a creature that was sunk in such dulness and sold to such trivialities in your bondage to the world, were all this time related to God and the ancient orders of His kingdom in a being so majestic!

How great a terror to some of you may that discovery be! I cannot say exactly how it will be with the bad minds now given up finally to their disorders. Powers of endless life they still must be; but how far shrunk by that stringent selfishness, how far burned away as magnitudes by that fierce combustion of passion, I do not know. But if they diminish in volume, and shrink to a more intensified power of littleness and fiendishness, eaten out, as regards all highest volume, by the malice of evil and the undying worm of its regrets, it will not be so with the righteous. They will develop greater force of mind, greater volume of feeling, greater majesty of will and character even for ever. In the grand mystery of Christ and His eternal priesthood—Christ who ever liveth to make intercession—they will be set in personal and experimental connexion with all the great problems of grace and counsels of love comprised in the plan by which they have been trained and the glories to which they are exalted. Attaining thus to greater force and stature of spirit than we are able now to conceive, they have exactly that supplied to their discovery which will carry them still further on with the greatest expedition. Their subjects and conferences will be those of principalities and powers, and the conceptions of their great society will be correspondent, for they are now coming to the stature necessary to a fit contemplation of such themes. The Lamb of Redemption and the throne of law, and a government comprising both, will be the field of their study, and they will find their own once petty experience related to all that is vastest and most transcendent in the works and appointments of God's empire.   Oh, what thoughts will spring up in such minds, surrounded by such fellow intelligences, entered on such themes, and present to such discoveries!   How grand their action!   How majestic their communion!   Their praise how august!   Their joys how full and clear!   Shall we ever figure, my friends, in scenes like these?   Oh, this power of endless life!—Great King of Life and Priest of Eternity! reveal Thyself to us, and us to ourselves, and quicken us to this unknown future before us!

XVI.

RESPECTABLE SIN.

JOHN viii. 9—"*And they which heard it, being convicted by their own conscience, went out one by one, beginning at the eldest, even unto the last; and Jesus was left alone, and the woman standing in the midst.*"

IT is with sins as with men or families, some have pedigree and some have not; for there are kinds and modes of sin that have, in all ages, been held in respect, and embalmed with all the honours of history; and there are others that never were and never can be raised above the level even of disgust. The noble sins will, of course, be judged in a very different manner from the humble, base-born sins. The sins of fame, honour, place, power, bravery, genius, always in good repute, will not seldom be admired and applauded. But the low-blooded sins of felony, and vice, and base depravity, are associated with brutality, and are universally held in contempt. Whether the real demerit of the two classes of sin is measured by such distinctions is more questionable. Such distinctions certainly had little weight with Christ. He was even more severe upon the sins of learning, wealth, station, and religious sanctimony, than upon the more plebeian, or more despised class of sins. Indeed, He seems to look directly through all the fair conventionalities, and to bring His judgment down upon some point more interior and deeper. He appears, in general, to be thoroughly disgusted with all the mere respectabilities, whether men or sins. The hypocrisies of religion, the impostures of learning, the gilded shows of wealth gotten by extortion, the proud airs of authority and power employed in acts of oppression, provoke His indignation, and He deals with them in such terms of emphasis as indicate the profoundest possible abhorrence.

Hence the jealousy with which He was watched by the elders, and priests, and rulers; for every few days some rabbi, scribe, lawyer, or committee of such, was sent out to observe Him, or question Him, or draw Him, if possible, into some kind of treason in His doctrine ; because they feared His influence with the people, lest He might put Himself at their head and raise a great revolution that would even subvert the present social order.

The cunning plot His enemies are working, in my text, is instigated by this kind of fear. He is teaching, it appears, a great multitude of people in the temple, when suddenly a company of Scribes and Pharisees are seen hustling in through the crowd, leading up a woman, to set her before Him. She has been guilty, they say, of a base crime, which the law of Moses punishes with public stoning and death, and they demand of Him what shall be done with her ; hoping that, out of the same perverse favour He is wont to shew to low people, He will take the woman's part, and so give them the desired opportunity to throw contempt on His character, and exasperate the popular superstition against Him.

Christ, apparently perceiving their design, determines to put them to confusion. He remains a long time silent, making no answer, and, of course, none that can be taken hold of. They press Him for a reply ; still no reply is given. They wait; and still it is not given. There they stand in the centre of the great concourse, all looking *at* them, and, as they soon begin to fancy, looking directly *into* them. It is a most uncomfortable position for them. To give still greater pungency to their thoughts, Christ withdraws His eyes from them, and, as if waiting for their complete confusion, writes abstractedly on the pavement. At length they grow perplexed, and begin to ask themselves how they shall get out of their very awkward predicament. They press Him still more vehemently, but He refuses to speak, save simply to say, Let the man of you that is without sin throw the first stone at the woman, if she is guilty ; and immediately falls to writing abstractedly on the ground again. The arrow sticks, and the suspense of silence makes them more and more conscious of the pain; till finally they can bear it no longer. Convicted thus by their own conscience, " they went out," as the text has it, one by one, " beginning at the eldest, even unto the last ; and Jesus was left alone, and the woman standing in the midst."

Look upon them now, as they withdraw, and follow them with your eye, as probably Christ and the whole assembly did. Observe the mannerly order of their shame—"beginning at the eldest, even unto the last!" See how carefully they keep the sacred rules of good breeding and deference to age, even in their snivelling defeat, and the chagrin of their baffled conspiracy, and you will begin to find how base a thing may take on airs of dignity, and how contemptible, in fact, these airs of dignity may be.

The subject thus presented is *respectable sin, sin that takes on the semblance of goodness, and judges itself by the dignity of its manner and appearance.* Almost all the really great or sublime sins of the world are of this class, and I shall undertake to shew that this more respectable type of sin is often, if not generally, deepest in the spirit of sin, and, in the sight of God, most guilty.

Just this, I think, has been the impression of you all, in the remarkable scene referred to in my text. These plausible accusers, pressing in with their victim in such airs of dignity, and retiring in such careful deference to age as not to allow even a year's difference to be disregarded, have yet been virtually detected and foiled in a thoroughly wicked conspiracy. Had they been a gang of thieves, their transaction would have been more base only in the name; for it was, in fact, a kind of dramatic lie, deliberately planned, to snare an artless, worthy, and visibly holy man. Accordingly, now that they are gone, driven out by the recoil of their own base trick, the Saviour, without using any word of reproach, quietly proceeds to bring out the scene just where their real character will be most impressively displayed. He says to the woman, "Where are thine accusers? Hath no man condemned thee?" "No man, Lord." "Neither do I; go, and sin no more." Sinner that she was, not even these sanctimonious conspirators could stand the challenge of their own sins long enough to accuse her. And the result is, that we are left by Christ in the impression, and that designedly, that on the whole, the woman, in her most shameful sin, was really less of a sinner than they. Her, therefore, we pity. Them we denounce and despise. How many things are we ready to imagine that might soften our judgment of her fall, if we only knew the secret of her sad history. Our judgment of their stratagem, on the other hand, permits no softening, but we approve ourselves only the more confidently, the more heartily we despise, and the more unrestrainedly we detest their hypocrisy in it. In pursuing now this very serious subject, we need,

First of all, to clear the influence of a false or defective impression, growing out of the fact that we ourselves are persons that live so entirely in the atmosphere of character and decency. Our range of life is so walled in by the respectability of our associations, that what is on the other side of the wall is very much a world unknown. Hence we have no such opinion or impression of sin anywhere as we ought to have. It is with us all our life long and in all our associations, much as it is with us here in our assembly for worship. The offensive and repulsive forms of sin are almost never here, by so much as any one sign or symptom. The sin is here, and sin that wants salvation; but it is sin so thoroughly respectable, as to make it very nearly impossible to produce any just impression of its deformity. Sitting here in this atmosphere of decency and order, how can you suffer any just impression of the dreadful nature of that evil which, after all, wears a look so plausible. If there came in with you, to mingle in your audience, a fair representation only of the town; if you heard, in the porch, the profane oaths of the cellars and hells of gambling; if you looked about with a cautious feeling, right and left, in the seat, lest some one might rifle your dress, or pick your pocket; if the victims of drink were seen reeling into the seats, here and there, and their hungry, shivering children were crying at the door, for bread; if the diseased and loathsome relics of vice, recognised sometimes as the sons and daughters of families once living in respect and affluence, were sprinkled about you, tainting the air you breathe; in a word, if actual life were here, in correct representation, how different a matter would it be for me to speak of sin, how different for you to hear! And the same holds true of the associations of your life generally. Sin, in its really revolting, shocking forms, seldom gets near enough to you to meet your eye. What you know of it is mostly gotten from the newspapers, and is scarcely more of a reality to you, many times, than the volcanoes you hear of in the moon.

Q

Secondly, we need also to clear another false or defective impression, growing out of the general tendency in mankind to identify sin with vice; and, of course, to judge that whatever is clear of vice is clear also of sin; which, in fact, is the same as to judge that whatever sin is respectable is no sin at all. Or, sometimes, we identify sin with acts of wrong, or personal injury, such as deeds of robbery, fraud, seduction, slander, and the like. In this view, again, whatever sin is respectable enough to be clear of all such deeds of wrong is, of course, no sin; whereas, there may be great sin where there is no vice, bitter and deep guiltiness before God where there is never one act of personal wrong or injury committed. All vice, all wrong, presupposes sin, but sin may be the reigning principle of the life, from childhood to the grave, and never produce one scar of vice, or blameable injury to a fellow-being. Indeed we must go further, we must definitely say that even virtue itself, as the term is commonly used, classes under sin, or has its root in sin. Virtue, as men speak, is conduct approved irrespectively of any good principle of conduct; and it is, for the most part, a goodness wholly negative, consisting in the not doing, the abstaining, and keeping off from whatever is confessedly base and vicious. Sin, on the other hand, is the negation of good as respects the principle of good. Anything is sin, as God judges, which is not in the positive, all-dominating power of universal love. Anything called virtue, therefore, which consists in barely not doing, is sin of course; because it is not in any positive principle of love or duty to God. Half the sin of mankind, therefore, consists, or is made up of virtue; that is, of what is generally called virtue, and passes for a virtuous character in the common speech of men. It is, in fact, respectable sin, nothing more; and has exactly the same root with all sin, even the worst—viz., the not being in God's love and a state of positive allegiance to God.

Consider now, thirdly, and make due account of the fact, that respectable sin is not less guilty because it has a less revolting aspect. A feeling is very generally indulged, even by such as are confessedly blameable for not being in the Christian life, that their blame or guilt is a thing of higher and finer quality than it would be under the excesses and degrading vices many practise. They measure their sin by their outward standing and conduct ; whereas all sin is of the same principle. The sin of one class is, in fact, the sin of the other, as respects everything but manner and degree. There are different kinds of vice, but only one kind of sin—viz., the state of being without God, or out of allegiance to God. All evil and sin, as we just now saw, are of this same negative root ; the want of any holy principle ; the state set off from God, and disempowered and degraded by the separation. The respectable sin, therefore, shades into the unrespectable, not as being different in kind, but only as twilight shades into the night. The evil spirit called sin may be trained up to politeness, and made to be genteel sin ; it may be elegant, cultivated sin ; it may be very exclusive and fashionable sin ; it may be industrious, thrifty sin ; it may be a great political manager, a great commercial operator, a great inventor ; it may be learned, scientific, eloquent, highly poetic sin ; still it is sin, and, being that, has, in fact, the same radical or fundamental quality that, in its ranker and less restrained conditions, produce all the most hideous and revolting crimes of the world.

There is a very great difference, I admit, between a courteous man and one who is ill-natured and insulting, between a generous man and a niggard, a pure and a lewd, a man who lives in thought and a man who lives in appetite, a great and wise operator in the market and a thief ; and yet, taken as apart from all accidental modifications or degrees, the sin-quality or principle is exactly the same in all. As in water face answereth to face, so one class of hearts to the other. The respectable and the disgusting are twin brothers ; only you see in one how well he can be made to look, and in the other how both would look, if that which is in both were allowed to have its bent and work its own results unrestrained.

Again, fourthly, it is often true that what is looked upon as respectable sin is really more base in spirit, or internal quality, than that which is more and more universally despised. And yet this is not the judgment of those who are most apt to rule the judgments of the world. The lies of high life, for example, are the liberties asserted by power and respectable audacity. The lies of commoners and humble persons are a fatal, irredeemable dishonour. The fashionable, who spurns the obligation of an honest debt, is only asserting the right and title of fashion; but the merchant or the tradesman who avoids the payment of his bond, loses his honour and becomes a knave. The conqueror who overruns and desolates a kingdom will be named with respect or admiration by history, when, probably enough, God will look upon him with as much greater abhorrence than if he had robbed a hen-roost, as his crime is bloodier and more afflictive to the good of the world. How very respectable those learned impostors the Scribes, and those sanctimonious extortioners the Pharisees! How base those knavish tax-gatherers and sinners in low life! But Christ, who respected not the appearance, but judged righteous judgment, had a different opinion. It is not the show of a sin, my friends, which makes it base, but it is its interior quality—what it is in motive, feeling, thought. It is the gloat of inward passion, the stringent pinch of meanness, the foulness of inward desire and conception, the fire of inward malignity, the rot of lust and hypocrisy. It is not for me, as public inspector of sins, to pass on their relative quality, or fix the brand of their degree. I will only say that the outwardly-respectable look of them is no good test of their quality; leaving it, as a question between you and your God, whether, if all the inward shapes of your thought, motive, feeling, desire, and passion were brought out into the open sight of this community, and all the false and factitious rules of judgment accepted by us were swept away, it might not possibly appear that there are characters here, in this very respectable assembly, as base in real demerit as many that are classed among the outcasts of the town.

It is obvious, fifthly, that what I am calling respectable sin is commonly more inexcusable — not always, but commonly. Sometimes the most depraved and abandoned characters are those who have cast themselves down, by their perversity, from the highest standing of privilege. But, however this may be, it cannot be denied that the depraved and abject classes of society have, to a great extent, been trained up to the very life they lead; to be idle and beg, to be cunning, sharp, predatory, in one way or another, thieves; to look upon the base pleasures of self-indulgence and appetite as the highest rewards of existence. They are ignorant by right of their origin, brutal in manners and feeling, accustomed only to what is lowest in the possible range of human character. Sometimes, alas! the real want of bread has made them desperate. I will not become the sponsor of their crime; enough that they are criminal, and consciously so. But who is there of you that does not pity their hard lot? who of you that, considering their most sad history, is not often more ready to weep over than to judge them? Is it incredible to you that, in your own respectable and decent life of sin, taken as related to your high advantages, there may even be a degree of criminality, which, as God estimates crime, is far more inexcusable than that for which many are doomed to suffer the severest and most ignominious penalties of public law?

I add a single consideration further—viz., that respectable sin is more injurious, or a greater mischief, than the baser and more disgusting forms of vicious abandonment. The latter create for us greater public burdens, in the way of charity and taxation for the poor, and of judicial proceedings and punishments for public malefactors. They annoy us more, too, by their miseries and the crimes by which they disturb the security and peace of society. And yet it is really a fair subject of doubt, whether, in a moral point of view, they have not a wholesome influence and are not a social benefit. They tempt no one. Contrary to this, they repel and warn away from vice every one that looks upon them. They hang out a flag of distress upon every shoal of temptation. They shew us the last results of all sin, and the colours in which they exhibit sin are always disgusting, never attractive. In this view they are really one of the moral wants of the world. We should never conceive the inherent baseness of sin, if it were not shewn by their experiment; revealed in their delirium, their rags, their bloated faces, and bleared eyes and tottering bodies, and, more than all, in the extinction of their human feeling, and the substitution of a habit or type of being so essentially brutal. We look down into this hell that vice opens, and with a shudder turn away! Meantime, respectable sin,—how attractive, how fascinating its pleasures. Its gay hours, its shows and equipages, its courteous society, its entertainments, its surroundings of courtly form and incident —how delicious to the inspection of fancy. Even its excesses seem to be only a name for spirit. The places of temptation, too, are not the hells and brothels, but the saloons of pleasure and elegant dissipation. Vice is the daughter of pleasure; all

unrespectable sin the daughter of respectable. Nay, if we go
to the bottom, church-going sin is the most plausible form of
sin that was ever invented, and, in that view, the most dangerous. For, if a man never goes to the place of worship, we take
his sin with a warning, or at least with some little sense of
caution; but, if he is regular at church, a respectful hearer of
the Word, a sober, correct, thoughtful man, still, (though never
a Christian,) a safe, successful, always respected, never-faltering
character—then how many will be ready to imagine that there
is one form of sin that is about as good as piety itself, and
possibly even better than piety. And so this church-going sin
gives countenance and courage to all other—all the better and
more effective countenance because no such thing is intended.
There is, in short, no such thing as taking away the evil of sin
by making it respectable. Make it even virtuous, as men speak,
and it will only be the worse in its power as regards the entice-
ments it offers to evil. It will not shock any one by deeds of
robbery and murder, it will not revolt any one by its disgusting
spectacles of shame and misery, but how many will it encourage
and shield in just that rejection of God which is to be their
bitter fall and their eternal overthrow.

It is scarcely possible, in closing this very serious subject, to
name and duly set forth all the applications of which it is
capable, or which it even presses on our attention.
With how little reason, for example, are Christian people,
and indeed all others, cowed by the mere name and standing of
men who are living still under the power of sin, and resisting or
neglecting still the grace of their salvation. Doubtless, it is
well enough to look on them with respect and treat them with
a just deference, but however high they may seem, allow them
never to overtop your pity. For what is the fair show they
make but a most sorrowful appeal to your compassions and
your prayers? How can a true Christian, one who is consciously ennobled by the glorious heirship in which he is set,
ever be intimidated, or awed, or kept back in his approaches
or his prayers by respect to that which is only respectable sin?
If he goes to God, entering even into the holiest with boldness,
how much more will he be able to stand before these princes of
name, and title, and power, and speak to them of Christ and

His great salvation. To falter in this boldness, brethren, is even a great wrong to our Master's gospel, which puts us, even the humblest of us, in a higher plane of dignity, far, far above any most honoured sinner of mankind.

Again, it is impossible, in such a subject as this, not to raise the question of morality—what it is, and is worth, and where it will land us in the great allotments of eternity. Morality, taken as apart from religion, is but another name for decency in sin. It is just that negative species of virtue which consists in not doing what is scandalously depraved or wicked. But there is no heart of holy principle in it any more than there is in the worst of felonies. It is the very same thing as respects the denial of God, or the state of personal separation from God, that distinguishes all the most reprobate forms of character. A correct, outwardly virtuous man is the principle of sin well dressed and respectably kept—nothing more. And will that save you? You can, I am sure, be in no great danger of believing that. A far greater danger is that the decent, outwardly respectable manner of your sin will keep you from the discovery of its real nature as a root of character in you. If we undertake to set forth the inherent weakness and baseness of sin, to open up the vile and disgustful qualities which make it, as the Scriptures declare, abominable and hateful to God ; if we speak of its poisonous and bitter effects within, and the inevitable and awful bondage it works in all the powers of choice and character, who of you can believe what we say? Such representations you will think, if you do not openly say, partake of extravagance. What can you know of sin, what can you feel of your deep spiritual need when you are living so respectably and maintain, in the outward life, a show of so great integrity and even so much of refinement often in what is called virtue? True conviction of sin, how difficult is it, when its appearances and modes of life are so fair, when it twines itself so cunningly about, or creeps so insidiously into our amiable qualities, and sets off its internal disorders by so many outward charms and attractions !

If, then, we are right in this estimate of morality and the very great dangers involved in it, how necessary is it, for a similar reason, that every man out of Christ, not living in any vicious practice, should set himself to the deliberate canvassing of his own moral state. Make a study of this subtle, cunningly veiled character, the state of reputable sin, and study it long enough to fathom its real import. Look into the secret motives and springs of your character; inspect and study long enough really to perceive the strange, wild current of your thoughts; detect the subtle canker in your feeling; comprehend the deep ferment of your lusts, enmities, and passions; hunt down the selfish principle which instigates, and misdirects, and turns off your whole life from God, setting all your aims on issues that reject Him; ask, in a word, how this respectable sin appears when viewed inwardly; how, if unrestrained by pride, and the conventional rules of decency and character, it would appear outwardly. Fathom the deep hunger of your soul, and listen to its inward wail of bondage, its mournful, unuttered cry of want after God. Ask it of the enlightening Spirit of God, that He will open to your view yourself, and make you know all that is inmost, deepest, most hidden, in the habitually veiled deformity of your sin. Make it your prayer even to God, " Search me, O God, and try me !"

You have a motive also in making this inquest that is even more pressing than many of you will suspect. For no matter how respectable your sin is, you never can tell where it will carry you, how long it will be respectable, or where it will end. Enough to know that it is sin, and that the principle of all sin is one and the same. In its very germ you have, potentially, whatever is abhorrent, abominable, disgusting; and when the fruit is ripe, no man can guess into what shape of debasement and moral infamy, or public crime, it may finally bring him. If he hears of a murder, like that of Webster, for example, he may be very confident that, in his particular and particularly virtuous case of unreligious living, there is no liability to any such result. And perhaps there is not. Perhaps the danger is different. Avoiding what is bloody, he may fall into what is false or low— some damning dishonesty or fraud, some violation of trust, some falsification of accounts, some debauchery of lust or appetite, some brutality which makes his very name and person a disgust. Sin works by no set methods. It has a way of ruin for every man that is original and proper only to himself. Suffice it to say that, as long as you are in it and under its power, you can never tell what you are in danger of. This one thing you may have as a truth eternally fixed, that respectable sin is, in principle, the mother of all basest crime. Follow it on to the bitter end and there is ignominy eternal. There is a law of retribution that keeps it company, and is never parted from it ; by which law the end is being shaped and the hideous result prepared. If the delicate, pretentious, always correct sinner keeps to his decency here, the proper end will shew itself hereafter, and then it will be seen how dark, after all, how deep in criminality, how bronzed in guilty thought, is every soul becoming under even the fairest shows of virtue, coupled with neglect of God, and separated from His personal love.

Advancing now a stage, observe, again, that it is on just this view of the world and of human character under sin, that the whole superstructure of Christianity is based. Christ comes forth to the world as a lost world. He makes no distinction of respectable and unrespectable as regards the common want of salvation. Nay, it is plain, from His searching rebukes laid on the heads of the priests, the rulers, and others in high life, that He is sometimes moved with greatest abhorrence by the sin of those who are most respectable and even sanctimonious. Hence the solemn universality of His terms of salvation. Hence the declared impossibility of eternal life to any, save by the same great radical change of character—a fact which He testifies directly to Nicodemus, the conscientious inquirer after truth, the sober and just senator, one of the very highest, noblest men in the nation—"Except a man be born again, he cannot see the kingdom of God." He asks not how you appear, but whether you are human. Nay, if you come to Him, like the young ruler, clothed in all such comely virtues, that He is constrained to look on your ingenuous, conscientious character with love, He will tell you, when you ask Him what you are to do to have eternal life, that you must forsake all, and come and follow Him. Decency, correctness, praise—all these are but the guise of your sin, which guise He will tell you must be for ever

abandoned as a ground of confidence before God, and the sin
which it now only adorns and covers must be itself removed,
and for ever taken away by the blood of the Lamb.

Have I now in my audience any forlorn one, like the woman
of my text, any youth, or older person, who is consciously sinking into the toils of vice, and beginning to taste its bitter humiliations; any that has consciously lost or begun to lose the
condition of respect and reputable living; any that begins to
scorn himself, or seems to be sinking under the pitiless scorn
of the world's judgments?   To such a one I rejoice to say, in
the name of Jesus Christ, that there is no scorn with Him.
He does not measure sin by our conventional and often false
rules of judgment.   The basest sin He was even wont to find,
in many cases, under the finest covering of respect.   He will
judge you rightly, not harshly.   If you have fallen, or begun
to fall, He wants to raise you.   He offers you His free sympathy and support, and, if others lay their look of contempt
upon your soul, He invites you kindly, whispers love and
courage, and if you are ready to receive Him, waits also to
say—"Thou art mine; go, son; go, daughter; sin no more!"

Brethren professed in the name and gospel of our Lord Jesus
Christ, it is Him I follow, and not any want of charity I in-
dulge, when I remind you that a still more mournful application of this subject is possibly required.   What, alas! and apart
from all severity of judgment, is the profession of many disciples but a state of serious and reputable sin?   They are
virtuous persons, as that term is commonly used; good always
on the negative side of prudence and caution; they have no
vices; they bring no scandal on the cause of Christ by their
walk.   But to what does all this amount, if there be nothing
further and more positive to go with it?   Does the mere keeping out of vice and scandalous misdoing—does the exactest
possible life, in fact, if we speak only of its correctness, constitute a living and true piety?   What is it, even at the best, but
a reputable, or possibly a somewhat Christian-looking state of
sin?   The Pharisees and other religious persons of the Saviour's
time were abundantly and even sanctimoniously exact persons.
And yet the Saviour discovered in them, if we can judge from

the tone of His rebukes, the worst and most incurable type of moral abandonment. They had so little sense of holiness, and so little sympathy with it, that they were His bitterest enemies, and even became His betrayers and murderers. He saw all this beforehand, wrapped up in their character; their washings, sacrifices, long prayers, and scrupulous tithings did not conceal it. You certainly have no such ceremonies; you do not believe in them, but you have covenants, communions, baptisms, family altars. Have you, in company with these, and answering to these, the new man of love, created anew in Christ Jesus unto good works? If you have not, if you live a dumb, unpositive life, under the power of the world, selfish still as before, and self-pursuing; if the old man is not crucified, and the new man, Christ, is certainly not being formed within you, then your profession signifies nothing but the mere respectability of your sin. What is your supposed piety but this, if it have no spiritual and inwardly transforming power? Christ is redemption only as He actually redeems and delivers our nature from sin. If He is not the law and spring of a new spirit of life, He is nothing. Beware, let me say to you in Christ's name, "beware of the leaven of the Pharisees and Sadducees." The true principle, my brethren, is this; and if this will yield us no just title to the Christian name, what we call our piety is in honest truth nothing more or better than a decent shape of sin—"For as many as are led by the Spirit of God, they are the sons of God"—as many, no more. Are we so led? Do we so live?

To dismiss this subject without some prospective reference, or glance of forecast on the future, is impossible, however painful and appalling the contemplations it will raise. When you go to stand before God, my friends, it will not be your dress, or your house, or your titles, or your wealth, no, nor even your virtues, however much commended here, that will give you a title of entrance among the glorified. Respectable sin will not pass then and there as here. The honour, the nobility of it is now gone by. The degrees, indeed, of sin are many, but the kind is one, and that a poor, dejected, emptied form of shame and sorrow. How appalling such a thought to any one who is capable of thought, and not absolutely brutalised by his guilt!

Furthermore, as sin is sin everywhere and in all forms, the respectable and the unrespectable the same in principle, and when the appearances are different, the same often in criminality, the world of future retribution must, of course, be a world of strange companionships. We are expressly told, and it seems a matter of reason also to suppose, that the spirits of guilty men will not be assorted there by their tastes, but by their character and demerits. Death is the limit and end of all mere conventionalities. The fictitious assortments of the earthly state never pass that limit. Rank, caste, fashion, disgust, fastidiousness, delicacy of sin—these are able to draw their social lines no longer. Proximity now is held to the stern, impartial principle of inward demerit—"That all may receive according to the deeds done in the body." This is the level of adjustment, and there appears to be no other. The standing of the high priests, the Scribes, and Pharisees, and the forlorn woman of my text, may be inverted now, or they may all take rank together. And so also many of you, that are now pleasing yourselves in the dignity of your virtues, and the honours of your social standing, may fall there into group and gradation with such as now you even look away from with profoundest distaste or revulsion. The subject is painful; I will not pursue it. I will only remind you that where the lines of justice lead, there you must yourselves follow ; and if that just award of respectable sin yields you only the promise of a scale of companionships from which your soul recoils with disgust, there is no wisdom for you but to be as disgustful of the sin as of the companionships, and draw yourself at once to Him who is purity, and peace, and glory, and, in all, eternal life.

XVII

1 CORINTHIANS i. 24—" *Christ the power of God.*"

THE cross and Christ crucified are the subject here in hand. Accordingly, when Christ is called the power of God, we are to understand Christ crucified; and then the problem is to conceive how Christ, dying in the weakness of mortality, and exhibiting, just there, if we take Him as the incarnate manifestation of God, the humblest tokens of passibility and frailty, is yet and there, as being the crucified, the power of God.

At our present point, and without some preparation of thought, we can hardly state intelligibly, or with due force of assertion, the answer to such a question. The two elements appear to be incompatible, and we can only say that the power spoken of is not the efficient or physical, but the moral power of God that, namely, of His feeling and character. But as this will be no statement sufficiently clear to stand as the ruling proposition of a discourse, I will risk a departure from our custom, and, instead of drawing my subject formally from my text, I will begin at a point external and draw, by stages, toward it; paying it, as I conceive, the greater honour, that I suppose it to be so rich and deep in its meaning, as to require and to reward the labour of a discourse, if simply we may apprehend the lesson it teaches.

Christ, then, the crucified, and so the power of God, this is our goal, let us see if we can reach it.

We take our point of departure at the question of passibility in God—is He a Being passible, or impassible?

It would seem to follow from the infinitude of His creatively-efficient power, and the immensity of His nature, that He is and must be impassible. There is, in fact, no power that is not in His hands. There are cases, it is true, where superiority in volume and physical force rather increases than diminishes passibility. Thus it is that man is subject to so great annoyance from the mere gnat; and the creature is able to inflict this inevitable suffering upon him, just because of his own atomic littleness. But there is no parallel in this for the relation of God to His creatures, or of theirs to Him, because they continue to exist only by His permission. Besides, He is spirit only, not a being that can be struck, or thrust upon, or any way violated by physical assault. What we call force, or physical power, cannot touch Him. And even if it could, He is probably incapable of suffering from it, as truly as even space itself. Like space, like eternity, He is, in His own nature, as spirit, essentially impassible—impassible, that is, as related to force.

But the inquiry is not ended when we reach this point, it is only begun. After all there must be some kind of passibleness in God, else there could be no genuine character in Him. If He could not be pained by anything, could not suffer any kind of wound, had no violable sympathy, He would be anything but a perfect character. A cast-iron Deity could not command our love and reverence. The beauty of God is that He has feeling, and feels appropriately toward everything done; that He feels badness as badness, and goodness as goodness—pained by one, pleased by the other. There must be so much or such kind of passibility in Him that He will feel toward everything as it is, and will be diversely affected by diverse things, according to their quality. If wickedness and wrong stirred nothing in Him different from what is stirred by a prayer, if He felt no disaffection toward a thief which He does not feel toward a martyr, no pleasure in a martyr faithful unto death which He does not in His persecutors, He would be a kind of no-character. We can hardly conceive such a being.

A very large share of all the virtues have, in fact, an element of passivity, or passibility in them, and without that element they could not exist. Indeed the greatness and power of character culminate in the right proportion and co-ordination of these passive elements. And just here it is, we shall see, that even God's perfection culminates. He is great as being great in feeling.

We raise a distinction, as among ourselves, between what we call the active and the passive virtues. Not that all virtues are not equally active, in the sense of being voluntary, or free, but that in some of them we communicate, and in some of them receive action. If I impart a charity, that is my active virtue; if I receive an insult without revenging, or wishing to revenge it, that is my passive virtue. All the wrong acts done us, and also all the good, are occasions of some appropriate, proportionate, and really great feeling, which is our passive virtue. And without this passive virtue in its varieties, we should be only no-characters, dry logs of wood instead of Christian men. Or, if we kept on acting still, we should be only active machines, equally dry as wood, and only making more of noise; for what better is the active giving of a charity if there be no fellow-feeling or pitying passion with it to make it a charity?

Now God must have these passive virtues as truly as men. They are the necessary soul of all greatness in Him. How, then, shall we conceive Him to have them and to have His sublime perfection culminate in them, when He is, in fact, impassible?

This brings us to the true point of our question. We discover, first, that God is and must be physically impassible. We discover, next, that He ought to feel appropriately to all kinds of action, and must have, in order to His real greatness in character, all the passive virtues. He must in one view be impassible and in some other passible, infinitely passible. And how is this, where is the solution?

It is here; that God, being physically impassible, impassible as relates to violating force, is yet morally passible. That is, He is a Being whose very perfection it is that He feels the moral significance of things, receives all actions according to their moral import, whether as done to Himself, or by one created being to another. In this latter sense, He feels actions intensely according to the moral delicacy of His nature, deeply according to the depth of His nature. In this point of view, He is just because He is perfect and infinite, infinitely passible. He has just that sense of things which infinite holiness must have—loves the tears of repentance in His child just as infinite mercy must—turns away from all wrong as profoundly revolted by it, as His infinite, eternal chastity must be.

It will be seen at once, that God can receive the sense of actions morally, in this manner, when they cannot touch Him as force or physically. He can feel ingratitude when He cannot feel a blow. He can loathe impurity, when He cannot be injured by any assault. He can be sore displeased by the cruelty of man to his fellow, when He could not suffer the cruelty Himself. He is pleased and gratified by acts of sacrifice, when He could not be comforted or enriched by the ministries of benevolence. All acts affect Him just according to their quality. A thermometer is not more exactly and delicately passive to heat, than He is to the merit and demerit of all actions. So, as regards what lies in character and pertains in that way to spirit, He is the most intensely passible of all beings, and has it for His merit that He is.

This, accordingly, is the representation given of Him in the Scriptures, or, as it will more assist my subject to say, in the Old Testament Scriptures. Thus He is blessed, or said to be, in all the varieties of agreeable affection, according to the merit and beauty of whatever is done that is right. He smelled a sweet savour, we are told, in Noah's sacrifice. He has pleasure in them that hope in His mercy. He is affected with joy over His people, as a prophet represents, even to singing, in the day of their restored peace. He is tender in His feeling to the obedient, pitying them that fear Him as a father pitieth his children. His very love is partly passive; that is, it is a being affected with complacency by those who are in the truth, and a being affected with compassion by the bitter and hard lot of those under sin. On the other hand, by how many unpleasant varieties or pains of feeling does He profess to suffer, in His relation to scenes of human wrong, ingratitude and disgusting baseness. The sighing of the prisoner comes before Him to command His sympathy. He calls after His people as a woman forsaken and grieved in spirit. He testifies, " I am pressed under you as a cart is pressed that is full of sheaves." His repentings are kindled together in view of the sins of His people. In all the afflictions of His people He is afflicted Himself. And, in the same manner, He is said to be exercised by all manner of disagreeable and unpleasant sentiments in relation to all manner of evil doings ; displeased, sore displeased, wroth, angry, loathing, abhorring, despising, hating, weary, filled with abomination, wounded, hurt, grieved; and even protests, like one sorrowing, that He could do nothing more for His vineyard that He has not done in it. There is, in short, no end to the variety of unhappy or disagreeable sentiments that must be excited in God's breast of infinite purity by the various complexities of guilt, wrong, shame, and loathsomeness, that are blended in the societies and scenes of our fallen world. If God could look on these things without disgust and abhorrence He would not be God. He would want all that is most amiable, freshest, most delicate, purest in love, everything that most commends Him to our reverence.

But these movings of disgust and abhorrence, all these sentiments that put Him in a just relation with evil, are painful. Simply to say that one is displeased is to say that he is disagreeably affected; or merely to say that one dislikes a character is to allege that he is unpleasantly affected by it. What, then, shall we think of God, when all these varieties of displeasure and dislike must as certainly be living experiences in Him as He is a holy and a living God? So far He is a Being subject to pain by reason of His very perfections. Nay, His pains do themselves enter into and make up a consubstantial part of His perfections.

And what is this, some will ask, but to assume the unhappiness, or, at least, the diminished happiness, of God. Is, then, God unhappy? Is He less than infinitely blessed? Pressed by this difficulty, it has been the manner of many teachers to fall back on the physical impassibility of God, imagining that there, at that fixed point, the true solution must begin. God, they say, is impassible. We are, therefore, to understand that, in all these Scripture expressions, these abhorrings, loathings, hatings, displeasures, angers, wearinesses, indignations, and the like, the Bible is only speaking of God after the manner of men. Yes, but supposing it to speak thus, what does it mean? Does it mean nothing? When it declares that God abominates sin, does it mean that He has no feeling at all in respect to it? Does it mean that He has a pleasant or pleased feeling? Neither; we mock the dignity of Scripture, nay, we mock the beauty itself of God, when we turn away, in this manner, all credit of right feeling and true rationality in Him.   No, this is what we mean : we mean, if we understand ourselves, that the figures in question are transferred from human uses and applied to God ; and that, when so applied, they express something true concerning God—viz., the great fact that God has the same kind of displeased, disaffected, abhorrent, and revolted feeling toward sin as the purest and holiest man has, only it is God's feeling, in God's measures, and according to God's purity, that His disgust is deep as the sea, that His indignation is a storm vast as the world, that His whole infinitude is moved with dislike, distaste, disgust, offended purity, abhorrence, and revolted love.   It would even be a a discredit to God to suppose anything less.

And so we come back on the difficulty, a hundredfold increased, and we ask again, how shall we save the infinite blessedness of God ?   By just dropping out our calculations of arithmetic, I answer, and looking at facts.   It seems to be good arithmetic and logically inevitable that, if any subtraction is made from God's infinite happiness, He cannot be infinitely happy.   No, it is not inevitable.   On the contary, He may even be the more blessed because of the subtraction, for to see that He feels rightly toward evil, despite of the pain suffered from it, to be conscious of long-suffering and patience toward it, to know that He is pouring, and ever has been, the fulness of His love upon it, to be studying now, in conscious sacrifice, a saving mercy—out of this springs up a joy deeper and more sovereign than the pain, and, by a fixed law of holy compensation, the sea of His blessedness is kept continually full.   All moral natures exist under this law of compensation; so that every being is made more blessed in all the passive virtues.   To receive evil rightly is to master it, to be rightly pained by it is to be kept in sovereign joy.   To suffer well is bliss and victory.

Probably no one ever thought of compassion as being any thing less than a joy, a holy bliss of feeling.   And yet it is *co-passion*.   It suffers with its objects, takes their burdens, struggles with their sorrows—all which is pain, a loss of happiness. Still it is no loss, because there is another element in the conscious greatness of the loss, and the man is even raised in order by the inward exaltation he feels.   So in respect to pity, long-suffering, patience with evil, and meekness under wrong. They have all a side of loss, and yet they are the noblest augmentations of blessedness. There is a law of moral compensation in them all, by which their suffering is married to inevitable joy.

Nor is this fact of compensation wholly confined to moral actions; a similar return keeps company with loss, and is expected to do so in other matters. The hearer of a tragedy, for example, goes to be afflicted, to have his soul harrowed and torn, that in so deep excitement he may feel the depth of his nature, and be exalted in the powerful surging of its waves. He suffers a great subtraction, but no diminution.

We need not, therefore, be troubled or concerned for God's happiness, because He feels toward evil, and with all His feeling, exactly as He should. That, if only we can drop the stupid computations of arithmetic, and look into the living order of mind, or spirit, is the sublimity even of His blessedness, as it is the necessary grace of His perfection.

Thus far I have spoken of God's passive virtue, principally as concerned in feeling toward what is moral, just according to its quality; in being affected pleasantly or disagreeably according to the good or evil of what He looks upon. But there is a moral passivity in all perfect character that is vastly higher than this and reaches further—viz., a passivity of mercy or sacrifice. In this a good or perfect being not only feels toward good or evil according to what it is, but willingly endures evil, or submits to its bad quality and action to make it what it is not—to recover and heal it. No extraordinary purity is necessary to make any one sensible of disaffection, or disgust, or pain, in the contemplation of what is vile and wicked; but to submit one's ease and even one's personal comfort and pleasure to the endurance of wickedness, in order to recover and subdue it, requires what is far more difficult. I can be disgusted easily enough by the ingratitude, offended by the treachery, wounded by the wrongs of an enemy; but to bear that enemy, and put myself in the way of receiving more injury in order to regain his friendship and restore him to a right feeling is quite another matter. I am never perfect in my relation to him till I can. All perfect virtue will do this; and none is perfect but this, whether in man, or in angel, or in God.

Just here, then, we begin to open upon the true meaning of my text, "Christ the power of God." There is no so great power even among men, as this of which I now speak. It conquers evil by enduring evil. It takes the rage of its enemy and lets him break his malignity across the enduring meekness of its violated love. Just here it is that evil becomes insupportable to itself. It can argue against everything but suffering patience, this disarms it. Looking in the face of suffering patience, it sinks exhausted. All its fire is spent.

In this view it is that Christ crucified is the power of God. It is because He shews God in self-sacrifice, because He brings out and makes historical in the world God's passive virtue, which is, in fact, the culminating head of power in His character. By this it is that He opens our human feeling, bad and blind as it is, pouring Himself into its deepest recesses and bathing it with His cleansing, new-creating influence. There is even a kind of efficiency in it, and that the highest—viz., moral efficiency; for it is moral power, not physical, not force. It is that kind of power which feeling has to impregnate feeling, that which one person has in good, to melt himself into and assimilate another in evil. Hence it is that so much is said of Christ as a new-discovered power—the power of God unto salvation; the Son of God with power; the power of Christ; Christ the power of God and the wisdom of God. The power spoken of here is conceived to be such that Christ is really our new Creator. We are His workmanship created unto good works; new creatures therefore in Him, transformed radically by our faith in Him, passed from death unto life, born of God, renewed in the spirit of our mind, created after God in righteousness and true holiness. All the figures of cleansing, sprinkling, washing, healing, purging, terminate in the same thing, the new creating efficacy of Christ the power of God. It is the power of character, feeling, a right passivity, a culminating grace of sacrifice in God.

But how does it appear that any so great efficacy is added to the known character of God by the life and death of Christ? Was not everything shewn us in His death explicitly revealed, or in language formally ascribed to God, by the writers of the Old Testament? God, I have already shewn, was certainly represented there as being duly affected by all evil; that is, He was shewn to be affected according to its true nature ; displeased, abhorrent, hurt, afflicted, offended in purity, burdened with grief and compassion.   But to have these things said, or ascribed formally to God, is one thing, and a very different to have them lived and acted historically in the world.   Perfections that are set before us in mere epithets have little significance, no significance but that which we give them by thinking them out.   But perfections lived, embodied physically, and acted before the senses, under social conditions, have quite another grade of meaning.   How much, then, does it signify when God comes out from nature, out of all abstractions and abstractive epithets, to be acted personally in just those glorious and Divine passivities that we have least discerned in Him and scarcely dare impute to Him.   By what other method can He meet us, then, so entirely new and superior to all past revelations, as to come into our world-history in the human form ; that organ most eloquent in its passivity, because it is at once most expressive and closest to our feeling ?

And if this be true respecting God's mere passivities of sensibility to right and wrong, how much truer is it, when we speak of Him in sacrifice.   No such impression or conception of God was ever drawn out, as a truth positive, from any of the epithets we have cited.   And what we call nature gives it no complexion of evidence.   Nature represents inexorable force, a God omnipotent, self-centred, majestic, infinite, and, as almost any one will judge, impassible.   Such are the impressions it gives, and it encourages no other.   We could almost as soon look for sacrifice in a steam-engine as in nature.   The only hint of possible relaxation we get from it is that which we borrow from the delay of punishment ; for this one thing is clear, that justice here is not done, and therefore we may guess that other ideas enter into God's plans.   So strongly opposite, therefore, is nature to any conception of flexibility in God, that we are continually put away from Christianity by its suggestions.   So closely holden are we by its power, that God, as in sacrifice, appears to be quite inconceivable to many of us, even though we look on the passion of the Lord Jesus itself.

To know Him thus we therefore need the more.   If the Old Testament gives us only verbal epithets concerning God, and nature sets us off from the conception of any real passivity in

these, how necessary, original, powerful is the God of sacrifice—
He that endures evil and takes it as a burden to bear—when
we see Him struggling under the load. And if still we cannot
believe, if we reduce our God in speculation still to a dry, un-
moving, negative perfection which escapes suffering by feeling
nothing as it is, only the more wonderful is the Power that can
be a power so great upon us when obstructed by such unbelief.
Still the fact is fact; the Christ has lived. His great and
mighty passion has entered into the world, and we do get impressions from it, even when we are shutting its most central
truth away. Somewhere still there is (how often do we say it?)
a wondrous power hid in the Cross! It penetrates our deepest
nature; and when our notional wisdoms are, at some time, left
behind—when we are merely holding the historic fact in practical trust unexplained—nothing meets our feeling so well as to
call it the great mystery of godliness. We do it because we
feel a somewhat in it more than we can reason out of it;
because it penetrates and works in our deepest nature with a
wondrous incomprehensible efficacy.

But in all this we are supposing that Christ suffered, and
that He is indeed the incarnate Word of God's eternity—God
manifest in the flesh. And the suffering is, by the supposition,
physical—a suffering under force. If, then, God is in His very
nature physically impassible, as we have said, how does it
appear that He is any way expressed in the passion of Christ?
how does the passion present Him as in sacrifice? Ah! that is
a difficulty! I confess, in all humility, that I cannot reason it.
I can only so far answer as to make out a case for faith, unob-
structed by the veto of reason.

And, first of all, it is not asserted, when we assert the physical impassibility of God, that He cannot suffer by consent or
self-subjection, but only that He cannot be subjected involun-
tarily. We know nothing of the liberty possessed by the
Divine nature to exist under assumed conditions whenever
there are any sufficient reasons for so doing. To deny that
God has such kind of liberty in the Word might even be a
greater infringement of His power than to maintain His natural
passibility.

In the next place, we can clearly enough see that there is no difficulty in the passion of Christ which does not also exist in the incarnation itself. It is indeed the incarnation or one of the included incidents. And the incarnation is, by the supposition, a fact abnormal, inconceivable, speculatively impossible. How can the Infinite Being God exist under finite conditions? How can the All-Present be localised? How (for that is only another form of the same question) can the impassible suffer? And yet it would be a most severe assumption to say that God cannot, to express Himself and forward His negotiation with sin, subject Himself, in some way mysteriously qualified, to just these impossible conditions.

Be this all as it may, there are ways of knowing and perceiving that are shorter and, in many things, wiser than the processes of the head. In this passion of Jesus it must be enough that I look on the travail of a Divine feeling, and behold the spectacle of God in sacrifice. This I see and nothing less. He is visibly not a man. His character is not of this world. I feel a divinity in Him. He floods me with a sense of God, such as I receive not from all God's works and worlds beside. And when I stand by His cross, when I look on that strong passion, and shudder with the shuddering earth and darken with the darkening sun, enough that I can say, "My Lord and my God!" I ask no sanction of the head; I want no logical endorsement; enough that I can see the heart of God, and in all this wondrous passion know Him as enduring the contradiction of sinners. No matter if I cannot reason the mystery; no matter if the whole transaction is a doing of the impossible when so plainly the impossible is done!—when I have the irresistible verdict in me self-pronounced! Why should I debate the matter in my head when I have the God of sacrifice in my heart? I will give up my sins. He that endures me so, subdues me, and I yield. O thou Lamb of God, that takest away the sin of the world! what Thou didst bear in Thy blessed hands and feet I cannot bear. Take it all away. Hide me in the depths of Thy suffering love—mould me to the image of Thy Divine passion!

Here now, my friends, and at this point I close. Here let us learn to conceive more fitly the greatness of God. His greatness culminates in sacrifice. He is great because there is a moral passivity so great in His perfections. All which the cross of Jesus signifies was central, eternally in His majestic character. Nothing superlative is here displayed, nothing is done which adds so much as a trace to God's personal glories. All that is done is simply to express or produce in real evidence what His glories were from eternity. All that is discovered to us in the passion was in Him from eternity. The cross was the crown of His perfection before the worlds were made. He was such a Being as could feel toward evil and good according to what they are—such a Being, too, as could suffer an enemy, endure his wrong in royal magnanimity, and subdue him by His patience. Oh, if He were only wise, omnipotent—a great architect piling immensity full of His works—fixed in His eternity—strong in His justice—firm in His decrees—that were doubtless something; even that would present Him as an object worthy of profoundest reverence, but in the passion of Jesus He is more. There His power is force; here it is sacrifice. There He creates by His fiat; here He new-creates by the revelation of sacrifice. There He astonishes the eye; here He touches and transforms the heart. Is it wrong to say that here is the summit of His greatness? Were He, then, the mere ideal that figures in our new literature; some great no-person; some vast To PAN sleeping back of the stars; some clear fluid of impersonal reason, in which both we and the stars are floating, having neither will nor feeling—a form of stolidity made infinite—would He be a greater Being, more admirable, warmer to our love, and worthier to be had in reverence? Oh, these great possibilities! this sorrowing love! this enduring patience that bears the sins of the world! He that groans in the agony, He that thirsts on the cross, this is the real and true—the Lord He is the God! the Lord He is the God! The God of mere amplitude will do to amuse the fancy of the ingenious—the God of sacrifice only can approve Himself to a sinner.

And here it is that our gospel comes to be so great a power. It is not, on one hand, the power of omnipotence, or of a naked, ictic force, falling in secretly regenerative blows, like a slung shot in the night. Neither is it, on the other hand, any mere appeal of gratitude, or newly-impressed obligation, drawing the soul to God by the consideration of what He has done, in the cross, to purchase a free remission. Bonds of gratitude, alas! have never been so great a power on human souls. And how does it appear that any such bond has been even admitted, when as yet the remission itself is rejected, and the want of it unfelt? No; this power, this wonderful power! is God in sacrifice. It is measured, and expressed, and incorporated in the historic life of the world as a power new-creative in the passion of Jesus, the incarnate Word of God; for it is here that God pours out into the world's bosom His otherwise transcendent perfections, and opens, even to sight, the otherwise inaccessible glories of His love. It is even the official work, therefore, and mission of the Holy Spirit to be Christ in men, taking the things of Christ's passion and shewing them unto men's hearts; for Christ himself is, in His sacrifice, the mighty power of God. This is the power that has new-created and sent home, as trophies, in all the past ages, its uncounted myriads of believing, new-created, glorified souls; the power that established, propagates, perpetuates, a kingdom; the power that has tamed how much of enmity, dissolved how many times the rock of obstinacy, cleansed, purified, restored to heaven's order, comforted in heaven's peace how many guilty, otherwise despairing souls. It can do for you, O sinner of mankind! all that you want done. It can regenerate your habits, settle your disorders, glorify your baseness, and assimilate you perfectly to God. This it will do for you. Go to the cross, and meet there God in sacrifice. Behold Him, as Jesus, bearing your sin, receiving the shafts of your enmity! Embrace Him, believe in Him, take Him to your inmost heart. Do this, and you shall feel sin die within you, and a glorious quickening— Christ the power of God, Christ in you the hope of glory—shall be consciously risen upon you, as the morn of your new creation.

And you, my brethren, that have known this dawning of the Lord, what a certification have you, in this sacrifice, of God's sympathy! How intensely personal is He to you! Go to Him in your every trouble. Go to Him most confidently in all the troubles of your inward shame, and the struggles even of your defeated hope. When the loads of conscious sin are heaviest on you, and you seem even to be sinking in its mires, address Him as the God of sacrifice. Have it also as your lesson, that you yourself will be most in power when readiest in the enduring of evil; that you will bear fruit and be strong, not by your force, not by your address, not by your words, but only when you are with Christ in sacrifice. Strange that any one who has ever once felt the power of God in Christ, should, for so much as a moment, miss or fall out of this glorious truth. It comes of that delusion of our selfishness, which is, in fact, a second nature in us,—the seeing only weakness in patience, and loss in sacrifice. But if God's own might and blessing are in it, so also are yours. Look for power, look for the fulness of joy where Christ himself reveals it. Take His cross, that same which He brought forth out of the bosom of God's eternal perfections, and go back with Him in it, to be glorified with Him in the height of His beatitude.

XVIII.

DUTY NOT MEASURED BY OUR OWN ABILITY.

LUKE ix. 13—"*But He said unto them, Give ye them to eat.*"

WHEN Christ lays it thus upon His disciples, in that solitary and desert place, to feed five thousand men, He cannot be ignorant of the utter impossibility that they should do it. And when they reply that they have only five loaves and two fishes, though the answer is plainly sufficient, He is nowise diverted from His course by it, but presses directly on in the new order that they make the people sit down by fifties in a company, and be ready for the proposed repast. Debating in themselves, probably, what can be the use of such a proceeding, when really there is no supply of food to be distributed, they still execute His order. And then when all is made ready, He calls for the five loaves and two fishes, and, having blessed them, begins to break, and says to them, "Distribute." Marvellous loaves! broken, they are not diminished! distributed, they still remain! And so returning, again and again, to replenish their baskets, they continue the distribution, till the hungry multitude are all satisfied as in a full supply. In this manner the original command—"Give ye them to eat"—is executed to the letter. They have made the people sit down, they have brought the loaves, they have distributed, and He at every step has justified His order, by making their scanty stock as good as a full supply.

This narrative suggests and illustrates the following important principle—

That men are often, and properly, put under obligation to do that for which they have, in themselves, no present ability.

This principle I advance, not as questioning the truth that ability, being necessary to an act, is necessary to complete obligation toward the same, but as believing and designing to

shew that God has made provision, in very many things, for
the coming in upon the subject of ability, as he goes forward
to execute the duties incumbent on him.   God requires no
man to do, without ability to do ; but He does not limit His
requirement by the measures of previous or inherently contained ability.   In many, or even in a majority of cases, the
endowment of power is to come after the obligation, occurring,
step by step, as the exigencies demand.   Of what benefit is it
that the subject have a complete ability in himself, provided he
only has it where and when it is wanted?   When, therefore, I
maintain that men are often required to do that for which they
have no present ability in themselves, I do it in the conviction
that God has made provision, in many ways, for the enlargement of our means and powers so as to meet our emergencies.
And He does this, we shall see, on a large scale, and by system
—does it in the natural life, and also in the works and experiences of the life of faith.

Thus, to begin at the very lowest point of the subject, it is the
nature of human strength and fortitude bodily to have an elastic
measure, and to be so let forth or extended as to meet the exigencies that arise.   Within certain limits, for man is limited in
everything, the body gets the strength it wants, in the exercise
for which it is wanted.   The body is not like mechanical tools
and engines, which never acquire any degree of strength by use
and the strain to which they are put, but rather begin to fail as
they begin to be used ; but it gains power for exertion by exertion, and sustains its competency in the same way.   It is able
to endure and conquer, because it has endured and conquered.
God, therefore, may fitly call a given man to a course of life that
requires much robustness and a high power of physical endurance, on the ground that when he is fully embarked in his calling, the robustness will come, or will be developed in it and by
means of it, though previously it seemed not to exist.   Indeed
the physical imbecility of some men will be the great crime of
their life, and they will be held answerable for it, on the simple
ground that they had too little courage and were too self-in-
dulgent to throw themselves on any such undertaking as a true
Christian manliness required.

There is yet another law pertaining to bodily capacity, which
is more remarkable—viz., that muscular strength and endurance

are often suddenly created or supplied by some great emergency for which they are wanted. What feats of giant strength have been performed under the stimulus of danger, or some impulse of humanity or affection. What sufferings have men supported in prisons, in deserts, on the ocean, sustained by hope, or nerved by despair. When the occasion is passed, and the man looks back upon the scene, how impossible does it seem that he should ever have done or suffered such things. It is indeed impossible to do it now. But then it was possible, in virtue of a great appointment of nature and Providence, by which the very occasions to be met shall so excite the nerves of action as to give us power to meet them. They do it suddenly and just for the time. In an instant, they endue us with what appears to ourselves to be preternatural strength; and when the great exigency is over, vanquished by the very powers it has itself supplied, we sit down to rejoice in a tremor of weakness.

So also it is the nature of courage to increase in the midst of perils and because of them, and courage is the strength of the heart. Often does the coward even become a hero by the accident of condition. How a man is able, not seldom, to proceed with firmness and heroic self-possession, when thrown amid difficult and perilous exposures or conflicts, who by no effort of courage could bring himself to engage in them, is well understood. Nor is it anything strange for a woman, in some terrible and sudden crisis, to be nerved with firmness and dauntless self-possession, then even to faint with terror when the crisis is past.

Intellectual force, too, has the same elastic quality, and measures itself in the same way, by the exigencies we are called to meet. Task it, and, for that very reason, it grows efficient. Plunge it into darkness, and it makes a sphere of light. It discovers its own force by the exertion of force, measures its capacity by the difficulties it has overcome, its appetite for labour by the labour it has endured. So that here again, as in respect to the body, a man may have it laid upon him to be forward in some greatest call of duty, when as yet he seems to have no capacity for it; on the ground that his capacity will so be unfolded as to meet the measures of his undertaking. How many persons who thought they had no ability to teach a class of youth in the Scriptures have gotten their ability by doing it.

And just so all great commanders, statesmen, lawgivers, scholars, preachers, have found the powers unfolded in their calling, and by it, which were necessary for it.

Here, too, great occasions beget great powers, and prepare the man to astonishing, almost preternatural, acts of mental energy. In great occasions, when a principle, or a kingdom, or some holy cause of heaven is at stake, an inspiration seizes him that fires the imagination, swells the high emotions, exalts and glorifies the will, and sends the spirit of the living creatures into every wheel of the mind before inert and lifeless. Thus electrified and penetrated by the great necessity, it becomes ethereal, rapid, clear, a fire of energy, a resistless power. What reasonings, what bursts of eloquence, what living words of flame, does it send forth to kindle and glow in the world's history for generations and ages to come.

The same also is true, quite as remarkably, of what we sometimes call moral power. By this we mean the power of a life and a character, the power of good and great purposes, that power which comes at length to reside in a man distinguished in some course of estimable or great conduct. It is often this which dignifies the great senator, so as to make even his common words, words of grave wisdom, cr perchance of high eloquence. It is this which gives a power so mysterious often to the preacher of Christ, such a power, that even his presence in any place will begin to disturb the conscience of many, even before they have heard him. No other power of man compares with this, and there is no individual who may not be measurably invested with it. Integrity, purity, goodness, success of any kind in the humblest persons, or the lowest walks of duty, begin to invest them finally with a character, and create a certain sense of momentum in them. Other men expect them to get on, because they are getting on, and bring them a repute that sets them forward, give them a salute that means—success. This kind of power is neither a natural gift nor properly an acquisition, but it comes in upon one and settles on him like a crown of glory, while discharging with fidelity his duties to God and man. It is a power contributed silently by others, a throne built for the victor, an eminence appointed him by the world. When contemplated in this light, how marked is the provision of God for letting down power upon a man who will act his part well. The world comes to him, of its own accord, to exalt him with its tributary breath.

And here again, also, it is to be noted that the power in question, this moral power, is often suddenly enlarged by the very occasions that call for it. Not seldom is it a fact that the very difficulty and grandeur of a design, which some heroic soul has undertaken to execute, exalts him at once to such a pre-eminence of moral power that mankind are exalted with him, and inspired with energy and confidence by the contemplation of his magnificent spirit. How often, indeed, is a man able to carry a project simply because he has made it so grand a project. He strikes, inspires, calls to his aid, by virtue of his great idea, his faith, his sublime confidence in truth, or justice, or duty.

It is only a part, or rather a generalisation of the truths already illustrated, that the great and successful men of history are commonly made by the great occasions they fill. They are the men who had faith to meet such occasions, and therefore the occasions marked them, called them to come and be what the successes of their faith would make them. The boy is but a shepherd, but he hears from his panic-stricken countrymen of the giant champion of their enemies. A fire seizes him, and he goes down, with nothing but his sling and his heart of faith, to lay that champion in the dust. Next he is a great military leader; next the king of his country. As with David, so with Nehemiah,—as with him, so with Paul,—as with him, so with Luther. A Socrates, a Tully, a Cromwell, a Washington,—all the great master-spirits, the founders and law-givers of empires and defenders of the rights of man, are made by the same law. These did not shrink despairingly within the compass of their poor abilities, but in their heart of faith they embraced each one his cause, and went forth, under the inspiring force of their call, to apprehend that for which they were apprehended. They had all their enemies and their obstacles—such enemies and obstacles as they had in themselves no force to conquer. But their confidence in their cause gave them a force. For, as it is said that ferocious animals are disarmed by the eye of man, and will dare no violence, if he but steadily look at them, so it is when right looks upon wrong. Resist the devil, and he will flee from you; offer him a bold front, and he runs away. He goes, it may be, uttering threats of rage, but yet he goes.

So it is that all the great, efficient men of the world are made. They are not strong, but out of weakness they are made strong.

I have dwelt thus at length on these illustrations that are offered us in the natural life, simply because they will, for that reason, be most convincing to many. You see, as a fact, that the ability we have to suffer, and do, and conquer, is never an ability previously existing in ourselves. It is an ability that accrues, or comes upon us, in the exigencies and occasions of life. How childish, then, is it in religion, to imagine that we are called to do nothing save what we have ability to do beforehand; ability in ourselves to do. We have, in fact, no such ability at all—no ability that is inherent, as respects anything laid upon us to do; our ability is what we can have, and then our duty is graduated by what we can have. Indeed we may affirm it as a truth universal, respecting vital natures of every kind, whether vegetable, animal, intellectual, or spiritual, that they have no rigidly inherent ability to do anything whatever. No plant or tree can grow by any inherent ability, apart from sun, soil, moisture, heat, and the like. No animal can do as simple a thing as breathing by inherent ability; he must have air—he can walk, or run, or climb, or fly, only by conditions external that must be supplied. So also the mind or intelligence can remember only as fit associations are supplied to assist the recall of things gone by; or discover laws only when stimulated by the suggestions of appropriate facts; or maintain a power of high command only when there are great occasions and perils to be mastered. In just the same way, passing to what is spiritual, God cannot be loved, save as He is offered to love in qualities that will awaken and support love. And, for the same reason, no sinner of mankind can regenerate himself by any inherent ability, apart from conditions powerfully presenting God, and pouring His radiance into the soul; for the regenerate state is only the new revelation of God within, whence before He was excluded; so that now the life proceeds from Him as its actuating impulse and law.

This whole question of ability in man—of natural ability as opposed to moral inability, or qualified by it—of gracious ability as a substitute for natural, or the equivalent of its restoration—is the discussion of a false issue, which consequently never can be settled. For there is really no such thing, and never was, as an ability for holiness, or moral perfection, that is inherent. If we speak of natural ability for good, a soul has no more natural ability to maintain the state of perfect goodness than a tree to grow without light, or heat, or mois-ture. Dependence is the condition of all true holiness, even in sinless minds, if such there be. They feed on what their God supplies, they are radiant with His light, they are warm by His heat, they are blessed and exalted by the participation of His beatitude; nay, His all-moving Spirit is the conserving and sustaining life of their perfections. So if we speak of a gracious ability given to souls under sin, conceiving that it is some com-mon bestowment given to raise them up into a plane of freedom, or the possibility of a new life, which gracious ability is a something inherent and precedent to the obligations of repent-ance, that also is a pure fiction; no such ability is given, and none is wanted. All such inventions are unnecessary; as also all the supposed difficulties involved in the reconciling of re-sponsibility and dependence—they are all superseded and for ever passed by the moment we discover and fully come into the truth that all our powers and responsibilities are complet-ed in and by our conditions; or, what is the same, by God's arrangements to bring in increments of grace and impulse of all kinds just when they are wanted. There is no difficulty here which is not found in all those examples which have been already cited from the natural life; for God has arranged, in the spiritual or supernatural, to administer helps of grace, occasions, impulses, and secret ministries of love, so as to com-plete our possibilities and keep us in bonds of obligation to do continually what we can as little do, without such conspir-ing helps, as we can breathe without air, or maintain life with-out breathing.

This, it will accordingly be found, is the Christian doctrine everywhere. Christianity has no conception of any such thing as a holy virtue wrought out and maintained by a responsible agent, acting from his own centre, as a self-centred and merely self-operative force; holy virtue, it conceives, even apart from sin, to be the drinking out of God's fulness, receiving and living in His deific impulse, and having even its finiteness comple-mented by His infinite wisdom and majesty. As little concep-

s

tion has it of something done to raise a fallen creature into some inherent capacity or ability to choose freely, that so he may be made responsible for choice. It boldly, undisguisedly declares to every human being under sin, that he has no complete power beforehand, as in reference to anything really good. And then it calls him to good, on the express condition always that he is to have powers, stimulants, increments, accruing as he wants them; that on these, or the promise of them, he may rest his faith and so go forward. It says to the struggling and misgiving penitent, " Let him take hold of my strength, that he may make peace with me; and he shall make peace with me." It calls every man to earnest and hopeful endeavour, by the consideration of an all-supporting grace that cannot fail; " Work out your salvation with fear and trembling; for it is God that worketh in you." It shews the Christian testifying in sublimity of confidence, " When I am weak, then am I strong; I can do all things through Christ, which strengtheneth me." It promises the faithful man all the support needed for his exigencies as they arise, " They that wait upon the Lord shall renew their strength; they shall mount up with wings as eagles; they shall run, and not be weary; they shall walk, and not faint." It also establishes, in a manner to comprehend everything, a doctrine of Divine concourse by the Holy Spirit, which carries in it the pledge of all accruing grace, and light, and might, and holy impulsion, "Ask, and ye shall receive; seek, and ye shall find; knock, and it shall be opened." Indeed, the doctrine or fact of the Holy Spirit is only another way of generalising the truth that God will co-work invigoratively, correctively, and directively in all the good struggles of believing souls; and so will bring in, at all times and junctures, those increments of power that are necessary to success.

It might also be added that Christianity itself is a grand empowering force in souls, and is designed to be—that when we were without strength Christ died for us. For He came forth into the world groping in its darkness, "as the brightness of the Father's glory," that the light of the knowledge of the glory of God in the face of His great life and passion might shine into our hearts. As when the returning sun of the spring warms out the torpid creatures, and sets them creeping forth revitalised and re-empowered with life, so this Sun of righteousness quickens the benumbed perceptions and imparts new warmth to the dead affections, placing us in new conditions of power; where, as we more fully believe and more faithfully work, we are ever to find new increments of light and help conspiring with us.   It only remains, in gathering up this summary of the Christian doctrine concerning ability, to say that, taken comprehensively, it is all included in that favourite and more than once asserted maxim of Christ—"For to him that hath shall be given, and he shall have more abundantly."   In this maxim He affirms the truth that every man is to expect his increments of power just as they are wanted.

In this very simple manner all the great speculative difficulties and supposed mysteries of freedom and dependence are despatched in the New Testament.   And it is a remarkable fact that no Christian there is ever found to be in any speculative trouble on this subject.   It is never even so much as a question of curious debate.   They see nothing wanted there but just to go into their places and take their responsibilities, and let God bear them out by His conspiring help, as they certainly know that He will.   Paul came directly down upon the discovery that he had ability to will, as a matter of choice, and yet could not find how to perform; but, instead of seeing any difficulty in such a condition, he only glories that in Christ and the Spirit he gets accruing helps that enable him both to will and to do. And just there, where he might have sunk himself in one of the abysses of theology, he begins, instead, to sing, "I thank God through Jesus Christ."

I will only add that all the simplest, most living, and most genuine Christians of our own time are such as rest their souls, day by day, on this confidence and promise of accruing power, and make themselves responsible, not for what they have in some inherent ability, but for what they can have in their times of stress and peril, and in the continual raising of their own personal quantity and power.   They throw themselves on works wholly above their ability, and get accruing power in their works for others still higher and greater.   Instead of gathering in their souls timorously beforehand upon the little sufficiency they find in possession, they look upon the great world God has made, and all the greater world of the Saviour's kingdom in it, as being friendly and tributary, ready to pour in

help, minister light, and strengthen them to victory, just according to their faith. And so they grow in courage, confidence,
personal volume, efficiency of every kind, and instead of slink-
ing into their graves out of impotent lives, they lie down in the
honours of heroes.

Let me express the hope, in closing this very important subject that a class of persons who generally compose a large body
in every Christian assembly, will find their unhappy mistake
corrected in it. I speak of such as make no beginning in the
Christian life, just because they want ability and assurance
and all evidence given them beforehand. They would be quite
ready to embark if the voyage were as good as over. They
cannot put themselves on God's Word, or trust Him for anything. They must be strong before they get strength. They
must have evidence of discipleship before they dare to be disciples. They act upon no such principle in any of their worldly
adventures. Here they get power by using it—throw themselves
upon the water and learn to swim by swimming. Dismiss, I
beseech you, one and all, and that for ever, this unpractical,
this really unmanly timidity. Commit the keeping of your
soul to God, as to a faithful Creator. Believe that He is faithful, and love to trust Him for His faithfulness. The moment
you can let go your misgiving, spiritless habit and cast yourself on God, to go into your duty, you are free. If the wind is
high and the water looks deep, and you have no courage to
venture on a holy life, behold Jesus coming to you, treading
lightly on the crests of the billows, and He comes to say, "It
is I." What assurance more do you want after that?

But there is a more general use of this subject which demands our notice. There are two great errors which, though
opposite to each other, are yet both corrected by the view I
have been seeking to impress. The error—viz., of those who
think the demands of the religious life so limited and trivial as
to require but little care and small sacrifices ; and the error of
those who look upon them as being so many and great that
they are discouraged under them. The former class is the more
numerous and generally the more worthless. They are worldly
disciples who have much Christian delight, as they think, in

magnifying salvation by grace. God, they suppose, will not be very exact with them ; for He is a gracious and long-suffering God, and does not expect much of man in the way of goodness or effect. They take a certain pleasure, for reasons more artful than they themselves suspect, in dwelling on the weakness of men and their deep dependence on God. This is their reverence, they imagine, their humility ; yes, it is even a very considerable part of their religion. Of course they undertake nothing, throw themselves upon no great work of duty. They are so respectful to their human weakness that they measure their obligations by it, and really undertake nothing that makes them feel their weakness, or demands any gift of grace and power transcending it.

How different is the view of duty that God entertains for us, and everywhere asserts in the Scriptures. In His sight we are all under obligation continually to undertake and do what is above our power, and to have this as the acknowledged rule of our life. He requires of us to be doing what we shall feel, to be carrying loads of duty, and responsibility, and sacrifice, under which, as men, we must tremble and faint ; and so to be proving always that, to them that have no might, He increaseth strength. We are to undertake cheerfully and do with a ready mind all which, under His provisions of nature and grace, we may become able to do.

Feeble, are we ? Yes, without God we are nothing. But what by faith every man may be, God requires him to be. This is the only Christian idea of duty—measure obligation by inherent ability. No, my brethren, Christian obligation has a very different measure. It is measured by the power that God will give us, measured by the gifts and possible increments of faith. And what a reckoning will it be for many of us, when Christ summons us to answer before Him, under this law, not for what we were, but for what we might have been. Then how many of us possibly that bore the name of Jesus will find ourselves before God, as the mere residuary substances of a dry and fruitless life—without volume, without strength, or any proper Christian manhood. The souls whom it was given us to lead to the Saviour are not there ; the religious societies we ought to have gathered, the temples of worship we ought to have erected and left as monuments of our fidelity, the charities we ought to have founded and consecrated to the blessing of the coming ages — all these good things that we might have done,. and which God was ready to empower us for doing, nowhere appear. And is that the kind of reckoning in which we are to be accepted as good and faithful servants? My brethren, God has little part with you, or you with Him, in such a kind of life. A very delicate and critical question it is, whether you have any part with Him at all. That only is Christian faith that lives in the power of faith; in that does its works, makes its sacrifices, sustains its hopes, and measures its holy obligations. Almost everything a Christian is to do for his times and the sphere in which he lives transcends his ability; and the very greatness and joy of his experience, (shall I not say the reality also?) consists in the fact that he is exalted above himself, and made a partaker, in his works, of a Divine power, as in his character of the Divine nature. He is a man who lives in God, and by God is girded to his duties and his triumphs—God in nature, God in the gospel, God in the spirit, God in the plenitude of His promises.

I named another error, that viz., of those who really think that the way of duty is too hard for them—who faint because the demands of God appear to be so high above their power. They forget or overlook the provision God has made to bring in increments of power, and support them in what appears to be too high for them. They hear the call, "Give ye them to eat," and remember only their five loaves and two fishes; and what are these among so many? They seem not to notice, or, if they notice, not to believe those words of promise by which God encourages and supports the insufficiency of men. Thus, if any one, trying to make higher attainments, and achieve some higher standing in religion, is overwhelmed with the infirmity and bitter evil of his own heart, and cries, "My iniquities have taken hold upon me, so that I am not able to look up;" what is there in such a discovery to break down his confidence? Just there is the place for him to believe and begin to sing with Paul, "I thank God, through Jesus Christ my Lord." The very first thing to be held by a true Christian is, that he has no inherent sufficiency for anything; and then, upon the top of that, he should place, as the universal antidote of discouragement, the great principle of accruing grace, sealed by the promise, "My grace is sufficient for thee."

So, again, there are many who faint when they look on almost any duty or good work, because they are so consciously unequal to it. Why, if they were not unequal, or felt themselves to be equal, they had better, for that reason, decline it; for there is nothing so utterly weak and impotent as this conceit of strength. Brethren, the day is wearing away, this is a desert place, there are hungry, perishing multitudes round us, and Christ is saying to us all, "Give ye them to eat." Say not, "We cannot; we have nothing to give." Go to your duty, every man, and trust yourselves to Him; for He will give you all supply, just as fast as you need it. You will have just as much power as you believe you can have. Suppose, for example, you are called to be a Sabbath-school teacher, and you say within yourself, I have no experience, no capacity, I must decline. That is the way to keep your incapacity for ever. A truce to these cowardly suggestions. Be a Christian, throw yourself upon God's work, and get the ability you want in it. So, if you are put in charge of any such effort or institution; so, if you are called to any work or office in the Church, or to any exercise for the edification of others; say not that you are unable to edify; undertake to edify others, and then you will edify yourself, and become able. So only is it possible for Christian youth to ripen into a vigorous Christian manhood. All the pillars of the Church are made out of what would only be weeds in it, if there were no duties assumed above their ability in the green state of weeds. And it is not the weeds whom Christ will save but the pillars. No Christian will ever be good for anything without Christian courage, or, what is the same, Christian faith. Take upon you readily, have it as a law to be always doing, great works; that is, works that are great to you; and this in the faith that God so clearly justifies, that your abilities will be as your works. Make large adventures. Trust in God for great things. With your five loaves and two fishes He will shew you a way to feed thousands.

There is almost no limit to the power that may be exerted by a single church in this or any other community. Fill your places, meet your opportunities, and despair of nothing. Shine ·s lights, because you are luminous; let the Spirit of Christ and of God be visible in you, because you are filled therewith ; and you will begin to see what power is possible to weakness—"Have faith, O ye of little faith." Hear the good word of the Lord, when He says, "I have called thee by thy name ; thou art mine. Fear not, thou worm, Jacob. Behold, I will make thee a new sharp threshing instrument having teeth ; thou shalt thresh the mountains, and beat them small, and shalt make the hills as chaff." Such are God's promises. Let us believe them ; which, if we can heartily do, nothing is impossible.

XIX.

HE THAT KNOWS GOD WILL CONFESS HIM.

PSALM xl. 10—"*I have not hid thy righteousness within my heart; I have declared thy faithfulness and thy salvation: I have not concealed thy loving-kindness and thy truth from the great congregation.*"

WHAT any true poet will say is commonly most natural to be said, and deepest in the truth; for his art is to be unrestrained by art, and to let the inspiration of his inmost, deepest life vent itself in song. And this exactly is the manner of our great Psalmist. We are not to understand that, in using the indicative form, he is merely reciting an historic fact, and telling us that he has not hid God's righteousness in his heart. His meaning is deeper—viz., to say that he could not do it, but must needs testify of the goodness, and sing of the sweetness, and exult in the joy, he had found in the salvation of God and the secret witness of His Spirit. Nay, he must even send his song into the temple, and call on all the great congregation of Israel to sing it with him, and raise it as a chorus of praise to the great Jehovah. What I propose, accordingly, at the present time, is to speak of—

The necessary openness of a holy experience; or, in other words, of the impossibility that the inward revelation of God in the soul should be shut up in it, and remain hid or unacknowledged.

I shall have in view especially two classes of hearers that are widely distinguished one from the other; first, the class who hide the grace of God in their heart undesignedly, or by reason of some undue modesty; and secondly, the class who, pretending to have it, or consciously having it not, take a pleasure in throwing discredit on all the appropriate expressions of it, such as are made by the open testimony and formal profession of Christ before men.

The former class are certainly blameable in no such sense or degree as the others. They are naturally timorous and self-distrustful persons, it may be, and do not see that they are distrusting God rather than themselves. They seem to themselves to have been truly renewed in the love of God, but they have some doubts, and they make it appear to be wiser that they should not, just now, testify their supposed new experience. It is better, they think, to wait till they have had a long, secret trial of themselves, and learned whether they can endure, —better, that is, to see whether they can keep alive the grace under suppression; when it must be infallibly stifled and cannot live, except in the open field of duty and love and holy fellowship. They are not simple; they are unnatural; what is in them, in their feeling, their secret hope, their joy begun, they regulate and suppress. If they were placed in heaven itself, they would not sing the first month, pretending that they had not tried their voices, or perchance doubting whether it is quite modest in them to thank God for His mercy, till they are more sure whether it is really to be sufficient in them. There is a great deal of unbelief in their backwardness; a great deal of self-consciousness in their modesty; and sometimes a little will is cunningly mixed with both. Sometimes they wait to be exhorted and made much of by the sympathy of others. Sometimes the very wicked thought is cunningly let in, behind their seeming delicacy, that God should do more for them, and give them an experience with greater circumstance.

In opposition, now, to both these classes, and without assuming to measure and graduate the exact degree of their blame before God, I undertake to shew that, where there is a true grace of experience in the heart, it ought to be, must, and will be manifest. And I bring to your notice—

1. The evident fact that a true inward experience or discovery of God in the heart is itself an impulse also of self-manifestation, as all love and gratitude are—wants to speak and declare itself, and will as naturally do it, when it is born, as a child will utter its first cry. And exactly this, as I just now said, is what David means—viz., that he had been obliged to speak, and was never able to shut up the fire burning in his

spirit from the first moment when it was kindled. He speaks
as one who could not find how to suppress the joy that filled
his heart, but must needs break loose in a testimony for God.
And so it is in all cases the instinct of a new heart, in its experience of God, to acknowledge Him. No one ever thinks it a
matter of delicacy, or genuine modesty, entirely to suppress any
reasonable joy; least of all, any fit testimony of gratitude toward a deliverer and for a deliverance. In such a case no one
ever asks what is the use? where is the propriety? for it is the
simple instinct of his nature to speak, and he speaks.

Thus, if one of you had been rescued, in a shipwreck on a
foreign shore, by some common sailor who had risked his life
to save you, and you should discover him across the street in
some great city, you would rush to his side, seize his hand, and
begin at once, with a choking utterance, to testify your gratitude to him for so great a deliverance. Or, if you should pass
restrainedly on, making no sign, pretending to yourself that you
might be wanting in delicacy or modesty to publish your
private feelings, by any such eager acknowledgment of your
deliverer, or that you ought first to be more sure of the genuineness of your gratitude, what opinion must we have, in such a
case, of your heartlessness and falseness to nature. In the
same simple way, all ambition apart, all conceit of self forgot,
all artificial and mock modesty excluded, it will be the instinct
of every one that loves God to acknowledge Him. He will say
with our Psalmist, on another occasion, "Come and hear, all ye
that fear God, and I will declare what he hath done for my
soul. Verily God hath heard me ; he hath attended to the voice
of my prayer."

2. The change implied in a true Christian experience, or the
revelation of God in the heart, is in its very nature the soul
and root of an outward change that is correspondent. The
faith implanted is a faith that works in appropriate demonstrations, and must as certainly work, as a living heart must beat
or pulsate. It is the righteousness of God revealed within, to
be henceforth the actuating spring and power of a righteous and
devoted life. It will inform the whole man. It will glow in
the countenance. It will irradiate the eye. It will speak from
the tongue. It will modulate the very gait. It will enter into
all the transactions of business, the domestic tempers, the social

manifestations and offices. It will make the man a benefactor,
and call him into self-sacrifice for God and the truth. It will
send him forth to be God's advocate with men, and require
him, in that manner, to make full testimony, either formally or
by implication, of what God has done for him. Of this, now, a
true Christian experience is the root and beginning, else it is
nothing. The inward change is no reality, but a pure fiction, if
it does not issue in this. In this it will issue, when it is allowed
to act unrestrainedly, even though it be, at first, the smallest
seed of grace possible. And oh, what multitudes are there, in
whom God is just beginning to be revealed, who by some false
modesty, some morbid thought of prudence, refusing to be
natural and simple, take the mode of silence, secrecy, or suppression, and so, in a very few days or months, fatally stifle the
grace of their salvation. The result is worse, only in the fact
that the abuse is more wicked, when the subject dares, in the
hour of his holy visitation, deliberately to make up his mind
that he will have his new-born joy as a secret, and live in it
for some years, at least, until he has absolutely proved the
genuineness of his faith. It will not be long, in such a case,
before he gets evidence enough against it ; for the only and the
absolutely necessary proof of its genuineness *is* that it reveals
itself ; comes out into action, becomes a life and a confession.
The good tree will shew the good fruit. It cannot go on to
bear the old, bad fruit out of modesty, or a pretended shrink-
ing from ostentation ; it must reveal the righteousness of God
within, by the fruits of righteousness without, else it is only a
mockery.

3. If any one proposes beforehand, in his religious endeavours, or in seeking after God, to come into a secret experience
and keep it a secret, his endeavour is plainly one that falsifies
the very notion of Christian piety, and if he succeeds or seems
to succeed, he only practises a fraud in which he imposes on
himself. He proposes to find a grace or obtain a grace from
God that he will hide and will not acknowledge, a grace, too,
that will neither grow nor shine. Instead of taking up his
cross to follow Christ, sacrificing openly wealth, reputation,
friends, home, everything dear for his Master's sake, he is going
to find a grace that brings, in fact, no cross—requires no sacrifice. He is going to be saved in a more easy and more agree-

able way than to come out and take his Master's part and bear the rough work of his Master's calling. To meet the scorn of the world and endure the hardness that distinguishes a soldier is not in his thoughts. Perhaps he does not expect to be so much of a Christian, so high in his attainments, and so eminently useful, but he hopes to be just enough Christian, in this more delicate and secret way, to save him; beyond which he cares for nothing more. But you have only to look into his heart, in such a case, to see that his motive is bad, even beyond respect. He is only fawning about the cross to get some private token of grace, when he does not mean to make any expense, or suffer any loss or self-denial for it. To come out and be separate, to make the cause and truth of Jesus a care of his own, to live a life that witnesses for God, is not his plan. He means no such thing. He wants, in fact, to be saved by a fraud, that is, by a secret experience hid in the heart, which makes no open testimony— costs no sacrifice for God. To say that such a state of mind is untruth itself, and that any spiritual experience it may assume to have had is no better, would be an insult even to your understanding.

4. It is not less clear, as I have already said incidentally, and now say only more directly, that the grace of God in the heart, unmanifested or kept secret, as many propose that it shall be, even for their whole life, will be certainly stifled and extinguished. The thought itself is a mockery of the Holy Spirit. The heart might as well be required to live and not beat as the new heart of love to hush itself and keep still in the bosom. Nothing can live that is not permitted to shew the signs of life. Even a tree—a solid, massive oak, embracing the earth in roots equal to half its volume, and drawing out of the rich soil its needed nutriment—will be stifled and yield up its life if it cannot put on leaves at the extremities and grow. So let any, the best and ripest Christian, if such a one could be induced to do it, (as most assuredly he could not,) retire from all the acts and forbid himself all the duties by which he would manifest his love to God and declare God's love to men, and that love would very soon be so far smothered in his bosom as to leave no evidence there of its existence. Accordingly you will find that all that class of persons who take the turn described give the most abundant proofs ere long that God is not with them. How can

He be with them when they propose even to be disciples in such a way that, if all others were to follow and be like them, Christ would not have a Church or even one friend or follower on earth? Will He consent, by His Spirit, do you think, to uphold a race of secret, unacknowledged followers in this manner—followers who turn their back to Him, will not confess, will not even speak or act the grace they receive? Be it rather a faithful, as it is a most evident saying—"For if we be dead with Him, we shall also live with Him; if we suffer, we shall also reign with Him; if we deny Him, He also will deny us."

5. This is the express teaching of the gospel, which everywhere and in every possible way calls out the souls renewed in Christ to live an open life of sacrifice and duty, and so to witness a good confession. "Come and follow me," are the words of Jesus. "Deny thyself, take up thy cross, and follow me." If it is a lowly calling, if we cannot descend to it, then He says, "Blessed is he who is not offended in me." If our pride, or the pride of our position, is too great, then He says, " Whosoever shall be ashamed of me and of my words, of him shall the Son of man be ashamed, when he shall .come in his glory." To exclude any possible thought of a secret discipleship, He says, "I have chosen you and ordained you, that ye should bring forth fruit; I have chosen you out of the world, therefore the world hateth you, and will persecute you as it has persecuted me." In the same way His apostles call upon all that love Him to come out and be separate, to put on the whole armour of God, and stand, to fight openly the good fight, to endure hardness, to make a loss of all things for His sake, to be His witnesses before men; leading always the way by their own bold, faithful testimony. When you look, for example, on such a character as Paul, it is even difficult to conceive how there can ever be any real communion of spirit, in any future world, between him and one so opposite, as to think of living a secret, unavowed piety. Between that craven way of secrecy and mere self-saving, on one hand, and his great heart of love and labour, on the other, can any bond of sympathy ever exist? Scarcely does an open transgressor, acting out, with strong audacity, the unbelief and wickedness of which he dares to take the responsibility, appear to be as far removed, or as radi-

cally unlike. It never once occurs to Paul that he can keep the grace hid in his heart. He does not appear to come forth and speak because he has it as a point of obligation, as perhaps Daniel opened his window to let his prayer be heard, but he has a testimony to give for Jesus that he must give, because of the fire it kindles in his heart. So before the Areopagus, and Felix, and Agrippa, and Cæsar, and on every shore touched by his feet, he goes preaching the Word and telling the story of his wonderful experience on the way to Damascus. Who that looks on this heroic figure, and sees how the heavenly ardour raised in this man's breast by the revelation of Jesus, impels him forth and sends him through the world, in a life-long testimony which no sacrifices or perils are able to arrest, can descend, for one moment, to so mean a thought, as the possibility of being saved by a secret piety. Again—

6. It deserves to be made a distinct point that there is no shade of encouragement given to this notion of salvation by a secret piety in any of the Scripture examples or teachings. If there is to be a large body of the secret heirs of salvation, such as will greatly surprise the more open, more pretentious friends of God, when they see the number, there ought to be at least some examples in the Scripture to encourage such an expectation. The nearest approach to such encouragement anywhere given, is that which is afforded by the case of the two senators, Joseph and Nicodemus. One of them, we are told, was a disciple secretly, for fear of the Jews. And the other came to Jesus by night, to inquire of Him, that he might not be counted a disciple. Both of them appear to have kept silence on His trial before the council, letting the decision go against Him there, and taking no responsibility on His account. But after He was crucified, they came to ask the body, and brought spices to embalm it. They were good, as disciples, to bury Jesus, but not to save His life, or serve Him while living. Indeed, if they had truly embalmed Him in their hearts, so that we could hear of them afterward making common cause with the disciples, it would greatly comfort us concerning them. Shall we ever hear anything more of them in that world where God's true witnesses are gathered and crowned? The truth is, that there is a very heavy shade over these two delicate and courtly friends of Jesus. They were men of society, and there-

fore saw the dignity of Jesus; but if you would like to be reasonably confident of your salvation, it certainly becomes you to do something a great deal more positive than to let your Master die, making no stand for Him even in the council where His death is voted, and then come in with spices to bury Him. The most fragrant spices are those that honour one's life, and not the posthumous odours that embalm His body. How singular is it, too, that not even the Pentecost calls out these disciples of the tomb. It is as if they had been buried with their Master and had not risen. In that wondrous scene of fellowship, where so many from all parts of the world are surprised to find themselves confessing and embracing, in open brotherhood, strangers of all climes and orders, and selling even their goods to relieve the common wants, it does not appear that any spices of the heavenly charity are brought in by these two secret friends of Jesus. When all beside are of one accord, rejoicing in acts of communion such as the world has never seen, they have no part in it. Ananias and Sapphira had as much, or even more.

Is it such examples that give encouragement to a secret piety? These two had certainly some notion of such a discipleship, but who will care to receive it from them? No, the real disciple is different ; he is thought of as a man who stands for his Master, and is willing to die for his Master. "Ye are the light of the world ;" and the light of the world is lighted up, of course, to shine. "Men do not light a candle," He says, "and put it under a bushel. Let your light so shine, that others, seeing your good works, may glorify your Father which is in heaven."

Drawing our subject now to a conclusion, we notice, first of all, in a way of practical application, the very absurd pretence of those who congratulate themselves on having so much of secret merit, which they even count the more meritorious because they keep it secret. Some persons of a generally correct life are put on this course by the flatteries of others, who love to let down the honours of religion, and hold them up as a foil in doing it. Some do it wilfully and scornfully, hinting that people who make so great a noise about religion would do well to be more modest, and that, if they were willing to proclaim their own merits, perhaps they might make as good a show themselves.

And yet how many are there, if we may trust the world's report, of these secret saints—not the least, but the greatest of all saints! It is very much as if a nation, fighting for its liberties, had vast armies of secret patriots, who did not believe in making so great a noise in the dust and carnage of the field, but, since they are too modest to put their superior bravery forward, and rush to the onset shouting for their country, are to be counted, for their modesty's sake, the bravest and truest patriots of all.

The real truth is, in respect to almost all these pretenders to a secret religion, that they are persons who know nothing of it. They are moralists, it may be, practising at what they call a virtue by themselves, but they do nothing that brings them into any relationship with God. It is not the righteousness of God which they have hidden so carefully, but it is their own—which, after all, is not hid. They never pray, they have no experience of God, they are as ignorant as the worst of men of any such thing as a divine joy in the heart. They do not break out and confess the Lord, simply because He is not in them. Nothing is in them but themselves, and they do confess themselves, they even boast themselves. Just as naturally would they boast and testify the love of God, if they felt its power. They really publish all the merit they have now, and, when religion dawns in their heart, they will as certainly declare the grace of God in that.

And this again brings us to notice the significance of the profession of Christ, when, and why, and with what views, it should be made. It should be made, because where there is anything to be professed it cannot but be made. If a man loves God he will take his part with God, just as a citizen who loves his country will take the part of his country. He will draw himself to all God's friends and count them brothers, rejoicing with them in the fellowship of the common love. He will set himself, in every manner, to strengthen, comfort, edify, stimulate them in their fidelity and application to good works. All this he will do by the simple instinct of his love to God. If there were no such thing enjoined upon the disciples of Christ as a formal profession, or church organisation, there would yet be generated, within six months, exactly the same

T

thing. The disciples would come out of the world in a body, testifying what God has done for them in the quickening grace of Christ shed abroad in their hearts, and claiming their fellowship with each other. As our fathers, in the "Mayflower," bound themselves in a kind of civil covenant on their passage, they would band themselves together in holy covenant before God, to co-operate in a form of spiritual order—a church. They would have their officers and leaders. They would watch for each other. They would have terms adjusted by which to separate themselves from hypocrites and impostors—all that we now have in our formal polities and church compacts. Co-operation is the strength of such as have a common cause, and organisation is the certain requisite of this. In this way the followers of Jesus must and will be set in solid phalanx to co-operate in the maintenance of their common cause.

This matter of professing Christ appears to be regarded by many as a kind of optional duty. Just as optional as it is for light to shine, or goodness to be good, or joy to sing, or gratitude to give thanks, or love to labour and sacrifice for its ends. No, my friends, there is no option here, save as all duties are optional, and eternity hangs on the option we make. Let no one of you receive or allow a different thought. Expect to be open, outstanding witnesses for God, and rejoice to be. In ready and glorious option, take your part with such, and stifle indignantly any lurking thought of being a secret follower.

Following in the same train, we notice, again, what value there may be in discoveries of Christian experience, and the legitimate use they may have in Christian society. Some of the best and holiest impulses ever given to the cause of God in men's hearts are given by testimonies of Christian experience. Like all other things, they are capable of abuse. They may run to a really pitiful conceit, being not only misconceived by the subjects themselves, but even made a gospel of and thrust forward on occasions where they are out of place and against all holy proprieties. Still there will be times, more or less private, when the humblest and weakest disciples can speak of what God has done for them, with the very best effect. Nor is there anything so unpractical and destitute of Christian respect as the shyness of some fastidious people in this matter. It never exists in a truly manly character, or in connexion with a full-toned, living godliness. That will be no such dainty affair, it will speak out. It will declare what God has done, and shew the method by which He works. The new joy felt will be a new song in the mouth, and every new deliverance will be fitly, gratefully confessed. There will be no shallow affectation of delicacy shutting the lips, and sealing them in a forced dumbness, as if the righteousness of God had been taken by a deed of larceny. How often will two disciples help and strengthen each other by shewing, each the other, in what way God has led him, what his struggles have been, and where his victories. And, if there should be three or four included, or possibly, and in fit cases, more, a whole church, what is there to blame? "They spake often, one to another," says the prophet; "and God hearkened and heard it." God listens for nothing so tenderly as when His children help each other by their testimonies to His goodness and the way in which He has brought them deliverance. Besides, there is a higher view of these personal testimonies and confessions. All these experiences, or life-histories of the faithful, will be among the grandest studies and most glorious revelations of the future,—a spiritual epic of wars, and defeats, and falls, and victories, and wondrous turns of deliverance, and unseen ministries of God and angels, that, when they are opened to the saints, will furnish the sublimest of all their discoveries of Christ and of God. Exactly as an apostle intimates in those most hopeful, inspiring words of his, "When He shall come to be glorified in His saints, and to be admired in all them that believe." May He not be glorified in them here, and, in some feebler measure, admired for the testimonies yielded by their experience, as their warfare goes on. ·

And now, last of all, let this one thing be impressed, for everything I have been saying leads to this, that the true wisdom, in all these matters of holy experience, is to act naturally. If you seem to yourself to have really passed from death unto life, and to have come into God's peace, interpose no affectations of modesty, no restrictions of mock prudence, but in true natural modesty and a sound natural discretion testify the grace you have received. Take upon you promptly every duty, enter the Church, obey the command of Christ, in the confession of His name and the public remembrance of His death.

Oh, if we could get rid of so many affectations in religion, and so many unnatural, artificial wisdoms, how many more real Christians would there be, and these how much better and heartier. How many are there in our Christian communities that are living afar off and apparently quite inaccessible, who if, at a certain time in their life, they had gone forward and taken the places to which they were called, would now be among the shining members of the great body of saints. And how many in the Church cripple themselves and all but extinguish their life, by allowing nothing good or right in them to be naturally acted out. They stifle every beginning of grace by their over-persistent handling, scrutinising, and testing of it. They read " Edwards on the Affections," it may be, till their affections are all worn out and killed by so much jealousy of them, when, if only they could give them breath in the open life of duty and sacrifice, they would flame up in the soul as heavenly fires, indubitable and irrepressible.

If any of you, either out of the Church or in, have lost ground in these artificial and restrictive ways, come back at once to your losing point and consent to be natural, to act out whatever grace God will give you, and when you are conscious of His love to you, or His new creating presence and peace in your heart, be as ready to trust your consciousness as you are the consciousness that you think, or doubt, or do anything else. In a word, do not hide the righteousness of God in your heart lest you make a tomb of your heart and bury it there. Go forward and act out naturally, testify freely, live openly the grace that is in you.

Thus it was, I have already said, with the sturdy warriors of the faith in the first ages of the Church. They were men who took the grace in them as a call. The love that broke into their hearts burned up all their false modesty. Their humble position was exalted by the faith of Jesus, and they stood forth in all the singularity of the cross, cowed by no superiors, daunted by no perils. God made them heroes by simply making them natural, and the time of Christly heroism will never be restored till men can take their lives in their hands and go forth, in downright good faith, to follow their Master, acting out the spirit He has kindled in them, and testifying to mankind the riches of the grace they have found in His gospel.

What we want above all things in this age is heartiness and holy simplicity; men who justify the holy impulse of grace in their hearts, and do not keep it back by artificial clogs of prudence and false fear, or the sham pretences of fastidiousness and artificial delicacy. These are they whom God will make His witnesses in all ages. They dare to be holy, dare just as readily to be singular. What God puts in them, that they accept, and when He puts a song, they sing it. They know Christ inwardly, and therefore stand for Him outwardly. They endure hardness. They fight a fight. And these are the souls, my brethren, who shall stand before God accepted. And we shall be accepted as we stand with them—otherwise never. It will be a gathering of the true soldiers—a gathering of them that have made sacrifices, conquered perils, and lived their open testimony for God and His Son. They will come in covered with their dust and scars, and Christ will crown them as heroes that have stood and kept their armour. And then how deep and piercing are those words of His — will they slay us for ever, or will they make us alive? " Whosoever therefore shall confess me before men, him will I confess also before my Father which is in heaven. But whosoever shall deny me before men, him will I also deny before my Father which is in heaven."

XX.

THE EFFICIENCY OF THE PASSIVE VIRTUES.

REV. i. 9—"*The kingdom and patience of Jesus Christ.*"

KINGDOM and patience! a very singular conjunction of terms, to say the least, as if in Jesus Christ were made compatible authority and suffering, the impassive throne of a monarch and the meek subjection of a cross, the reigning power of a prince and the mild endurance of a lamb. What more striking paradox! And yet in this you have exactly that which is the prime distinction of Christianity. It is a kingdom erected by patience. It reigns in virtue of submission. Its victory and dominion are the fruits of a most peculiar and singular endurance. I say the fruits of endurance, and by this I mean, not the reward, but the proper results or effects of endurance. Christ reigns over human souls and in them, erecting there His spiritual kingdom, not by force of will exerted in any way, but through His most sublime passivity in yielding Himself to the wrongs and the malice of His adversaries. And with Him, in this most remarkable peculiarity, all disciples are called to be partakers; even as the apostle in his exile at Patmos writes, "I, John, who also am your brother and companion in tribulation, and in the kingdom and patience of Jesus." I offer it accordingly to your consideration, as a kind of first principle in a good life, which it will be the object of my discourse to illustrate—

That the passive elements, or graces of the Christian life, well maintained, are quite as efficient and fruitful as the active.

It is not my design, of course, to discourage or restrain what are called active works in religion. Christ himself was active beyond almost any human example. All great and true servants of God have been men of industry, and of earnest and strenuous application to works of duty. I only design to exhibit what many are so apt to overlook or forget, the sublime

efficacy of those virtues which belong to the receiving, suffering, patient side of character.   They are such as meekness,
gentleness, forbearance, forgiveness, the endurance of wrong
without anger and resentment, contentment, quietness, peace,
and unambitious love.   These all belong to the more passive
side of character, and are included, or may be, in the general
and comprehensive term, patience.   What I design is to shew
that these are never barren virtues, as some are apt to imagine,
but are often the most efficient and most operative powers that
a true Christian wields; inasmuch as they carry just that kind
of influence which other men are least apt and least able to resist.

We too commonly take up the impression that power is
measured by exertion; that we are effective simply because of
what we do, or the noise we make; consequently, that when
we are not in exertion of some kind, we are not accomplishing
anything; and that if we are too humble, or poor, or infirm, to
be engaged in great works and projects, there is really nothing
for us to do, and we are living to no purpose.   This very gross
and wholly mistaken impression I wish to remove, by shewing
that a right passivity is sometimes the greatest and most effective
Christian power, and that if we are brothers and companions
in the kingdom and patience of Jesus, we are likely to fulfil the
highest conception of the Christian life.   Observe then—

First of all, that the passive and submissive virtues are most
of all remote from the exercise or attainment of those who are
out of the Christian spirit and the life of faith.   All men are
able to be active.   Most men do exert themselves in works that
are really useful.   A vast multitude of the race have excelled in
forms of active power that are commonly called virtuous, without any thought of religion.   They have been great inventors,
discoverers, teachers, law givers, risked their life, or willingly
yielded it up in the fields of war for the defence of their country
or the conquest of liberty, worn out every energy of mind and
body in the advancement of great human interests.   Indeed it
is commonly not difficult for men to be active or even bravely
so; but when you come to the passive or receiving side of life,
here they fail.   To bear evil and wrong. to forgive, to suffer no
resentment under injury, to be gentle when nature burns with a
fierce heat, and pride clamours for redress, to restrain envy, to

bear defeat with a firm and peaceful mind, not to be vexed or fretted by cares, losses, or petty injuries, to abide in contentment and serenity of spirit, when trouble and disappointment come—these are conquests, alas how difficult to most of us! Accordingly it will be seen that a true Christian man is distinguished from other men, not so much by his beneficent works, as by his patience. In this he most excels and rises highest above the mere natural virtues of the world. Just here it is that he is looked upon as a peculiar and partially divine character. The motives seem to be a mystery. What can set a man to the suffering of evil and wrong with such a spirit? Thought lingers questioning round him, asking for the secret of this mysterious passivity. Even if it be derided there is yet felt to be a something great in it; truly he is another kind of man and not of us, is the feeling of all who are not in Christ with him. By this he will be seen and felt to belong to a distinct order of being and character. He is set off by his patience to be a brother and companion in the kingdom and patience of Jesus.

Consider also more distinctly the immense power of principle that is necessary to establish the soul in these virtues of endurance and patience. Here is no place for ambition, no stimulus of passion, such as makes even cowards brave in the field. Here are no exploits to be carried, no applauses of the multitude to be won. The disciple, knowing that God forgives and waits, wants to be like Him; knowing that he has nothing himself to boast of but the shame of a sinner, wants to be nothing, and prefers to suffer and crucify his resentments, and, since God would not contend with him, will not contend with those who do him injury. He gets the power of his patience wholly from above. It is not human, it is divine. Hence the impossibility of it even to great men. Napoleon, for example, had the active powers in such vigour that he made the whole civilised world shake with dread. But when he came to the place where true greatness consisted only in patience, that was too great for him. Just where any Christian woman would have shone forth in the true radiance and sublimity of an all-victorious patience, he, the conqueror of empires, broke down into a peevish, fretful, irritable temper, and loosing thus, at once, all dignity and composure of soul, died before his time, because he had been resolved into a mere compost of faculty by the ferment of his ungoverned passions.   On the other hand, we have in Socrates an illustrious example of the dignity and sacred grandeur of patience.   The good spirit or genius he spoke of as being ever with him, was, in fact, the teacher of this noble and truly divine submission to wrong.   It wears no merely human look, and the world of all subsequent ages has been made to feel that here is a certain sublimity of virtue, which sets the man apart from all the great men of profane history. No ancient character stands with him.   He is felt to be a kind of sacred man, who, by means of his wonderful passivity to wrong, and his gentleness toward his enemies, is set quite above his kind, revealing as it were the gift of some higher nature. You perceive in his example that the passive virtues both involve and express a higher range of principles; hence they are necessary to all highest character in the active.   We can act out of the human, but to suffer well requires a participation of what is divine.   Hence the impression of greatness and sublimity which all men feel in the contemplation of that energy which is itself energised by a self-sacrificing and suffering patience. And accordingly there is no power over the human soul and character so effective and so nearly irresistible as this.

Notice, again, yet more distinctly, what will add a yet more conclusive evidence, how it is chiefly by this endurance of evil that Christ, as a Redeemer, prevails against the sin of the human heart and subdues its enmity.   Just upon the eve of what we call His passion, He says, in way of visible triumph, to His disciples, "The prince of this world is judged;" as if the kingdom of evil were now to be crushed, and His own new kingdom established by some terrible bolt of judgment falling on his adversaries.   It was even so; and that bolt of judgment was the passion of the cross.   We had never seen before the sublime passivities of God's character, and His ability to endure the madness of evil. We had seen Him in the smoke, and heard Him in the thunders of Sinai.   We had felt His judgments, we had trembled under His frown, we had seen the active management and sway of His providence.   But now, in the cross, we see Him bearing wrong, receiving the shafts of human enmity, submitting Himself, in His sublime patience, to the fury of the disobedient, and so, melting down by His gentleness what no terrors could intimidate, and no frowns of judgment could subdue. Thus our blessed Redeemer made Himself a king, and set up a kingdom. It is the kingdom of His patience. When law was broken, and all the supports of authority set up by God's majesty were quite torn away, God brought forth a power greater than law, greater than majesty, even the power of His patience, and by this He broke for ever the spirit of evil in the world. The sinner could laugh at God's thunders, and stiffen himself against all the activities of His omnipotent rule, when exerted to abase and humble him, but when He looks upon the cross of Jesus, and beholds the patience of God's love and mercy, then he relents and becomes a child. The new-creating grace of Christianity is scarcely more, in fact, than a divine application of the principle, that when nothing else can subdue an enemy, patience sometimes will.

Again, it is important to notice that men, as being under sin, are set against all active efforts to turn them, or persuade them; but never against that which implies no effort—viz., the gentle virtues of patience. We are naturally jealous of control by any method which involves a fixed design to exert control over us: therefore we are always on our guard in this direction. But we are none the less open, at all times, to the power of silent worth, and the unpretending goodness of those virtues that are included in patience. If a man is seen to live in content, and keep a mind unruffled by vexation, under great calamities and irritating wrongs, we have no guard set against that, we almost like to be swayed by such a kind of power. Indeed we should not have a good opinion of ourselves, if we did not admire such an example and praise it. And in just this way it happens, that many a proud and wilful soul will resist the most eloquent sermon, and will then be completely subdued and melted by the heavenly serenity and patience of a sick woman. For a similar reason, all the submissive forms of excellence have an immense advantage. They provoke no opposition, because they are not put forth for us, but for their own sake. They fix our admiration therefore, win our homage, and melt into our feeling. They move us the more, because they do not attempt to move us. They are silent, empty of all power but that which lies in their goodness, and for just that reason they are among the greatest powers that Christianity wields.

Once more, it is important for every man, when he will cast the balance between the powers of action and of passion, or when he will discover the real effectiveness of passive good, to refer to his own consciousness. See how little impression is often made upon you by the most strenuous efforts to exert influence over you, and then how often you are swayed by feelings of respect, reverence, admiration, tenderness, from the simple observation of one who suffers well ; receiving injury without resentment, gilding the lot of poverty and privation with a spirit of contentment and of filial trust in God ; forgiving, gentle, unresisting, peaceful, and strong, under great storms of affliction. How gently do these lovely powers of patience insinuate themselves into your respect and love. When some palpable assault of active endeavour, such as argument, advice, or exhortation, besieges you, how instinctively do you harden yourself against it, and offer yourself to it as a wall to be battered down if it can be. But when you see a Christian suffer well, strong in adversity, calm and happy in days of trouble, smiling on through months of pain, in a spirit of unmurmuring patience, contented with a hard lot of poverty and outward discouragement, how ready are you to feel the power of such examples, how welcome are they, as faces of blessing, to a place in you mind, and how often do they bend you, by their sacred power, to better purposes of life, that could not be extorted by any more obtrusive means. Let every Christian carefully observe his own consciousness here, and he will be in the least possible danger of disesteeming patience, as a barren or sterile virtue, or of looking upon effort and action as the only operative and fruitful Christian powers.

Let us notice now, in conclusion, some of the instructive and practical uses of the truth illustrated.   And

1. It is here that Christianity makes issue with the whole world on the question of human greatness.   That is ever looked on by mankind and spoken of as greatness which displays some form of active power. The soldier, the statesman, the inventor, the orator, the reformer, the poet—all great thinkers and doers, by whom, as mighty men and men of renown, great masses of people, or even nations, are swayed in their opinions, or their history, or profoundly moved, prepared to some higher future

—are taken as examples of the most real and highest form of greatness. It has never entered into human thought, unsanctified by religion, that there is or can be any such thing as greatness in the mere passive virtues, or in simply suffering well; least of all in suffering wrong and evil with a forgiving, unresentful spirit. Christianity is here alone, holding it forth as being, when required, the divinest, sublimest, and most powerful of all virtues to suffer well. Even the summits of deific excellence and glory it reveals, by the endurance of enemies, and the bitter pangs of a cross accepted for their good. It works out the recovery of transgressors by the transforming power of sacrifice. And so it establishes a kingdom, which is itself the reign of the patience of Jesus. The whole plan centres in this one principle, that the suffering side of character has a power of its own, superior, in some respects, to the most active endeavours. And in this it proves its originality by standing quite alone. The Stoics appear to have had a dim apprehension that something of this kind might be true, but the patience they inculcated was that of the will, and not the patience of love and trust. It was, in fact, obstinacy, without any consent to suffering at all; a will hardening itself into flint; a sensibility deadened by assumed apathy; and all this in the proud determination to be sufficient against all the evils of this life. It was not suffering well, therefore, but refusing to suffer, and, in that view, was a most active and strenuous form of effort. And there was a certain greatness in this we cannot deny, though it was only a mock-moral greatness and not that true, heaven-descended greatness, which belongs to Christian charity. To say—Let patience have her perfect work that ye may be perfect and entire, wanting nothing; to understand that character is even consummated in these passive virtues—this could only be taught by the gospel of the cross. And yet how manifestly true it is, when once it is seen in such an example as that of Jesus, that a suffering love is the highest conceivable form of greatness.

2. The office of the Christian martyrs is here explained. We look back upon the long ages of woe, the martyr ages of the Church, and we behold a vast array of active genius and power, that could not be permitted to spend itself in works of benefaction to the race, but was consecrated of God to the more

sacred and more fruitful grace of suffering. The design was, it would seem, to prepare a Christly past, to shew whole ages of faith populated with men who were able, coming after their Master and bearing His cross, to suffer with Him, and add their human testimony to His. And they overcame by the blood of the Lamb, and by the word of their testimony, and they loved not their lives unto the death. And so it has been ordered that the Church of God shall know itself to be the child of suffering patience. The scholars, the preachers, all the great and noted characters, who have served the Church by their labours, pass into shade—we think little of them ; but the men of patience, the holy martyrs, these we feel as a sacred fatherhood, charging it, oh, how seriously and filially upon our souls, to be followers of them who, through faith and patience, inherit the promises. Who that feels the power of these martyr ages descending on him, can ever think, even for a moment, that the passive virtues of the Christian life are sterile virtues, and that action is the only fruitful thing.

3. We see in this subject how it is that many persons are so abundantly active in religion, with so little effect ; while others who are not conspicuous in action accomplish so much. The reason is, that one class trust mainly to the virtues of action, while the others unite also the virtues of patience. One class is brother and companion in the kingdom and works of Jesus, the other in the kingdom and patience of Jesus. Accordingly there is something of the same distinction between them that there is between John the Baptist and the Saviour, as regards the extent and the subduing, permanent quality of their effects. Thus a man may be very active in warnings, exhortations, public prayers, plans of beneficence, contributions of time and money, and it may seem, when you look upon him, that he is going to produce immense effects by his life. But suppose him to be very much of a stranger to the patient virtues of Christ—railing at adversaries, blowing blasts of scorn upon those whom he wishes to reform in their practices, impetuous, wilful, irritable, hot—how much good is that man going to do by all his activity ? What can he do but irritate, and vex, and, as far as he is concerned, render the very name of religion, or possibly of Christ himself, odious. Or suppose him to be a petulant neighbour, or a harsh and passionate man to persons in his employ, resentful and

retaliatory against those who cross him in his interests, fretful and storming always with impatience, when providences do not work rightly, or when other men do not exactly fulfil their duties or engagements. How manifest is it that such a man will do little or nothing by his religious activity. The difference between him and a right-minded, healthy Christian, is the same as between Jehu and Jesus. So the woman who is zealous in the street, busy ever in the works of active charity, but ill-natured and fretful in her house, impatient with her children, given to harsh words and bitter constructions upon the character of others, implacable in her resentment of supposed injuries, jealous, envious—what can she accomplish by any possible degree of activity? And how many are there in the churches, who are really forward in all good works, but are continually thwarting all effect and reducing the value of their efforts as nearly as possible to nothing by just such defects of passive goodness as some of these which I have named.

On the other hand, have you never observed the immense power exerted by many Christian men and women whose lives are passed in comparative silence? You know not how it is, they seem to be really doing little, and yet they are felt by thousands. And the secret of this wonder is that they know how to suffer well—they are in the patience of Jesus. They will not resent evil, or think evil. They are not easily provoked. They are content with their lot, though it be a lot of poverty and affliction. They will not be envious of others. When they are wronged they remember Christ and forgive, when opposed and thwarted, they endure and wait. They live in an element of composure and sweetness, and cannot be irritated and fretted by men, because they are so much with God, and so ready to bear the cross of His Son, that human wrongs and judgments have little power to unsettle or disturb them. Now before these a continual flood of influence will be continually rolling. Their gentleness is stronger than the onsets and assaults of other men. They are in the kingdom of Jesus reigning with Him. because they are with Him in His patience.

4. The reason why we have so many crosses, trials, wrongs, and pains, is here made evident. We have not one too many for the successful culture of our faith. The great thing, and that which it is most of all difficult to produce in us, is a parti-

cipation of Christ's forgiving gentleness and patience. This, if we can learn it, is the most difficult and the most distinctively Christian of all attainments. Therefore we need a continual discipline of occasions, poverty, sickness, bereavements, losses, treacheries, misrepresentations, oppressions, persecutions; we can hardly have too many for our own good, if only we receive them as our Saviour did His cross. It is by just these refining fires of trial and suffering that we are to be most advanced in that to which we aspire. The first thing that our Saviour set Himself to, when He began His ministry, was the inculcation of those traits that belong to the passive or patient side; for these He well understood were most remote from us, highest above us, and most of all cross to the impatient stormy spirit of sin within us. He opened His mouth and taught them for His first lesson, "Blessed are the poor in spirit; blessed are the meek; blessed are the peace-makers; blessed are they that are persecuted for righteousness' sake;" and afterward, in the same discourse, "Resist not evil; whosoever shall smite thee on thy right cheek, turn to him the other also. Love your enemies, bless them that curse you, do good to them that hate you, and pray for them that despitefully use you and persecute you; that ye may be the children of your Father which is in heaven." And then, going on to unfold this latter idea, shewing how God reveals His impartial, unresentful patience, He comes to this; at last, as the summit of all—"Be ye therefore perfect, even as your Father in heaven is perfect;" as if it were the crown of all perfection, whether in God or man, to endure evil well. Or, in other words, as if it were his opinion that all good character is consummated and crowned in the virtues included under patience.

Therefore, I said we have not too many occasions given us for the exercise of patience; which is yet more evident, when we consider the Christian power of patience. How many are there who, by reason of poverty, obscurity, infirmity of mind or body, can never hope to do much by action, and who often sigh at the contemplation of their want of power to effect anything. But it is given to them, as to all, to suffer; let them only suffer well and they will give a testimony for God which all who know them will deeply feel and profoundly respect. It is not necessary for all men to be great in action. The greatest and sublimest power is often simple patience; and for just that reason we need sometimes to see its greatness alone, that we may embrace the solitary, single idea of such greatness, and bring it into our hearts unconfused with all other kinds of power. Whoever gives to the Church of God such a contribution—the invalid, the cripple, the neglected and forlorn woman, —every such person yields a testimony for the cross that is second in value to no other.

Let this be remembered, and let it be your joy, in every trial, and grief, and pain, and wrong you suffer, that to suffer well is to be a true advocate, and apostle, and pillar of the faith—

"They also serve who only stand and wait."

And here, let me add, is pre-eminently the office and power of woman. Her power is to be the power most especially of gentleness and patient endurance. An office so divine let her joyfully accept and faithfully bear—adding sweetness to life in all its exasperating and bitter experiences, causing poverty to smile, cheering the hard lot of adversity, teaching pain the way of peace, abating hostilities and disarming injuries by the patience of her love. All the manifold conditions of human suffering and sorrow are so many occasions given to woman to prove the sublimity of true submission and reveal the celestial power of passive goodness.

Finally, there is reason to suspect that men not religious are commonly averted from the Christian life, more by their dislike of the submissive and gentle virtues, than by any distaste of sacrifice and active duty. They could enter as companions into His kingdom, if only they could be excused from the patience. Their life of sin is a life of will or self-will, therefore a life centred in themselves. They have undertaken to hew their own way; therefore to thrust, and push, and fret themselves against obstructions, and resent oppositions, to envy, and hate, and revenge themselves on enemies, is the luxury, in great part, of their sin. They can admire and praise benevolence, truth, disinterestedness of conduct, but to bear evil, and love enemies, and be patient—that is wholly distant from the temper they are in. They are not without admiration for these gentle kinds of excellence when displayed by God himself; they will even be affected by what they perceive to be the sublimity of

His greatness in them; but they cannot think of such in themselves without distaste or a feeling of disesteem. There is a want of spirit, something tame and weak in such ways, something too hard upon human pride to be endurable.

And yet how plain it is, my friends, that for the want of just these passive virtues your character is all disorder and confusion. There can be nothing, as you have seen, of the highest, truest greatness in you without the virtues of patience; you are not called to descend to these, but, if possible, to ascend. Christ commands you to take up His cross and follow Him, not that He may humble you, or lay some penance upon you, but that you may surrender the low self-will and the feeble pride of your sin, and ascend into the sublime patience of heavenly charity. You begin to reign the moment you begin to suffer well. You are only degraded when you suffer and groan, writhing under pains God lays upon you, in the manner of a slave. Renounce what is real degradation, and the pride that now detains you will not be left. Choose what will most exalt you, and these gentle virtues of the cross will be accepted first. And then it will not be left us to exhort you; for you will even claim it as your joy to be brother and companion in the kingdom and patience of Jesus.

XXI.

JEREMIAH xlviii. 11—"*Moab hath been at ease from his youth, and he hath settled on his lees, and hath not been emptied from vessel to vessel, neither hath he gone into captivity; therefore his taste remained in him, and his scent is not changed.*"

THERE is a reference here, it will be seen, to wine, or to the process by which it is prepared and finished. It is first expressed from the grape when it is a thick, discoloured fluid or juice. It is then fermented, passing through a process that separates the impurities, and settles them as lees at the bottom. Standing thus upon its lees or dregs, in some large tun or vat, it is not further improved. A gross and coarse flavour remains, and the scent of the feculent matter stays by and becomes fastened, as it were, in the body of the wine itself. To separate this, and so to soften or refine the quality, it is now decanted or drawn off into separate jars or skins. After a while it is done again, and then again; and so, being emptied from vessel to vessel, the last remains of the lees or sediment are finally cleared, the crude flavours are reduced, the scent itself is refined by ventilation, and the perfect character is finished.

So it has not been, the prophet says, with Moab. He hath been at ease from the first, shaken by no great overturnings or defeats, humbled and broken by no captivities, ventilated by no surprising changes or adversities. He has lived on, from age to age, in comparative security, settled on his lees: and therefore he has made no improvement. What he was, he still is; his taste remains in him, and the scent of his old idolatries and barbarities of custom is not changed. Accordingly, the prophet goes on to declare, in the verses that follow, that God will now deal with him in a manner better adapted to his want; that He will cause him to wander, empty his vessels, break his bottles, give him all the agitation he needs, and so will make him to be ashamed of the idolatries of Chemosh, even as Israel was ashamed of Bethel, their confidence.

There has all along been a kind of mental reference, it will be seen, in his language, to the singular contrast between Moab and Israel, which here in these last words comes out. Israel, the covenanted people, have had no such easy and quiet sort of history. They have been wanderers, in a sense, all the while; shaken loose or unsettled every few years by some great change or adversity—by a state of slavery in Egypt, by a fifty years' roving and fighting in the wilderness, by a time of dreadful anarchy under the judges, by overthrows and judgments under the kings, by a revolt and separation of the kingdom, then by a captivity, then by another; and so, while Moab, heaved and loosened by no such changes, has retained the scent of its old customs and abominations, Israel has become quite another people. The calves of Bethel were long ago renounced; the low superstitions, the coarse and sensual habit, all the idolatrous fashions and affinities which corrupted their religion have been gradually fined away.

Similar contrasts might be instanced among the states and nations of our own time; in China, for example, and England; one standing motionless for long ages, and becoming an effete civilisation, absolutely hopeless as regards the promise of a regenerated future; the other emptied from vessel to vessel, four times conquered, three times deluged with civil war, converted, reformed and reformed in religion, and finally emerging, after more than one change of dynasty, into a state of law, liberty, intelligence, and genuinely Christian manhood, to be one of the foremost and mightiest nations of the world.

But my object is personal, not political or social, and the principle that underlies the text is one that may be universalised in its applications. It is this :—

That we require to be unsettled in life by many changes and interruptions of adversity, in order to be most effectually loosened from our own evils, and prepared to the will and work of God.

We need, in other words, to be shaken out of our places and plans, agitated, emptied from vessel to vessel, else the flavours of our grossness and impurity remain. We cannot be refined on our lees, or in any course of life that is uniformly prosperous and secure. My object will be to exhibit this truth, and bring it into a just application to our own personal experience. Observe, then—

1. How God manages, on a large scale, in the common matters of life, to keep us in a process of change, and prevent our lapsing into a state of security such as we desire. No sooner do we begin to settle, as we fancy, and become fixed, than some new turn arrives by which we are shaken loose and sorely tossed. When the prophet declares that He will overturn, overturn, overturn, he gives in that single word a general account of God's polity in all human affairs. The world is scarcely turned on its axle more certainly than it is overturned by the revolutions of Providence. It seems even to be a law, in every sort of business or trade, that nothing shall stand on its lees. Credit is a bubble bursting every hour at some gust of change. What we call securities are as well called insecurities. Titles themselves give way, and even real estate becomes unreal under our feet. Nor is it only we ourselves that unsettle the security of things. Nature herself conspires to loosen all our calculations, meeting us with her frosts, her blastings, her droughts, her storms, her fevers, and forbidding us ever to be sure of that for which we labour. Markets and market prices faithfully represent the unsteadiness of our objects. We look upon them as we might upon the sea, and it even makes one's head swim, only to note the fluctuations of all human goods and values represented there. Nothing in the world of business is allowed to have a base of calculable certainty. Unforeseen disasters wait on our plans, in so many forms and combinations, that we are sure of nothing, and commonly bring out nothing exactly as we expected to do.

The very scheme of life appears to be itself a grand decanting process, where change follows change, and all are emptied from vessel to vessel. Here and there a man, like Moab, stands upon his lees, and commonly with the same effect. Fire, flood, famine, sickness in all forms and guises, wait upon us, seen or unseen, and we run the gauntlet through them, calling it life. And the design appears to be to turn us hither and thither, allowing us no chance to stagnate in any sort of benefit or security. Even the most successful, who seem, in one view, to go straight on to their mark, get on after all, rather by a dexterous and continual shifting, so as to keep their balance and exactly meet the changing conditions that befall them. Nor is there anything to sentimentalise over in this ever-shifting, overturning process, which must be encountered in all the works of life; no place for sighing—vanity of vanities. There is no vanity in it, more than in the mill that winnows and separates the grain.

But we must hasten to points more immediately religious, carrying with us, as we may, a lesson derived from these analogies. Observe, then—

2. That the radical evil of human character, as being under sin, consists in a determination to have our own way, which determination must be somehow reduced and extirpated. Hence the necessity that our experience be so appointed as to shake us loose continually from our purpose, or from all security and rest in it. Sin is but another name for self-direction. We cast off the will of God in it, and set up for a way and for objects of our own. We lay off plans to serve ourselves, and we mean to carry them straight through to their result. Whatever crosses us, or turns us aside, or in any way forbids us to do or succeed just as we like, becomes our annoyance. And these kinds of annoyance are so many and subtle and various, that the very world seems to be contrived to baffle us. In one view it is. It would not do for us, having cast off the will of God, and set up our own will, to let us get on smoothly and never feel any friction or collision with the will cast off. Therefore God manages to turn us about, beat us back, empty us from vessel to vessel, and make us feel that our bad will is hedged about, after all, by His almighty purposes. Sometimes we seem to bend, sometimes to break. Be it one or the other, we lose a part of our stiffness. By and by, to avoid breaking, we consent to bend, and so at last become more flexible to God, falling into a mood of letting go, then of consent, then of contrition. The coarse and bitter flavour of our self-will is reduced in this manner, and gradually fined away. If we could stand on our lees, in continual peace and serenity, if success were made secure, subject to no change or surprise, what, on the other hand, should we do more certainly than stay by our evil mind, and take it as a matter of course that our will is to be done; the very thing above all others of which we most need to be cured.

It would not answer even for the Christian, who has meant to surrender his will, and really wants to be perfected in the will of God, to be made safe in his plans and kept in a continual train of successes. He wants a reminder every hour; some defeat, surprise, adversity, peril; to be agitated, mortified, beaten out of his courses, so that all remains of self-will in him may be sifted out of him, and the very scent of his old perversity cleared. Oh, if we could be excused from all these changes and somersaults, and go on securely in our projects, it would ruin the best of us. Life needs to be an element of danger and agitation,—perilous, changeful, eventful; we need to have our evil will met by the stronger will of God, in order to be kept advised, by our experience, of the impossibility of that which our sin has undertaken. It would not even do for us to be uniformly successful in our best meant and holiest works, our prayers, our acts of sacrifice, our sacred enjoyments; for we should very soon fall back into the subtle power of our self-will, and begin to imagine, in our vanity, that we are doing something ourselves. Even here we need to be defeated and baffled, now and then. that we may be shaken out of our self-reliance and sufficiency, else the taste of our evil habit remains in us, and our scent is not changed.

3. Consider the fact that our evils are generally hidden from us till they are discovered to us by some kind of trial or adversity. This is less true of vicious and really iniquitous men. They see every hour with their eyes what is in them, or, at least, they may, by the acts they do. Their profanities, frauds, and lies, their deeds of impurity and violence, all that comes out of them shews them to be defiled. Not so with a generally correct man, still less so with a genuine, faithful Christian endeavouring after greater sanctification and a closer conformity to the will of God. Every such man living a life outwardly blameless, and desiring earnestly to grow in all true holiness, is, by the supposition, correct outwardly, and, therefore, the evils that remain in his spirit are, to a great extent, latent from himself. Sometimes, in a frame of high communion with God, he imagines that he is much more nearly purified than he is. And when he knows, from his poverty and spiritual dulness, that something is certainly wrong in him, he will have great difficulty in detecting the precise point of his infirmity. It is in him like some scent in the air, the source of which is hidden, and cann

be traced. Perhaps he will never definitely trace it so as to have it as a discovery, and yet God will manage, by the gusts of adversity and change, to winnow it away, even though it be undiscovered. More commonly, however, every such turn of adversity will bring out some particular fault in him which before was hid, and which he greatly needed to have discovered, and he will be able to set himself to the very work of purification by a direct endeavour. What good man ever fell into a time of deep chastening who did not find some cunning infatuation by which he was holden broken up, and some new discovery made of himself. The veils of pride are rent, the rock of self-opinion is shattered, and he is reduced to a point of gentleness and tenderness that allows him to suffer a true conviction concerning what was hidden from his sight. Nor is anything so effectual in this way as to meet some great overthrow that interrupts the whole course of life; all the better if it dislodges him even in his Christian works and appointments. What was I doing, he now asks, that I must needs be thrown out of my holiest engagements? for what fault was I brought under this discipline? He has every motive now to be ingenuous, for the hand of God is upon him, and what God declares to him he is ready to hear. And ah! how many things that were hidden from him start up now into view! How could he be allowed to go on prosperously when there was so much in him and his engagements that required rectification, and ought, if it be not removed, for ever to exclude him from these engagements. Perhaps he will be thrown out of them entirely, and turned to something else, that he may there discover, in a second overthrow, other evils that are still hidden from his knowledge. Oh, it is a great thing with us that our God is faithful, and will not spare to set us in order before our own eyes. If He should let us be as Moab from our youth, then should we be as Moab in the loss of all valuable improvement. Better is it, far better, that He empties us about on this side and on that, and passes us through all sorts of captivities; for then we are, at least, learning something which is valuable to be known.

4. It is another point of advantage in the changes and surprises through which we are continually passing, that we are prepared in this manner for the gracious and refining work of the Spirit in us. When we are allowed to stand still, and are

agitated by no changes, we become incrusted, as it were, under
our remaining faults or evils, and shut up in them as wine in
the vat where it is kept.   And the Spirit of God is shut away,
in this manner, by the imperviousness of our settled habit.
But when great changes or calamities come, our crust is broken
up, and the freshening breath of the Spirit fans the open chamber of the soul, to purify it.   Now the prayer, "Cleanse Thou
me from secret faults," finds an answer which before was impossible.   Providence, in this view, is an agitating Power to
break the incrustations of evil, and let the gales of the Spirit
blow where they list in us.   Under some great calamity or
sorrow, the loss of a child, the visitations of bodily pain, a
failure in business, the slanders of an enemy, a persecution for
the truth or for righteousness' sake, how tender and open to
God does the soul become!   "Search me, O God, and try me,
and see if there be any evil way in me," is now the ingenuous
prayer, and the Spirit of God comes in to work the answer,
finding everything ready for an effectual and thorough purgation.   And so, by a double process, Providence and the Spirit
both in unity, (for God is always one with Himself), we are perfected in holiness and finished in the complete beauty of Christ.
We could never hope to have our secret evils cleared by any
process of particular discovery and sanctification, but God's own
Spirit can reach every most hidden fault, and all the innumerable, undiscoverable vestiges of our depravity, doing all things
for us.   And so, at last, even the scent of it will be finally
changed.   These holy ventilations of grace, it is our comfort to
know that nothing can finally escape.   Again—

5. Too great quiet and security, long continued, are likely to
allow the reaction or the recovered power of our old sins, and
must not therefore be suffered.   As the wine standing on its
dregs or lees contracts a taste from the lees, and must therefore
be decanted or drawn off, so as to have no contact longer with
their vile sedimentary matter, so we, in like manner, need to be
separated from everything pertaining to the former life, to be
broken up in our expectations, and loosened from the affinities
of our former habit.   In our conversion to God we pass a crisis
that, like fermentation, clears our transparency and makes us
apparently new; we are called new men in Christ Jesus; still
the old man is not wholly removed.   It settles like dregs at the

bottom, so to speak, of our character, where it is, for the present, unseen. One might imagine, for the time, that it is wholly taken away ; and yet it is there, and is only the more likely to infect us that it is not sufficiently mixed with our life to cloud our present transparency. Our sanctification is not to be completed save by separation from it. And therefore God, who is faithful to us, continues to sever us, as completely as possible, from all association with the old life and condition ; breaks up our plans, compels a readjustment of our objects, empties us about from vessel to vessel, that our taste may not remain. Otherwise the hidden sediment of the old man will some time flavour and corrupt the new even more than at first. Suppose a man is converted as a politician—there is nothing wrong certainly in being a politician—but how subtle is the power of those old habits and affinities in which he lived, and how likely are they, if he goes straight on by a course of prosperous ambition, to be finally corrupted by their subtle reaction. When he is defeated, therefore, a little further on, by untoward combinations, and thrown out of all hope in this direction, let him not think it hard that he is less successful now in the way of Christ, than he was before in the way of his natural ambition. God understands him, and is leading him off, not unlikely, to some other engagement, that He may get him clear of the sediment on which he stands. In the same way, doubtless, it is that another is driven out of his business by a failure, another out of his family expectations by death and bereavement, another out of his very industry and his living by a loss of health, another out of prayers and expectations that were rooted in presumption, another out of works of beneficence that associated pride and vanity, another out of the ministry of Christ, where, by self-indulgence, or in some other way, his natural infirmities were rather increased than corrected. There is no engagement, however sacred, from which God will not sometimes separate us, that He may clear us of our sediment and the reactions of our hidden evils. Were it not for this, were everything in our trade or engagement to go on perfectly secure and prosperous, how certainly would the old man steal up in it from the bottom where it lies, to corrupt, and foul, and fatally vitiate the new. This our God will not suffer, and therefore He continues to unsettle us, tear us away from our works, our gains, our plans, our pleasures, our associations, and not seldom even from our recollections, that our change may go on to completion.

Once more, we are most certainly finished, when we are brought closest to God, and we are never brought so near to God as when we are most completely separated from our personal schemes and objects, and from all the works of the flesh. How tender do we become, when we are loosened by some great and sore disappointment ; even as Israel was finally cured of its last vestiges of idolatry by its bitter captivities. Having nothing left of all our expectations, driven out of our places, and plans, and works, and all that our pride cherished, possibly out of our prayers themselves, because of the pride so cunningly veiled in their guises of sanctity, what can we do but confess that God himself is our all, and take Him as the total blessing of our life. How closely now are we drawn to Him, receiving, as it were, a divine flavour from His purity. And when He is thus brought nigh, how rapidly are we changed in all the secret scents and flavours of our defilement.

And now, let me suggest, as in reference to all these illustrations, how much more they would signify if it were a day with us of great public calamity, a day, for example, of religious persecution, a day when fathers or sons are hunted or dragged to prison, or when possibly we ourselves are expecting every hour to be seized and arraigned for the faith of the gospel—and so to be witnesses for it, even by the sacrifice of our lives. Oh, these times of persecution, what Christians do they make! How little hold has this world, or its sins, of men who have laid even their lives upon the altar! We complain, how often, that in these days of security and liberty, Christian piety grows thin and feeble, that it loses tone, and appears even to want a character of reality. The difficulty is that our opinions, our faith, our Christian life, cost us nothing, and the church slides into the world because there is no broad, palpable line of suffering and sacrifice to separate the two. And for just this reason, how many in our time that have practically lost the distinction, are beginning to be chiefly occupied with Christianity, as a gift to this world ; admiring it as a civiliser of society and a promoter of what is called human progress. How many even seem to expect that the modern conditions of political liberty and security, coalescing with and patronising the gospel, are going to set it onward, and that henceforth the world must be growing into a kind of perfect state, by its own vital forces. Alas! I mistrust this millennium of Moab! it will never be seen. It is not in man, or human society, to be purified, exalted, and finally consummated by any such comfortable and even process. And there is nothing in our present indications to favour such a hope. These times of security and ease, when rightly viewed, are but the lull of the ocean between storms. It were hard to say that times of public fear and persecution are better. God knows what is better and will temper the ages Himself. But, alas! for poor human nature, what does it shew more evidently even now, in this short holiday of peace, than the inevitable tameness and feebleness of devotion, when the fires of great public adversity are smothered. Or if we seek to dress up still our giants and heroes in the faith, how shadowy and meagre do they look. And what can we rationally promise, but that our condition of ease and humanitarianism must finally run itself into the ground, preparing some terrible reaction, some war of Gog and Magog that shall empty the Church from vessel to vessel, leaving her again, as of old, nothing to hope for and look after on earth, but that she may win a better world in the sacrifice and loss of this.

The applications of this subject are many and various.

First of all, it brings a lesson of admonition to the class of worldly men who are continually prospering in the things of this life. One may be continually prospering in some things when he is not in all. He may be uniformly successful in his business engagements and enterprises, for example, when, in fact, he is tossed by many and sore disappointments, and shaken by intense agonies of heart. And by these he may be kept in that airing of right conviction which is needed to winnow his bad tempers and sober his confidence. Far otherwise will it be with you, if you prosper in everything and are agitated by no kind of adversity. This is the blessing of Moab, and the danger is that, standing thus upon the lees from your youth, disturbed by no crosses, unsettled by no changes, you will finally become so fast-rooted in pride and forgetfulness of God, as to miss everything most dear in existence. Nothing could be more perilous for you than just that which you deem your happiness. Nor is any word of God more pointedly serious than this,

" Because they have no changes, therefore they fear not God."
I commend it to your deepest and most thoughtful attention.

Others, again, have been visited by many and great adversities, emptied about from vessel to vessel all their lives long,
still wondering what it means, while still they adhere to their
sins.   There is, alas! no harder kind of life than this, a life of
continual discipline that really teaches nothing.   Is it so with
you, or is it not?   Scorched by all manner of adversities, are
you still unpurified by the fires you have passed through?
Defeated, crossed, crushed, beaten out of every plan, baffled in
every project, shut away from every aspiration, blasted in every
object your soul has embraced, are you still unprofited?   I have
known such examples,—fig-trees that God has dug about every
year, and that still remain as barren as if no hand of care had
touched them.   Is there anything more strange, in all the subjects of knowledge, than that a man, an intelligent being, should
be nowise instructed by the sufferings of a life?—separated in
no degree from the world and self, and the scent of his manifold
evils, by that which God has sent upon him to correct his
understanding, and purify his love, and fashion him even for
the angelic glory?   So he plods on still, contriving, and failing,
and groping with his face downward, and hoping against hope,
and wondering that the earth will not consent to bless him.
Oh, poor, weather-worn, defeated, yet unprofited man,—he cannot see when good cometh!   There is no class of beings more
to be pitied than defeated men, who have gotten nothing out of
their defeat but that dry sorrow of the world which makes it
only more barren, and therefore more insupportable.

It is necessary, in the review of this subject, to remind any
genuine Christian what benefits he ought to receive in the trials
and changes through which he is called to pass.   How many
are there who are finally driven out of every plan they have laid
for their course of life.   Their families are dissolved and recon-
structed.   Their location is dislodged.   Their business ends in
defeat.   No kind of settlement is attempted which is not broken
up by some kind of change or adversity.   And even where there
is a measure of prosperity, how many are the changes, losses,
trials, surprises, and pains.   Do you find, my brother, that, when
you are thus emptied about, dislodged, agitated, loosened, you
are purified?   Or, does the bad flavour of your worldly habits,

the scent of your old ambition, or your earthly pride, remain? There could not be a worse sign for you as regards the reality of your Christian confidence. And it will be a worse sign still, if you are habitually irritated by your defeats, and even dare to murmur impatiently against the strange severity of God,—as if it were a strange thing for you that your faithful God will try to bring you off the lees on which you stand! A far more strange thing is it that, having no great persecutions to suffer for Christ, you cannot find how, as a follower, to endure these common trials. God forbid that you so little understand your privilege in them. Receive them meekly, rather, and bow down to them gladly. Bid them welcome when they come, and, if they come not, ask for them; lift up your cry unto God, and beseech Him that by any means He will correct you, and purify you, and separate you to Himself.

But there is a use of this subject that has many times occurred to you already, and to this, in conclusion, let us now come.* By the visitation of God upon us—upon you, that is, and upon me—the tenure and security of our relation as pastor and people has been interrupted now for two whole years. Whether it was God's design, by this interruption, to refine us and purify us to a better use of this relation, or to bring it to a full end, remains now to be seen. The former is my earnest hope and my constant prayer. Was there nothing in us, on one side or on both, that required this discipline, and made it even necessary for us? Is there no reason to suspect that, in our state of confidence and security, we were beginning to look for the blessing of Moab and not for the blessing of Israel? For myself, I feel constrained to admit that I had come to regard my continuance here too much as a matter of course, an appointment subject to no repeal or change. I had learned to trust you implicitly as my friends, and knew that you could never be less. I had let my roots run out and downward among you, in a growth of nearly a quarter of a century. There was stealing on me thus, as I now discover, a feeling of security and establishment which is not good for any sinful man, and will not let him be the pilgrim on earth that he ought. Under the

* This discourse was so far coloured, as a whole, by the peculiar interest of the occasion referred to here in the close, that retaining the occasional matter appears to be required.

semblance of duty and constancy, I had undertaken to die here and nowhere else, knowing no other people, place, or work. And under this fair cover crept a little foolish pride, it may be, that really needed chastisement. As if it were for me to say where I would stay or die! Just here, unwittingly, my imagined constancy became presumption. Furthermore, I had always been too much like Moab, as I now see, and bitterly needed some kind of captivity more real, some change more crippling than the trivial adversities I had heretofore tossed aside so lightly.

Meantime, was there nothing on your part or in you that required a similar discipline? Having seen your church almost uniformly prosperous for a long course of years, and growing steadily up from a feeble and small one to a condition of strength, were there not many of you that were losing a righteous concern for it, and beginning to leave it practically to me, as if I could take care of it? ceasing in that manner from their trust in God, by which they had before upheld me, and from those personal responsibilities for it which are the necessary condition of all earnestness in the Christian life? I should do wrong not to say that I have many times been so far oppressed by this conviction as to doubt whether it might not even be better for you if I were entirely taken out of the way. You have been subjected to some uncommon trials on my account. Have you never slid from the Christian constancy and patience in which you stood into a temper of mere self-reliance, as if by some human sufficiency you had been able to stand unbroken? Were you touched by no subtle pride, were you betrayed into no undue self-confidence, were you slid unwittingly into no trust in a worm that you mistook for trust in God? Ah! if you had been cut down as a church by adversity, crippled, weakened, emptied from vessel to vessel, brought into captivity as regards all hope from man, how much might it have done for you. It is the blessing of Moab, as I greatly fear, that has injured you, and, as God is faithful, He would not let you suffer in this manner longer. And so, both for my sake and for yours, He has brought this heavy trial or adversity upon us. By this He takes us off our lees, and His design has been to ventilate us by the separation we have suffered. He means to purify us, to take away all our self-confidence, and our trust in each other, and bring us into implict, humble trust in Himself.

And the work He has begun, I firmly believe that He will prosecute till His object is gained. If two years of separation will not bring us to our places and correct our sin, He will go further—He will finally command us apart, and tear us loose from all our common ties and expectations. For myself, I am anxious to learn the lesson He is teaching, and I pray God that a similar purpose may enter into you. Let not this happy return, which God has vouchsafed me, and the congratulations of the occasion, drive away all the sober and searching truths God was trying to enter into our hearts. Be jealous of any such lightness. As you rejoice with me and give thanks unto God for His undeserved goodness, consent with me to God's corrections also, and join me in the prayer that other and heavier corrections may not be made necessary by the want of all fruit in these. For be assured that, as you are Israel and not Moab, God will deal with you as He deals with Israel, and will not spare till your purification is accomplished. Let us go to Him as penitents in our common sorrow, and make our common confession before Him, determined, every one, that he will turn himself to God's correcting hand, and follow it. And as Thou hast smitten us, O Lord, do Thou heal us; as Thou hast broken, do Thou bind us up; that we may be established in holiness before Thee, and walk humbly and carefully in Thy sight, as those whom the Lord hath chastened.

XXII

HEB. vii. 26—"*Separate from sinners, and made higher than the heavens.*"

WITH us of to-day it is the commendation of Jesus that He is so profoundly humbled, identified so affectingly with our human state. But the power He had with the men of His time moved in exactly the opposite direction, being the impression He made of His remoteness and separateness from men, when He was, in fact, only a man, as they supposed, under all human conditions. With us it is the wonder that He is brought so low. With them that He could seem to rise so high, for they knew nothing as yet of His person, considered as the incarnate Word of the Father. This contrast, however, between their position and ours is not as complete as may, at first, seem to us, for that which makes their impression makes, after all, a good part of ours. For when we appeal thus to His humiliations under the flesh and as a man of sorrows, we really do not count on the flesh and the sorrows as being the Christly power, but only on what He brought into the world from above the world by the flesh and the sorrows—the holiness, the deific love, the self-sacrificing greatness, the everlasting beauty, in a word, all that most distinguishes Him above mankind and shews Him most transcendently separate from sinners. Here is the great power of Christianity—the immense importation it makes from worlds of glory outside. Hence the intimation of the text, that it became our Lord, as the priest of our salvation, to be not only holy, harmless, and undefiled, but separate also from sinners, and made higher than the heavens, that so He may be duly qualified for His transcendent work and office.

What I propose, then, for my present subject is—*The separateness of Jesus from men; the immense power it had and must ever have on their feeling and character.*

I do not mean by this that Christ was separated as being at all withdrawn, but only that, in drawing Himself most closely to them, He was felt by them never as being on their level of life and character, but as being parted from them by an immense chasm of distance.   He was born of a woman, grew up in the trade of a mechanic, was known as a Nazarene, stood a man before the eye, and yet He early began to raise impressions that separated Him, and set Him asunder inexplicably from the world He was in.

These impressions were not due, as I have said, to any distinct conceptions they had of Him as being a higher nature incarnate, for not even His disciples took up any such definite conceptions of His nature till after His death and ascension. It was guessed, indeed, that He might be Elias or some one of the old prophets, but we are only to see, in such struggles of conjecture, how powerfully He has already impressed the sense of His distinction or separateness of character, for such guesses or conjectures were even absurd, unless they were instigated by previous impressions of something very peculiar in His unearthly manner requiring to be accounted for.

His miracles had undoubtedly something to do with the impression of His separateness from ordinary men, but a great many others, who were strictly human, have wrought miracles without creating any such gulf between them and mankind as we discover here.

It is probably true also that the rumour of His being the Messiah—the great, long-expected Prince and Deliverer—had something to do in raising the impressions of men concerning Him.   But their views of the Messiah to come had prepared them to look only for some great hero and deliverer, and a kind of political millennium under His kingdom.   There was nothing in their expectation that should separate Him specially from mankind as being a more than humanly superlative character.

Pursuing, then, our inquiry, let us notice, in the first place, how the persons most remote and opposite, even they that finally conspired His death, were impressed or affected by Him.   They deny His Messiahship ; they charge that only Beelzebub could help Him to do His miracles ; they are scandalised by His familiarity with publicans and sinners and other low people ; they arraign His doctrine as a heresy against many of the most sacred laws of their religion; they charge Him with the crime of breaking their Sabbath, and even with excess in eating and drinking; and yet we can easily see that there is growing up, in their minds, a most peculiar awe of His person. And it appears to be excited more by His manners and doctrine and a certain indescribable originality and sanctity in both, than by anything else. His townsmen the Nazarenes, for example, were taken with surprise, by His discourses in the synagogue and elsewhere, knowing well that He had never received the aids of learning. Is not this the carpenter's son? they inquired. Do we not all know His brothers and sisters, living here among us? Whence then these gracious words that we hear Him speak? When His wonderful sermon on the mount was ended, what said the multitude? The very point of their astonishment was that He spoke with such an original and strong authority, and not as the Scribes, who were, in fact, the Sophists of Jewish learning, but were held in high respect as a learned order. The expressions made use of by these hearers of Jesus indicate, in fact, a raising of their own thoughts by what they had heard, and the sense they had of some sacred and even celestial freshness in His manner and doctrine. Without including the centurion at Capernaum among His enemies, we may gather something from Him, in respect to the probable impression made by the bearing and discourse of Jesus. He was a Roman, but appears withal to have been a man of religious worth and culture. He had even built a synagogue for the people of Capernaum, at his own expense. In that synagogue he had probably been rewarded in hearing Jesus speak; for the Saviour had been making Capernaum a kind of centre for some time past. But we observe that when he sends to Jesus to obtain the healing of his servant, he has been so deeply impressed with the Saviour's manner, that he does not presume on his military position as keeping guard over a vanquished country, takes on no high airs of negotiation, but even requests that Jesus will not think it necessary to come under his roof, for He is really not worthy of so great honour. He may have apprehended that Christ might have some religious scruples in respect to the implied defilement of such intercourse with a nominal pagan. If so, there was the greater respect in his delicacy.

Beginning with impressions like these, we can easily see that the public mind is gradually becoming saturated with a kind of awe of His person ; as if He might be some higher, finer nature come into the world.   This was the feeling that shook the courage of the traders and money-changers in the temple, and made them fly in such feeble panic before Him.   For the same reason it was that a band of officers, sent out at an early period to arrest Him, returned without having executed their commission ; for they said, "Never man spake like this man." Such words of clearness, and repose, and purity, fell on them, as excited their imagination, starting the conception apparently of one speaking out of eternity and worlds unknown.   He put them under such constraints of fear, in short, by His words and manner, that they did not dare to arrest Him.   And just this kind of feeling grew upon the people as His ministry advanced, till it became a general superstition ; for it is the way of minds infected by any such tendencies, to make ghosts of the fancy out of mere impressions of superior dignity, and even goodness. Hence, so far from supposing that He could be captured as safely as a lamb, and with less of resistance, they appear to have had a kind of suspicion that He would strike blind, or annihilate the first man that touched Him.   Indeed, one reason why they wanted to get Him in their power apparently was, that He was reported to have given out His determination to shake down the temple, and they were even much concerned lest He might do it.   Hence the problem with them was, not how to arrest any common man, or sinner of mankind, but a superior, mysterious, fearful one, and there wanted, as they imagined, some kind of magic to do it.   They took up thus an impression that, if they could suborn one of His followers, it would break the spell of His power, and they could proceed safely.   They bought off Judas accordingly, and he was to conduct them—not that they could not otherwise find the Saviour ; not that Judas could do anything physically in the matter of the arrest which they could not do themselves ; but they seem to have imagined that, if Judas would bring them directly before Him, and speak to Him, it would assure them, and be a kind of token to Him that His power was broken ; for they believed greatly in spells and other such conceits of the fancy.   And yet when they came upon Him—a large band of marshals and assistants, with torches and

lanterns, and all strong arms of defence—they were smitten with
such dread at the thought of being actually before Him, that
they even reeled backward and fell to the ground! He was
such a Being, in their apprehension, that their chances of living
another minute were doubtful!

It is easy also to see that Pilate, even after His arrest, is profoundly impressed with the sense of something superior, more
wise, or holy, or sacred, than he had seen before. The dignity
of Christ's answer, and also of His manner, had awakened
visibly a kind of awe in his mind. It was as if he had undertaken to question a king indeed; one superior in all majesty to
himself. Unaccountably to himself he grows superstitious, as if
dealing with some Divinity, he knows not who, and he cannot
so much as give his mere negative sentence of permission, pagan
though he be, without washing his hands as religiously as if he
were some Pharisee, to be clear of the guilt of the transaction.
The centurion, too, that kept guard by the cross, another
Roman, is so affected, or impressed by the majestic manner of
Jesus in His death, that he bears spontaneous witness, out of
his own feeling, probably in words which he had heard, but only
dimly understood as having some very mysterious and high
meaning, "Truly this was the Son of God!"

If now it should be objected here that the enemies of Jesus
would never have dared to insult His person so brutally in His
trial and crucifixion, if they had been really impressed, as we
are supposing, with the wonderful sacredness and separateness
of His character, it is enough to answer that exactly this is the
manner of cowardice. Only yesterday these same men were in
such awe of Him that they trembled inwardly at the sound of
His name; and now that they find Him strangely in their power,
submitting to them in the meekness of a lamb, they grow brave,
pleased to find that they can be; and, to make it sure, they
multiply their blows and other indignities in a manner of low
and really ignominious triumph over Him. But how soon does
the true shame and bitterness of their sin return upon them.
For, when they saw the funeral weeds of nature's sorrow hung
over the sun, and felt the shuddering ague of the world, their
spirit fell again. "And all the people," says Luke, "that came
together to that sight, beholding the things that were done, smote
their breasts, and returned."

Turn now, secondly, to the disciples, and observe how they were impressed or affected by the manner and spirit of Jesus. And here the remarkable thing is, that they appear to be more and more impressed with the distance between Him and themselves, the longer they know Him, and the more intimate and familiar their acquaintance with Him. He took possession of them strangely even at the very first, much as you will see in the case of Matthew the publican. The man is sitting at the receipt of custom, and Christ, who is passing by, says to him, " Come, follow me." That word has a mystery in it which cannot be withstood ; he forsakes all and follows at command. At first, however, the impression had of Jesus is more shallow in all the disciples. It fared with them much as with the woman at the well, who took Him first for a common traveller, then for a prophet, and finally as the great Messiah, having only the faintest conception of Him probably even then. But they grew more and more impressed with His greatness, and the strangeness of His quality ; for there was so much in His authority, purity, love, wisdom, that they could only spell Him out by syllables.

Thus we may take Peter as an example for all the others ; for in the surname, Peter, that was early given him by his Master, and also by the promise that on him, as the rock of its foundation, the Church was to be built, everything was done to keep him assured and help him to maintain a footing of confidence. How, then, was it, as he came into closer acquaintance with his Master ? At the first, when his brother Andrew conducted him to Jesus, he felt much as his brother did the day before, when he and his friend, having heard John's remarkable apostrophe, " Behold the Lamb of God," accosted Him freely, put themselves, as it were, upon Him, and spent, if we may judge, whole hours in their private questioning. Peter's exclamation, shortly after, at the miraculous draught of fishes, " Depart from me, O Lord, for I am a sinful man," might seem to indicate a very wide sense of distance already felt between him and Christ; but it rather signifies, after all, the violence of his wonder at the miracle, than any deep moral sense of the dignity, purity, and superior majesty of Christ. Accordingly it will be seen, some time after this, that he is bold enough to take the Saviour to account and rebuke Him, with a degree of emphasis not a little

offensive, for the conceit of it.   At the washing of the disciples'
feet he breaks out again less boldly, but as soon as he finds that
he is in a mistake, recalls his strong asseveration, saying in the
gentlest manner, "Not my feet only, but my hands and my
head."   Then again, at the scene of the table, where the revelation is, "One of you shall betray me," he has been so far
removed, sunk so low, by the wonderful discourses of Jesus to
which he has been listening, that he does not even dare to
accost his Master with a question spoken aloud, but beckons to
John to whisper it for him, as he lies reclining on the Saviour's
breast.   Then, once more, after having openly denied Him and
foresworn all connexion with Him, seeing that He is now
stripped of His power, and His very Messiahship is a virtually
exploded hope, Peter is nevertheless under such an habitual awe
of His person, that the simply catching a look of His eye, as He
goes out of the hall of Caiaphas, and seeing it turned full upon
him, breaks him quite down, and even overwhelms him with
sorrow.   He was in the most unlikely mood for it possible;
fresh in the wrong, flushed by the very oaths he has taken, all
in a tremor, unstrung for any consideration of truth by the inward disturbance of his falsity, and yet he is riven by that
mere look of Jesus as if it were a glance of the Almighty.

The same thing could be shewn by other examples, but it
must suffice to say that, while the miracles of Christ do not increase in grandeur with the advance of His ministry, His disciples are visibly growing all the while more and more impressed
with the sense of distance between Him and themselves, and of
some unknown transcendent mystery by which He is separated,
as another kind of being, from the world He is in.   This, in
part, is their blessing; for, as they are humbled in it, so they
are raised by it, feel the birth of new affinities, rise to higher
thoughts, and are wakened to a conscious struggle after God.

What now, thirdly, is the solution of this profound impression
of separateness made by Christ on the world?   That His
miracles and the repute of His Messiahship do not wholly
account for it we have already observed.   It may be imagined
by some that He produced this impression artificially, by means
of certain scenes and observances designed to widen out the
distance between Him and the race; for how could He other-

wise obtain that power over them which He was properly
entitled to have by His own real eminence, unless He took
some pains to set them in attitudes in which His eminence
might be felt. In other words, if He is to have more than a
man's power, He must somehow be more than a man. Thus,
when He says to His mother, "Woman, what have I to do with
thee? my hour is not yet come;" or when, being notified that
His mother and brethren are standing without waiting to see
Him, He asks, "Who, then, is my mother, and who are my
brethren?" it will be imagined that He is purposely suggesting
His higher derivation and His more transcendent affinities.
But, even if it were so, it must be understood only that He is
speaking out of His spiritual consciousness, claiming thus
affinity with God, and with those who shall embrace Him in
the eternal brotherhood of faith; not as boasting the height of
His natural Sonship.

So, again, in the scene of the baptism, and the vision of the
dove descending upon Him, introduced by the very strange out-
burst of prophetic utterance in John, when he sees the Saviour
coming,—"Behold the Lamb of God, that taketh away the sins
of the world!" it may be imagined that the design is to usher
Him into His ministry as a superior being. But what, in that
view, shall we say of the great soul-struggle previous, called the
temptation? It is not to be denied that the scene of the
baptism connects impressions of some very exalted quality in
the subject; and yet, if we bring in the temptation, and regard
the transaction as a solemn inaugural of Christ's great ministry,
—God's act of separation, His own act of assumption here
passed,—there is nothing in it to set Him off distinctly from
men, save as He is set off by His character and His con-
secration to His work. Indeed, no one took up the impression
from this inaugural scene that He was a being above the
human order.

On a certain occasion He is transfigured, and Moses and Elias
appear as only secondary figures in the scene; by which it may
be designed, some will fancy, to widen out the chasm between
Himself and men, shewing Himself to be the compeer and
more,—even the Lord of angels and glorified spirits. This may
have been the design, or rather it probably was; at least, so far
as to have that effect on the future ages; for it was important,

we may believe, to right impressions of His person, in the coming time, that His excellent glory should some time have been discovered or uncovered to men, and the facts reported as historical proofs of His divinity. But it does not appear that the three by whom the transfiguration was seen and reported ever disclosed the fact during the Saviour's lifetime; and it is remarkable that one of these, even after the fact, had such confidence and assurance toward his dear Lord, that he even dared to lay his head on that once transfigured breast! In which it is made clear that, however much we may imagine Christ to have been lifted in order by the scene of the transfiguration, He still remained a properly fellow nature, even to one who was present as a beholder; who felt in his deepest centre the separateness of Christ and the transcendent mystery of His character, but does not appear to have been at all removed or thrown out of confidence by the sacred awe in which he saw Him invested. He could never have laid his head on the bosom of a person regarded as being really deific.

But what shall we say of the really astounding assumptions put forth by Christ? Were they not designed as declarations or assertions of a superhuman order in His natural person? When He asks, "Who convinceth me of sin?" when He declares, "Ye are from beneath, I am from above. I am the bread that cometh down from heaven;" when He dares to use the pronoun *we*, as relating to Himself and the Father, "We will come unto him, and make our abode with him;" when He speaks of the glory He had with the Father before the world was; when He engages, Himself, to send down the Holy Spirit after His ascension, "I will send you another Comforter;" when He claims to be the judge of the world, and speaks of holding the world's throne; nay, when, to give His most ordinary and familiar mode of doctrine, He says, "I am the way, the truth, and the life; no man cometh unto the Father but by me;" it is most certainly true, that He is challenging, in all such utterances, honours and prerogatives that are not human. At the same time, if He had not before separated Himself heaven-wide from men, by His character, and produced, in that manner, a sense of some wonderful mystery in Him, He would have been utterly scouted and hooted out of the world for His preposterous assumptions. These very assumptions, therefore, presuppose a separation already realised, even more remarkable than that which is claimed or asserted.   Indeed, the minds of His disciples were so much occupied with the impressions they felt, under the realities of His character, that they scarcely attended to the strange assumptions of His words, and did not even seem to have taken their meaning till after His death.

The remarkable separation, therefore, of Christ from the sinners of mankind, and the impression He awakened in them of that separation, was made, not by scenes, nor by words of assertion, nor by anything designed for that purpose, but it grew out of His life and character—His unworldliness, holiness, purity, truth, love; the dignity of His feeling, the transcendent wisdom and grace of His conduct.   He was manifestly one that stood apart from the world in his profoundest human sympathy with it.   He often spent His nights in solitary prayer, closeted with God in the recesses of the mountains.   He was plainly not under the world, or any fashions of human opinion.   He was able to be singular, without apparently desiring it, and by the simple force of His superiority.   Conventionalities had no power over Him, learning no authority with Him.   He borrowed nothing from men.   His very thoughts appeared to be coined in the mint of some wisdom higher than human.   There was also this distinction in all His virtues, that they did not open, like those of men, at the larger end, growing less and less, the further in they might be penetrated; but at the smaller, as if no strain, or ostentation were possible, growing larger therefore, and wider, and fuller, the more conversant and the more familiar with them any one might be.   His whole ministry, therefore, was a kind of discovery and so a process of separation. The purity of His life grew greater; the truth of His doctrine more than mortal, or that of any mortal prophet; His love itself deific; and so—this is the grandeur and glory of His life—He rose up out of humanity or the human level into Deity and the separate order of uncreated life, by the mere force of His manner and character, and achieved, as man, the sense of a Divine excellence before His personal order as the Son of God was conceived.   And so it finally became established in men's feeling, as it stood in His last prayer, that there was some inexplicable oneness where His inmost life and spirit merged in the

Divine and became identical. His human fire had already
mingled its blaze with the great central sun of Deity.

Accordingly what we see in His resurrection and ascension,
and the scenes of intercourse between, is only a kind of final
consummation, or complete rendering of what was already in
men's hearts. There it begins to come out that He is the
King, even the Lord of Glory. Death cannot hold Him. The
earth cannot fasten Him. The parting clouds receive Him
and let Him through to His throne, not more truly but only
more visibly separate than before, in that He is made higher
than the heavens.

How great a thing now is it, my hearers, that such a Being
has come into our world and lived in it—a Being above mortality while in it—a Being separate from sinners, bringing unto
sinners by a fellow-nature what is transcendent and even deific
in the Divine holiness and love. Yes, we have had a visitor
among us, living out, in the moulds of human conduct and
feeling, the perfections of God! What an importation of glory
and truth! Who that lives a man can ever, after this, think
it a low and common thing to fill these spheres, walk in these
ranges of life, and do these works of duty which have been
raised so high by the life of Jesus in the flesh? The world is
no more the same that it was. All its main ideas and ideals
are raised. A kind of sacred glory invests even our humblest
spheres and most common concerns.

Consider, again, as one of the points deducible from the truth
we have been considering, how little reason is given us, in the
mission of Christ, for the hope that God, who has such love to
man, will not allow us to fail of salvation by reason of any mere
defect or neglect of application to Christ. What, then, does
this peculiar separateness of Christ signify? Coming into the
world to save it—taking on Him our nature that He may draw
Himself as close to us as possible—what is growing all the
while to be more and more felt in men's bosoms but a sense of
ever-widening, ever-deepening, and, in some sense, incommunicable separateness from Him? And this, you will observe,
is the separateness, not of condition, but of character. Nay, it
grows out of His very love to us in part and His profound one-

ness with us, for it is a love so pure and gentle—so patient, so disinterested, so self-sacrificing—that it parts Him from us in the very act of embrace, and makes us think of Him even with awe! How, then, will it be when He is met in the condition of His glory, and the guise of His humanity is laid off? There is nothing then to put Him at one with us or us at one with Him but just that incommunicable and separate character which fills us even here with dread. If, then, your very Saviour grows more and more separated from you, in all your impressions, the more you see of Him, how will it be when you drop the flesh and go to meet Him invested only in your proper character of sin? If before you thought of Him with awe, and even with a holy dread, how little confidence will be left you there when you see Him in the fulness of His glory, even that which He had with the Father before the world was? If He was separate before, how inevitably, insupportably separate now.

Consider, also, and accurately distinguish, as here we may easily do, what is meant by holiness, and what especially is its power, or the law of its power. Holiness is not what we may do or become in mere self-activity or self-culture, but it is the sense of a separated quality in one who lives on a footing of intimacy and oneness with God. The original word, repre-sented by our word *holiness*, means separation or separateness —the character of being drawn apart, or exalted, by being con-secrated to God and filled with inspiration from God. It supposes nothing unsocial, withdraws no one from those living sympathies that gladden human life. On the contrary, it quickens all most gentle and loving affinities, and brings the subject just as much closer in feeling to his fellow-man as he is closer to God and less centralised in himself. But it changes the look or expression, raising in that manner the apparent grade of the subject, and separating him from what-ever is of the world or under the spirit of the world. He is not simply a man as before, but he is more—a man exalted, hallowed, glorified. The Divine tempers are in him—the power of the world is fallen off—his words have a different accent— his acts an air of repose, dignity, sanctity—and the result is, that mankind feel him as one somehow become superior. It stirs their conscience to speak with him—it puts them under impressions that are consciously not of man alone. This is holiness—the condition of a man when he is separated visibly from the world and raised above it by a Divine participation. It is, in fact, the greatest power ever exerted by man, being not the power of man, but only of God himself manifested in him.

But the great and principal lesson derivable from this subject is, that Christianity is a regenerative power upon the world only as it comes into the world in a separated character—as a revelation or sacred importation of holiness.

We have in these times a very considerable and quite pretentious class, who have made the discovery that Christ actually eat with publicans and sinners! This fact indeed is their gospel. Christ, they say, was social, drew Himself to every human being, poured his heart into every human joy and woe, lived in no ascetic manner as a being withdrawn from life. And so it becomes a principal matter of duty with us to meet all human conditions in a human way and make ourselves acceptable to all. They do not observe that Jesus brought in something into every scene of society and hospitality which shewed a mind set off from all conformities. When He eat with publicans and sinners, He declared expressly that He did it as a physician goes to the sick, did it that He might so call sinners to repentance. So when he dined with Zaccheus, He there proclaimed Himself the Son of Man, who was come to save the lost. When He shared the assiduous hospitality of Martha, what did He but remind her of the one thing needful, quite passed by in her over-doing carefulness? And when He dined with one of the great rich men of the Pharisees, what did He but strike at the very usurpation of all high fashion, by openly rebuking those who seized on the highest places of precedence? and what did He propose to the host himself, but that true hospitality is that which is given with no hope of return?—in which also He touched the very quick of all heartlessness and all real mockery in what is called society. Yes, it is true that Jesus eat with publicans and sinners. He never stood apart from any advance of men. But how visibly separated was He there and everywhere from the shallow conventionalities of the world; how pure, majestic, free, and faithful to His great ministry of salvation!

We have also a great many schemes of philanthropy started in these days, that suppose a preparation of man or society to be moved directly forward, on its present plane, into some advanced or nearly paradisiac state. The manner is to address men at their present point, in their present motive, under their present condition, with some hope of development, some scheme, truth, organisation, and so to bring them into some compact or way of life that will discontinue the present evils and make a happy state. As if there were any such feasibility to good in man, that he can be put in felicity by mere invitation or consent! Christ and Christianity think otherwise. For the blessed Redeemer comes into the world in the full understanding that, in being identified with the world, He will become a great power only as He is also separated from it. And in this lies the efficacy of His mission, that He brings to men what is not in them, what is opposite to them, the separated glory, the holiness of God. Come, then, ye holiday saviours, ye reformers, and philanthropic regenerators of the world, send forth your invitations to society, summon the world to come near and make even a fixed contract to be happy, and one that shall be indissoluble for ever! Bring out your paper coaches and bid the sorrow-stricken peoples ride forth, down the new millennium you promise without prophecy ; do your utmost ; stimulate every most confident hope, and then see what your toy-shop apparatus signifies !

No, we want a salvation which means a grace brought into the world that is not of it. When the real Saviour comes, there will be great falling off, for the thoughts of many hearts will be revealed. He will not be a popular Saviour. He that puts men in awe, as of some higher spirit and more divine of which they know nothing; He that visits the world to be unworldly in it, and draw men apart from it and break its terrible spell—He, I say, will not be hailed with favour and applause. Indeed I very much fear that many who assume even now to be His disciples would not like Him, if he were to appear on earth. His unworldly manner, His profound singularity as a Being superior to sin and to all human conventionalities, would offend them and drive them quite away. Who of us here to-day would really follow Jesus and cleave to Him, if He were now living among us ?

This brings me to speak of what is now the great and desolating error of our times. I mean the general conformity of the followers of Christ to the manners and ways, and, consequently, in a great degree, to the spirit of the world. Christ had His power, as we have seen, in the fact that He carried the impression of His separateness from it and His superiority to it. He was no ascetic, His separation no contrived and prescribed separation, but was only the more real and radical that it was the very instinct or freest impulse of His character. He could say, "The prince of this world cometh, and hath nothing in me;" counting the bad kingdom to be only a paste-board affair, whose laws and ways were but a vain show, that He could not even so much as feel. This now is what we want, such a fulness of Divine participation, that we shall not require to be always shutting off the world by prescribed denials, but shall draw off from it naturally, because we are not of it. A true Christian, one who is deep enough in the godly life to have his affinities with God, will infallibly become a separated being. The instinct of holiness will draw him apart into a singular, superior, hidden life with God. And this is the true Christian power, besides which there is no other. And when this fails everything goes with it.

Neither let us be deceived in this matter by our merely notional wisdoms, or deliberative judgments, for it is not a matter to be decided by any consideration of results—the question never is, what is really harmful, and so wrong, but what will meet the living and free instinct of a life of prayer and true godliness? I confess that when the question is raised, whether certain common forms of society and amusement are to be indulged or disallowed, the argument sometimes appears to preponderate on the side of indulgence. What is more innocent? Must we take the morose and, as it were, repugnant attitude of disallowing and rejecting everything harmless that is approved by men? In what other way could we more certainly offend their good judgment and alienate their personal confidence? Ought we not even to yield a certain allowable freedom for their sake? So stands the computation. Let it be granted that, as a matter of deliberation, the scale is turned for conformity. And yet the decision taken will not stand; for there is no truly living Christian that wants or at all relishes such conformities. On the other hand, you will see that such as argue for them and make interest in them, however well disposed in matters philanthropic, have little or nothing in them of that which is the distinctively Christian power, and do not add anything to the living impression of the gospel; for the radical element of all great impression is wanting—viz., the sense of a separated life. Their instinct does not run that way. What they want is conformity, more conformity, to be always like the world, not different from it, and in that gulf they sink, lost to all good effect, nay, a hindrance to all.

There is no greater mistake, as regards the true manner of impression on the world, than that we impress it being homogeneous with it. If in our dress we shew the same extravagance, if our amusements are theirs without a distinction, if we follow after their shows, copy their manners, busy ourselves in their worldly objects, emulate their fashions, what are we different from them? It seems quite plausible to fancy the great honour we shall put on religion, when we are able to set it on a footing with all most worldly things, and shew that we can be Christians in that plausible way. This we call a liberal piety. It is such as can excel in all high tastes, and make up a figure of beauty that must needs be a great commendation, we think, to religion. It may be a little better than to be openly apostate; but, alas! there is how little power in such a kind of life! No; it is not conformity that we want, it is not being able to beat the world in its own way, but it is to stand apart from it, and produce the impression of a separated life: this it is, and this only, that yields any proper sense of the true Christian power. It is not the being popular that makes one a help to religion, no holy man was ever a truly popular character. Even Christ himself, bringing the Divine beauty into the world, profoundly disturbed the quiet of men by His very perfections. All really bad men adhering to their sin, hated Him, and their animosity was finally raised to such a pitch, that they crucified Him. And what does He say, turning to His disciples, but this very thing, "The servant is not greater than his lord; if they have persecuted me, they will persecute you. I have chosen you out of the world, *therefore* the world hateth you." We are certainly not to make a merit of being hated, for the worst and most wicked can do that; as little are we to make a merit of popularity and being even with the world in its ways. There is no just mode of life, no true holiness, or fruit of holy living, if we do not carry the conviction, by our self-denial, our sobriety in the matter of show, and our withholding from all that indicates being under the world, that we are in a life separated to God. Therefore His great call is—"Come out from among them, and be ye separate, and touch not the unclean thing, and ye shall be my sons and daughters, saith the Lord Almighty." And there is a most profound philosophy in this. If we are to impress the world we must be separate from sinners, even as Christ our Master was, or at least according to our human degree, as being in His Spirit. The great difficulty is, that we think to impress the world, standing on the world's own level and asking its approbation. We conform too easily and with too much appetite. We are all the while touching the unclean thing—bowing down to it, accepting its law, eager to be found approved in it. God therefore calls us away. Oh, that we could take our lesson here, and plan our life, order our pursuits, choose our relaxations, prepare our families, so as to be truly with Christ, and so, in fact, that we ourselves can say, each for himself, "The prince of this world cometh, and hath nothing in me."

And this exactly is our communion with Jesus ; we propose to be one with Him in it. In it we connect with a Power transcendent, the Son of Man in glory, whose image we aspire to, and whose mission, as the Crucified on earth, was the revelation of the Father's love and holiness. We ask to be separated with Him and set apart to the same great life. Our communion is not on the level of our common humanity, but we rise in it ; we scale the heavens where He sitteth at the right hand of God ; we send our longings up and ask to have attachments knit to Him—to be set in deepest, holiest, and most practical affinity with Him—and so to live a life that is hid with Christ in God. In such a life we become partakers of His holiness, and in the separating grace of that, partakers also of His power.

THE END.

BALLANTYNE, ROBERTS, AND CO., PRINTERS, EDINBURGH.

Check Out More Titles From HardPress Classics Series In this collection we are offering thousands of classic and hard to find books. This series spans a vast array of subjects – so you are bound to find something of interest to enjoy reading and learning about.

Subjects:
Architecture
Art
Biography & Autobiography
Body, Mind &Spirit
Children & Young Adult
Dramas
Education
Fiction
History
Language Arts & Disciplines
Law
Literary Collections
Music
Poetry
Psychology
Science
…and many more.

Visit us at www.hardpress.net

CPSIA information can be obtained
at www.ICGtesting.com
Printed in the USA
BVHW091752260819
556835BV00025B/4380/P